Resurrection

Resurrection

THE CONFIRMATION *of* CLARENCE THOMAS

John C. Danforth

VIKING

VIKING
Published by the Penguin Group
Penguin Books USA Inc., 375 Hudson Street,
New York, New York 10014, U.S.A.
Penguin Books Ltd, 27 Wrights Lane,
London W8 5TZ, England
Penguin Books Australia Ltd, Ringwood,
Victoria, Australia
Penguin Books Canada Ltd, 10 Alcorn Avenue,
Toronto, Ontario, Canada M4V 3B2
Penguin Books (N.Z.) Ltd, 182–190 Wairau Road,
Auckland 10, New Zealand

Penguin Books Ltd, Registered Offices:
Harmondsworth, Middlesex, England

First trade edition

Published in 1994 by Viking Penguin,
a division of Penguin Books USA Inc.

10 9 8 7 6 5 4 3 2

Copyright © John C. Danforth, 1994
All rights reserved

A leatherbound signed first edition of
this book has been published
by The Easton Press.

LIBRARY OF CONGRESS CATALOGING IN PUBLICATION DATA
Danforth, John C.
Resurrection : the confirmation of Clarence Thomas / John C. Danforth.
p.   cm.
Includes index.
ISBN 0–670–86022–0
1. Thomas, Clarence, 1948–   . 2. United States. Supreme Court—Officials and
employees—Selection and appointment. 3. Hill, Anita. 4. Sexual harassment of
women—Law and legislation—United States. I. Title.
KF8745.T48D36   1994
347.73'2634—dc20
[347.3073534]   94-25005

Printed in the United States of America
Set in Bodoni Book
Designed by Kathryn Parise

To Sally

Preface

All of us see the events of life in the light of our own experiences and values. I see the summer and early autumn of 1991 in the light of my religious tradition.

The heart of the Christian faith is the redemptive work of God in the death and resurrection of Jesus Christ. For a Christian, that action of God, accomplished at a particular time and place, can never be duplicated. Yet the Christ event is not remote from the lives of ordinary people. St. Paul tells Christians that if in baptism they have been united with Christ in his death, they will certainly be united with him in his resurrection.[1] Ordinary people experience the terrible reality of death. Ordinary people share in the ultimate victory of life.

The confirmation of Clarence Thomas is the most dramatic example I have seen of both weakness and strength, of the intensity of suffering and the power of God to make a new creation, all in a very short period of time. Yet, however dramatic, the example of Clarence Thomas is not unique. All kinds of people suffer. All kinds of people experience the loss of any sense of self-worth. All kinds of people become new creations by the power of God.

Thousands of people wrote to me during and after the Clarence Thomas–Anita Hill hearing. Most letters supported Clarence, and those in opposition were almost all of one kind, from women who told me of their own horrible experiences with sexual harassment. They,

too, saw the Thomas confirmation in the light of their own life histo-
ries. I believe that, for them, Clarence Thomas was a stand-in for men
who abuse women. If so, he quite literally bore the sins of others.

The passion narratives of all the Gospels say that when the crowd
came to arrest Jesus, a bystander (identified by John as Peter) took a
sword and cut off the ear of the high priest's slave.[2] It was a spirited
but stupid and obviously futile act, contributing nothing to the great
work that was taking place. Reflecting on my own activities on the
Sunday and Monday of Columbus Day weekend, 1991, I think of Peter and his sword.

I conducted the interviews that became the substance of this book in
late 1991 and early 1992. I am grateful for the time and candor of the
following people who spoke with me: Clarence and Ginni Thomas,
Sally Danforth, Ken Duberstein, Mike Luttig, Lee Liberman, Mark
Paoletta, Steven and Elizabeth Law, Kay James, Diane Holt, Ricky
and Larry Silberman, Nancy Altman, Janet Brown, Allen Moore, John
Bliss, Larry Thompson, Hank Brown, Orrin Hatch, Arlen Specter,
Alan Simpson, Rob McDonald, Jon Chambers, Peter Leibold, Steve
Hilton, Dick Leon, and John Mackey.

In addition, I am grateful to Joe Biden for sharing with me his own
memories of the events described in this book. At times, there were
differences between Joe's intentions and the interpretations of Clarence and his supporters. I have described those differences in the
Notes.

Contents

Resurrection

The Agony of Summer

The ordeal of Clarence Thomas began on the afternoon of June 27, 1991, the day Thurgood Marshall announced his retirement from the U.S. Supreme Court. The U.S. Court of Appeals for the District of Columbia had completed its session, and Clarence had returned to his chambers after a late lunch with his former law clerk, Chris Landau. Just before his luncheon appointment, he had gone to a mall with his son, Jamal, to buy training shoes for him. After an interesting and demanding year on the court of appeals, the new judge was looking forward to a leisurely summer.

On his return to the courthouse, one of his clerks told him that Justice Marshall had announced his retirement, and White House legal counsel Boyden Gray had phoned to ask him to come to the Justice Department at 4:30. That meeting was attended by Attorney General Richard Thornburgh, Gray, and Michael Luttig, the assistant attorney general in charge of the Office of Legal Counsel.

Luttig was thirty-seven years old, but his small stature and fair hair made him look younger. He was brilliant and held the most intellectually challenging job at the Justice Department. Despite his age, he had been nominated by President Bush for the U.S. Court of Appeals for the Fourth Circuit. Having worked on the nominations of Justices Sandra Day O'Connor and David Souter, he was asked by the White House and the attorney general to take responsibility for helping the next nominee prepare for his Senate confirmation hearing, even though this would mean that Luttig would have to delay taking his place on the court of appeals beyond his own July 31 confirmation date.

Clarence did not want to be nominated to the Supreme Court. He had already gone through four confirmation hearings: one for assistant secretary of education, one for each term as chairman of the Equal Employment Opportunity Commission (EEOC), and one for the court of appeals. He had served for eight years in very controversial jobs in controversial administrations, and he knew that there were people within the civil rights leadership who took strong exception to his opposition to race-based affirmative action programs. He believed that a Supreme Court confirmation would be "at least a replay of what I went through to get on the court of appeals," and that ordeal, while mild compared to what he would experience, was bad enough. Clarence doubted whether he had the constitution to go through it again. Moreover, he enjoyed the work and the quiet of the court of appeals. In his words, after a year on that court, he "was just beginning to regain a positive outlook on life."

The meeting in the attorney general's office lasted perhaps forty-five minutes. Its purpose was not to discuss the candidate's jurisprudence, since the administration was generally familiar with the positions Clarence had taken in writings and speeches, but to expose any personal problems or experiences that could prove embarrassing. As he recalls, the inquiry covered marijuana use, which was already mentioned in Clarence's existing FBI file, and his divorce from his first wife, Kathy.

None of these specifics, or any other facts known to him, caused any concern to Clarence or his questioners. His fear was not the known but the unknown. He remembers wondering, "What could they cook up against me? How could they blow something out of proportion against me?" Most of all, he was concerned about how his work at EEOC could be used against him. He recalled that he had made "hundreds of decisions [at EEOC] and actually thousands over my tenure. What were they going to find when they go through papers? Was there one policy dispute? Was there one person you fired? Was there one case that you voted the wrong way on? I thought they were going to dredge up all of the age stuff again." The "age stuff" referred to charges made while Clarence was a nominee for the court of appeals that he had been responsible while chairman of EEOC for allowing age discrimination cases to lapse beyond the statute of limitations.

According to Mike Luttig's recollection of the meeting in the attorney general's office, Clarence was "scared." Clarence told Luttig that he knew from his prior confirmations that his nomination would be controversial; there were a number of potential opponents who would stop at nothing to get at him personally. He knew that he was a rarity, a black conservative and, therefore, anathema to liberals who believed blacks to be their special cause. But what made him abhorrent to liberals was precisely what appealed to a conservative president. The Bush administration was well aware of the likelihood of controversy and, in Luttig's words, "expected what we got, up to the Anita Hill story." At no time prior to the nomination did Anita Hill's name enter into Clarence's discussion with the administration, and at no time did Anita Hill cross his mind. "That wasn't even on the charts," noted Clarence later.

The White House counsel's office assigned Mark Paoletta, one of its young lawyers, to the Thomas confirmation. Mark had worked on Clarence's court of appeals confirmation and had developed enduring respect and affection for the nominee. In preparation for the work ahead, Mark immediately began poring over Clarence's opinions and many of his speeches. He knew there would be a fight over the Supreme Court nomination but never anticipated the events that followed or the ferocity of the opposition. He had noted the opposition of liberal interest groups to the court of appeals nomination and was surprised that they had not made more of a fight at that time. What concerned him now were newspaper stories he remembered in which people were reported to have said, "That's just the D.C. Circuit. If he ever goes up to the Supreme Court, we are going to get him."

Because Clarence had been confirmed by the Senate on four previous occasions and therefore had been subjected to four previous background checks by the FBI, Mark was reasonably confident that there was nothing in his personal life that would cause difficulty. The problem would not be Clarence's actions, he thought, but his words. He had made speeches—many of them—as chairman of the EEOC and as a conservative black in the Reagan administration. The speeches contained rhetorical flourishes that may have served as good applause lines for Republican audiences but would seem excessive to the media and to Democratic senators. In fact, one of the favorite targets in Clarence's speeches was Congress, and it struck Mark that these remarks would be used against Clarence in the confirmation process.[3]

Early on the morning of June 28, 1991, Vice President Dan Quayle telephoned me at my house in Washington, D.C. He was about to go to a meeting to discuss possible replacements for retiring Supreme Court justice Thurgood Marshall and had one question to ask me: How far would I go in supporting the nomination of Clarence Thomas? My answer was instantaneous: I would go at least as far as Senator Warren Rudman had in supporting David Souter.

Rudman, a good friend and a highly regarded senator from New Hampshire, had set the standard for all-out support for a nominee the year before. He was a close personal friend of Souter, who had been his deputy and then successor as attorney general of New Hampshire. Rudman not only lent his own stature to the Souter nomination; he personally escorted Souter on visits to the offices of individual senators. To make a similar effort on behalf of Clarence Thomas would require a major commitment of time and of whatever standing I had in the Senate, for this was certain to be a controversial nomination if the president made it. I did not hesitate a second. That I would give this everything I had was the promise I made to the vice president.

My support for Clarence Thomas had nothing to do with Clarence the judge; it had everything to do with Clarence the person. I assumed that President Bush could nominate any number of qualified individuals who would share his conservative views on the role of the Supreme Court. I also assumed that there were many people more experienced and with better legal ability than Clarence. Certainly Clarence was intelligent enough to do the work of the Supreme Court, but he had served only a short time on the court of appeals, and most of his professional experience was not in the practice of law but in administering—the EEOC, and, before that, the Office of Civil Rights in the Department of Education.

Philosophically, Clarence was more conservative than I, especially in his strongly held view that affirmative action was not the way to achieve racial equality. But I did not think his political philosophy should be relevant to his nomination. Clarence espoused judicial restraint: the idea that a judge should apply the law and not use the court to further his or her own philosophical cause. I was confident that Clarence would not misuse the power of his office.

Clarence embodied the American dream: he had ascended from humble origins in Pinpoint, Georgia. But when I received the call from the vice president on June 28, it was no American dream that prompted my response. I had not known Clarence in Pinpoint, Georgia, and had not seen him endure deprivations during his youth. I first met him in the law school faculty lounge when he was a third-year law student at Yale, interviewing for a position in the Missouri attorney general's office. I promised him more work and less pay than anyone else in his class, and he has often reminded me that I was true to my word. He came to Jefferson City and did the work of my office and did it well. For me, Clarence Thomas was no idealized dream of rags to riches; he was a person whom I got to know seventeen years before his nomination and whom I had known ever since: in Jefferson City, as an assistant in my Senate office, as an official in the executive branch, and as a judge on the court of appeals. It was not the legend of Clarence Thomas, the poor kid from Pinpoint, that inspired my loyalty. It was the reality of Clarence Thomas here and now.

We all have people whose lives are intertwined with our own. We know them and love them for who they are, not for their political views or for the stories of their lives, however interesting. Clarence's life has been intertwined with mine. I know him and love him for who he is. That is why I answered the vice president's call without a pause and without a doubt.

The picture of the Clarence Thomas I know comes to me in flashbacks, not in biographical detail. It is Jefferson City on Christmas Eve 1974. Clarence's wife and son are away with her family, and I learn that he is alone in a new town. I ask him to our home for our family dinner. He declines. I press the invitation. Again, he declines. He thinks I am feeling sorry for him and does not want to be an object of pity. But I am the boss who will not take no for an answer. Finally, grudgingly, he relents and arrives at our home for Christmas turkey, still insisting that he does not want us to feel sorry for him. He can take care of himself. He is proud but warm.

It is the spring of 1990, and Clarence has just taken his place on the U.S. Court of Appeals for the District of Columbia. I am standing outside my office door, looking down the long corridor at a silhouetted figure pushing a cart that is used to deliver government papers to Senate offices. It is Robert Foster, the black employee of the Senate Commerce Committee responsible for office deliveries. Walking slowly beside Robert as he pushes his cart, engaged in animated and obviously friendly conversation, is the newest member of the second highest court of the land, making personal delivery to me of a photograph of his swearing-in ceremony.

It is Joe Biden's Russell Building Office immediately after Clarence's nomination to the Supreme Court. After courtesy calls on the majority and minority leaders of the Senate, it is the first of some sixty office visits Clarence will make, and it is a media spectacle. Senator Biden, chairman of the Judiciary Committee, leads Clarence to the side of the room. The door is opened, and one wave after another of television cameras pushes through. Joe Biden, always friendly and talkative, tries his best to make Clarence feel at ease, but Clarence does not know where to look or what to say. Somehow Robert Foster has come in with the media, and Clarence spots him in the crowd. Clarence erupts into his booming laugh, as though neither Senator Biden nor any reporter was in the room. "There's Robert," he shouts. "Hi, Robert!"

It is 1986, and Clarence has been nominated by President Reagan for a second term as EEOC chairman. We are walking across the parking area immediately in front of the Senate steps of the Capitol. Clarence is expecting a grueling confirmation process, especially at the hands of Senator John Melcher, who has been vociferous in complaining about the lapsing of age discrimination cases during the Thomas chairmanship. I ask Clarence why he allowed himself to be renominated for a job he never wanted in the first place and which had become a battleground of controversy. He replies, "Because I have to finish the job."

Proud but warm, exuberant but seriously committed to his job, there is nothing mean or petty about him. When he worked on my staff, first in Jefferson City and then in Washington, he delighted in speaking his mind and taking strong positions, yet he did not speak with anger, only with intensity and spirit. He was clearly the most popular person in the office. People loved him, and the people who loved him stood with him throughout his agony.

To the world, he was the poor black from Pinpoint who made good, or perhaps the conservative ideologue who would sit on the Supreme Court. To the little people in the corridors of the Senate or the courthouse—those who pushed the carts or guarded the doors—he was the one who knew their names.

On Monday, July 1, Clarence Thomas flew to Kennebunkport, Maine, where President Bush offered to nominate him to the U.S. Supreme Court. Clarence confirms what the president has said: no litmus test was administered, and no promises were asked for or made on the subjects that might come before the Court, including abortion.

If Clarence was "scared" about the confirmation fight as Mike Luttig has reported, if he thought his opponents would stop at nothing to destroy him, and if he was content with his service on the court of appeals, why did he accept the president's nomination? He had every right to decline the offer. Why did he not do so? That is a question he has asked himself, and here is how he answers it: "There is a lot that I didn't want to do. I didn't want to be reconfirmed for EEOC. I didn't want to go to EEOC. But sometimes you are called upon to do things that you don't want to do." Reflecting on the trip to Kennebunkport, Clarence refers to Jesus in the Garden of Gethsemane: "I always think I would like this cup to pass away; that it is not my will but God's that will be done. If the president asks you to be on the Supreme Court, you do not say no. You have an obligation to your country. If you think you can make a contribution, when the president calls, you say, 'Yes.' . . . It wasn't a matter of, 'Yes, I'm dying to do it. This is something I have wanted to do all my life.' It was, 'Yes. This is an honor, and it's a way that I can make a major contribution to my country.' But . . . I was not overwhelmed by the possibility of doing this work on the Supreme Court. Indeed, I never focused on it. I was petrified by having to go through the confirmation process and having to live through threats and having to live through people who are poring through files and documents with no purpose other than to destroy you as a person."

At dinnertime on July 1, after Clarence's return from Kennebunkport, I used the telephone in the Shrine Club of Kirksville, Missouri, to congratulate my friend. I recall both his expression of honor at his nomination and his concern about the ferocity of the opposition that would surely be mounted against him. I suggested that he read the twelfth chapter of the Epistle to the Romans: "Repay no one evil for evil, but take thought for what is noble in the sight of all. . . . Never avenge yourself, but leave it to the wrath of God. . . . If your enemy is hungry, feed him; if he is thirsty, give him drink."

Excellent advice for the new, frightened nominee. I was not able to follow it myself.

Shortly after the president announced the nomination, Mark Paoletta was on the telephone serving as the contact between the White House and people who had known Clarence. In his words, "It is really amazing how many people Clarence Thomas knew and how many people liked and loved him and were willing to help out. These were people who knew him long ago in the EEOC days, college friends, law school friends, people from all different walks of life, political persuasions—whoever knew him loved him."

Mark maintained a Rolodex of hundreds of people from Clarence's past. Typically callers would say that they had been referred to Mark by another Thomas friend, that they had read something about Clarence, and that they wanted to set the record straight. Some wanted to write letters; some offered to testify. When I asked Mark how many character witnesses he could have produced for Clarence he replied: "I would say every single person I talked to, hundreds. We could have had a hearing for three weeks of parading people up giving five-minute statements of Clarence Thomas that would all be laudatory."

Anticipating a difficult struggle, the White House chose the best person they could find to take principal responsibility for the Thomas confirmation: Ken Duberstein. This was the second time the Bush White House had turned to Ken to shepherd a Supreme Court nominee through Senate confirmation. His initial experience was with David Souter, a much easier case. I was delighted that Ken would be helping Clarence. I had known him for several years in a number of capacities: he was a respected Washington lobbyist, and he had served as White House chief of staff in the Reagan administration. I admired his ability and his strategic judgment. More than that, I like him. Ken can be funny and personable, but he is also straightforward and tough-minded. He does not hesitate to say exactly what he thinks and can be quite insistent, especially when asking for even greater commitments of time from his teammates. Throughout the summer, it seemed that Ken was always phoning me, always asking that I add one more senator to my list of calls or that I issue one more statement on behalf of Clarence.

On the afternoon of July 2, I was sitting on a bench using a pay telephone fixed to the exterior wall of a supermarket in Rolla, Missouri, while my wife, Sally, was buying groceries. It was my first conversation with Ken about the confirmation, and he was telling me that during the next months, Clarence Thomas would demand most of my time. Within days, Ken began to prove his point.

Beginning shortly after his nomination on July 1, Clarence Thomas had the strong feeling that someone was trying to kill him. His description of his fears resembles an extended nightmare or perhaps a scene from a movie thriller. By his account, "The feeling is as though you're waiting in the wilderness for someone with guns to find you and kill you. And that's the way I felt all summer. I felt under siege the entire summer."

The small town house the Thomases then owned in suburban northern Virginia had a tiny grass yard and a patio, and it was hemmed in by similar homes in the large development. Clarence spent most of the summer, especially August and early September, in his home, preparing for intensive questioning on the law in his confirmation hearing. He recalls peering through his window at the decks of surrounding houses to see if there was anyone there who was trying to kill him.

This fear of being stalked and murdered may seem paranoid unless we consider the context. Concern for physical survival was not new to a black male raised in the rural Georgia of the 1950s and 1960s. As a child, he heard terrifying tales of black men who had been abducted and thrown into the swamps, where their bodies were consumed by crabs. He remembers riding in a car when he was a boy and seeing a billboard that said, "The United Klans of America Welcomes You to North Carolina," and he knew the dangers of straying from the interstates onto rural roads. While he was in law school, continued concern for his childhood fears led him to literature on lynchings of southern blacks.

With this lifelong concern about the physical danger of black males, Clarence watched on television a press conference at which Florence Kennedy of the National Organization for Women said, "We're going to Bork him. We're going to kill him politically—this little creep. Where did he come from?"[4] Soon after hearing this statement, he imposed one restriction on himself to help him deal with the attacks he knew would come: he refused to read newspapers or watch television news. The process ahead would be hard enough without reading or hearing every negative or threatening thing said about him.

We could fault Clarence Thomas for confusing the Florence Kennedy threat to "Bork" or to "kill him politically" with a threat of physical violence. The meaning of the verb *to Bork* was well known to Clarence. It referred to the campaign that defeated Judge Robert Bork's Supreme Court nomination in 1987. To Clarence, *to Bork* meant the relentless effort by interest groups to wage a political campaign against a nominee, creating a grotesque image of the person in order to build public pressure by alarmed constituents on senators who would vote on the nomination. The campaign against Bork, waged in mass mailings, full-page newspaper ads, and television commercials, had nothing to do with the threat of physical violence. It did have to do with a concerted effort to destroy the reputation of the nominee.

In Clarence's description of his own state, physical death and destruction of his reputation are not clearly differentiated.[5] He recounts his fears from early July in these words: "These people are going to try to kill me. I hadn't done anything to them, but they are going to try to kill me. And so I was always waiting to be killed. I mean literally waiting to be destroyed in some way."

The attacks began the day after President Bush announced the nomination, on Tuesday, July 2. On that day, the delegates to the General

Synod of the United Church of Christ voted to denounce Clarence as a "severe opponent of civil rights and human rights." Later in the day, Kate Michelman, executive director of the National Abortion Rights Action League, held a news conference attacking Clarence for his alleged "opposition to privacy and the right to choose abortion."[6]

Mike Luttig remembers that in July, there was what he calls a "quasi crisis a day" as Clarence's opponents gave stories to the press, who immediately turned to the White House for confirmation or denial of everything or anything they heard.

Years earlier, Clarence had made speeches that referred favorably to Louis Farrakhan, the militant black leader of the Nation of Islam, now well known for his diatribes against Jews.[7] Was it true that Clarence was antisemitic?

Clarence had made various speeches in which he referred to "natural law." Natural law theory was a long-abandoned branch of jurisprudence that had been used by ultraconservative judges to strike down governmental regulation. Clarence's use of the phrase "natural law" might put him in the camp of extreme reactionaries.[8] Was this Clarence's legal philosophy as well?

As a judge, Clarence had decided a case involving Ralston Purina Company.[9] Since I was a friend of Clarence's and I held stock in Ralston Purina, was this unethical judicial behavior?

Clarence was reported to have made a cruel comment about his sister's being on welfare.[10] Was he heartless?

It was charged that Clarence had beaten his first wife. Had he?

Clarence belonged to a conservative church in which people speak in tongues.[11] Was this true?

Had Clarence claimed 4-F status to avoid the draft?

Did Clarence keep a Confederate flag in his office in Jefferson City?

While in law school, had Clarence watched pornographic movies?

While a youth, had Clarence tried marijuana?

And on, and on, and on.

It is a maxim of modern politics that if charges are not answered, they stick. Ken Duberstein and I believed that the maxim applied to the Thomas confirmation. If there was an answer, it should be given quickly, and to each charge, with the exception of the last two listed above (which we thought should be dismissed as the indiscretions of youth), there was an answer, and we did our best to provide it quickly:

At the time of Clarence's speeches, neither he nor the general public were aware of Louis Farrakhan's antisemitism. Clarence was referring to Farrakhan's encouragement of self-help for blacks.

Clarence's reference to natural law was that its principle that "all men are created equal" is embodied in the Declaration of Independence, predates the Constitution, and should have formed the basis of the great civil rights case *Brown* v. *Board of Education,* holding that racially separate facilities cannot be equal.

I had never heard of the Ralston Purina case before it was decided, and I had no interest in its outcome. When this issue arose in connection with the confirmation, we asked the opinion of two experts on judicial ethics, who told us there was no violation of ethical standards.[12]

Clarence had not made a public criticism of his sister and flew to Georgia to apologize to her when a reporter's story on Clarence's conversational remarks was published.

The father of Clarence's first wife answered numerous calls from the media with the assurance that Clarence did not beat his daughter.

Clarence attends an Episcopal congregation with a pro-life tradition. He does not speak in tongues.

Clarence received a draft notice, appeared for his physical examination, and failed the physical.

The flag in Clarence's office in Jefferson City was of Georgia, his native state, not the Confederacy.

The problem was how to get the responses to these petty and mean-spirited accusations to the media without Clarence's doing so personally. Since the day of his nomination, Clarence had refrained from saying more than one-sentence pleasantries to the media. He and Ken

Duberstein believed that any statements should be made directly to senators who would vote on his confirmation, either in personal courtesy calls in their office or in testimony before the Judiciary Committee, and that he should not embark on what could be an endless process of fielding media questions. On the other hand, responses were necessary. For example, the suggestion that he had embraced the antisemitism of Louis Farrakhan was so outrageous and so potentially damaging to Clarence that it could not go unanswered. The solution was that I became Clarence's surrogate, getting his views in telephone conversations with him and then representing his views in the media.

This method of responding to attacks was used as well to condemn unwanted assistance from would-be allies. On September 3, two conservative organizations, the Conservative Victory Committee and Citizens United, began running television commercials that were vicious personal attacks on two Democratic members of the Judiciary Committee, Joe Biden and Ted Kennedy, and on a third senator, Alan Cranston of California. In addition, senators who were not members of the committee told me that they were being attacked by Thomas supporters in their state media.

These commercials were disastrous; as a practical matter, they could do the Thomas nomination nothing but harm. The goal of our effort was to win the support of Democratic senators, not insult them. Until he announced his opposition on September 27, Ken and I thought that there was a good chance that chairman Biden would support the nomination. I was trying to convince Democrats to vote for Clarence Thomas until the time of the vote. If ever there was an accurate use of the phrase "With friends like these, who needs enemies?" it applied to the people who thought they were helping Clarence by attacking Democratic senators.

Clarence immediately and strongly expressed to me his abhorrence of these negative commercials, and I relayed these views to the media and to concerned senators.

Clarence's disdain for the negative commercials was far more than a pragmatic effort to disassociate himself from a blunder by conservative supporters. He made a point of raising the subject with me, even after the commercials had ceased being aired. He told me that what he called ad hominem attacks were wrong in principle and could not be condoned. If personal attacks were wrong against a nominee, so they were wrong in support of a nominee. This was more than a position stated with the intention that it be relayed to the press. This was a view stated strongly in personal, entirely off-the-record discussions Clarence had with me. The confirmation process had gone sour not simply because it had hurt Clarence Thomas but because hurting people on both sides of the issue became standard procedure. Clarence was deeply hurt by the confirmation process. He was also acutely sensitive to the hurt suffered by others.

As the attacks against Clarence mounted in early July, Ginni Thomas became concerned about their effect on her husband, to the point of worrying about his health. She recalls that he was "devastated" as each charge was made and convinced that his opponents were trying to destroy him. Each day, she and Clarence went to the Justice Department for meetings with Mike Luttig, Mark Paoletta, and Lee Liberman, deputy White House counsel and the niece and namesake of a friend of mine from St. Louis. Each night the couple would review in their home the allegation of the day. Ginni recalls that Clarence took each charge personally; each one was affecting him in a deeper and more personal way than she expected. She confirms that from the first days in July, Clarence believed that his opponents were trying to destroy him. With each charge, he would ask, "Why are they attacking me?"

Mike Luttig, who met with Clarence daily during July and August, describes him as "a man who truly treasures his privacy" and was progressively "stunned" by the personal nature of the inquiries and attacks. According to Mike, during the first weeks of July, Clarence "felt violated, and he used that term. He would feel violated at having to respond to these questions."

In an effort to prevent Clarence from becoming consumed by his offense at the stories circulated about him, Mike tried to persuade him that he was experiencing not a personal attack but a political debate and that no one cared about Clarence per se. Clarence refused to accept this interpretation and told Mike, "You just don't understand. These people are after me personally." In his interview with me, here is how he described his experience in the summer of 1991:

"[The attacks] were immediate. The attacks did nothing but make clear my foreboding. . . . It was like I was about to die. . . . I don't know if you have ever been close to a very bad accident and you have this flash of your whole life before you. . . . The whole summer was like a rerun of my life backwards and forward, freeze frame—forward; reverse. I mean everything was like that, and I was scared to death. I was frightened and I wanted to go home.

"I wanted to go back to Pinpoint. I wanted to go back to a simple life. I didn't want to be on the Supreme Court. I wanted my name. I wanted to go to . . . Hechinger's [a Washington hardware store]. . . . I loved to go to Hechinger's. I wanted to go for walks with my wife. I wanted to go to the movies with my wife. I wanted to go toss a football with my son. I wanted to go out and wash my car and then pull it back in the garage; go down the street and chat with my neighbors. I just wanted to go back to my life. That's all I wanted."

Reflecting on the accusations of early July, Clarence recalls, "My question was, What are they going to accuse me of next? I just agonized over it all summer. It's sort of like Herr K. in Kafka's *The Trial*. It is a terrifying experience."

Clarence was as uncertain about the identity of his accusers as he was about the nature of the accusations. Both he and I were convinced that various groups were working hard to defeat him, but we had no first-hand knowledge of who they were or how they were operating.[13] At the outset of the confirmation process, he thought that the same groups that opposed him for the court of appeals would lead this new campaign. He particularly expected that a civil rights organization founded by Norman Lear, People for the American Way, and the Alliance for Justice, a liberal group that targeted conservative judicial nominees, would be especially active in the opposition.

With this in mind, Clarence attempted in July and August to mollify the black leadership of the civil rights movement. His hope was that he could win their support, or at least reduce the intensity of their opposition, by a series of face-to-face meetings. Perhaps he could persuade them that although they would not have chosen him themselves, they could have done worse at the hands of a Republican president.

At the suggestion of black friends, Clarence attended small meetings with members of the NAACP board, with the NAACP Legal Defense Fund, and with the Southern Christian Leadership Conference. He met with black leaders from Alabama at the request of Senator Howell Heflin, a Democratic member of the Judiciary Committee, and with black leaders from South Carolina at the request of Senator Fritz Hollings.

Despite his willingness to meet with black leaders, substantial opposition did come from the civil rights organizations, especially after the unexpectedly strong and early action taken by the Congressional Black Caucus in July. That the caucus, with only its sole Republican, Gary Franks, supporting Clarence, came out against him served as a catalyst to opposition by black organizations.

Clarence did not anticipate or understand the opposition of the AFL-CIO. The widely held view among Clarence's supporters is that the AFL-CIO was responding to intense pressure from the Congressional Black Caucus, its most consistent ally in Congress, and that the AFL-CIO, in turn, put pressure on the board of the NAACP.

Most surprising to Clarence was the extent of animosity and the energetic involvement of women's organizations.[14] He believed that he had a good record of working with women's groups, especially in advocating their position on Title IX, which applies to sex discrimination in education, while he was assistant secretary of education. While chairman of EEOC, he supported litigation against sexual harassment,[15] and he had promoted women to top positions at the commission.[16] Although he had been a part of the Reagan administration that had opposed women's groups on comparable worth,[17] he felt that he had been a champion of women's issues.

Clarence knew that women's groups were riveted to a single issue sure to come before the Supreme Court in the immediate future: the fate of *Roe* v. *Wade,* the 1973 abortion decision. As a new justice, Clarence Thomas could prove to be the decisive vote on the subject they cared about most. They did not want a likely vote for overruling *Roe* v. *Wade* added to the Court.

Clarence would have understood the opposition of women's groups if he had a position on *Roe* v. *Wade.* In fact, he did not have a position, yet throughout the confirmation process, his opponents insisted that this could not be the case.[18] Surely everyone had a position on *Roe* v. *Wade,* and anyone who claimed the contrary must be a fool or a liar. Repeatedly, though, Clarence stood by his statement: he had not pre-judged and would not prejudge that issue.

Neither the Bush administration nor I had any knowledge of how Clarence would decide an abortion case. Speaking of the administration, Mike Luttig said, "We had no earthly idea how he would vote on *Roe* v. *Wade.* The issue was never broached at any time prior to the nomination, and at no time since has it been broached." Regardless, women's groups were convinced that Clarence Thomas must have had an opinion of the law of abortion, and this conviction sufficed to justify any means to defeat his confirmation.

Clarence did not anticipate that charges would be made by Anita Hill.

Mike Luttig recalls a day in July when he and one of his Justice Department assistants were at the Thomas house preparing Clarence for the confirmation process. During a discussion of a staffing matter at EEOC, Clarence mentioned the name Anita Hill. Looking ahead to the Judiciary Committee hearing, Mike was alert to names of people whom the administration could ask to appear before the committee on Clarence's behalf, and he asked Clarence whether they should contact Hill for that purpose. Clarence said that he would not necessarily think of Hill as a witness. Luttig asked, "Well, would she be a positive witness on your behalf?" Clarence responded, "I have every reason to think so." After the Anita Hill story broke, Mike asked his assistant whether there was any tinge of concern in Clarence's voice when Hill's name came up. In Luttig's words, "He and I both agreed that there was none whatsoever, just absolutely none. It was as if I had asked about a colleague or almost a friend, and he had no reservations at all about us contacting her or anything else."

A similar discussion took place with Lee Liberman of the White House. Liberman mentioned Anita Hill as a black law professor whom the administration might invite as a pro-Thomas witness before the Judiciary Committee. Again, Clarence expressed no concern about Anita Hill's testifying before the committee. Liberman places this conversation in early September, because she remembers reading a *Washington Post* article the following day that quoted Hill as criticizing Clarence for lacking sympathy for his sister on welfare, and on that basis Liberman struck Hill from the list of pro-Thomas witnesses.[19]

Similarly, both Clarence and Diane Holt recall a telephone conversation they had well before the Anita hill story broke. Neither is certain about the time of the call—late July, or August, or maybe September—but they agree on what was said. Holt, who continued at EEOC after Clarence went to the court of appeals, had been Clarence's personal secretary at both the Department of Education and EEOC. During the telephone call, Holt told Clarence of a conversation she had had with Dave Kyllo, a congressional liaison official at EEOC. Kyllo mentioned to Holt a rumor he had picked up on Capitol Hill that Anita Hill was being checked out as a credible witness against Clarence. Holt told Clarence that she assured Kyllo there was nothing to worry about with respect to Anita Hill, and in their call both Holt and Clarence agreed that there was no reason to be concerned.

Throughout July and until the Senate's summer recess that began in early August, Clarence Thomas and I together visited more than half the members of the Senate in their offices. Without exception, the senators were courteous to Clarence, and I was impressed by his candor and skill in responding to their questions.

From the outset of the confirmation process, Ken Duberstein was interested in the public image that Clarence projected. Ken recalls his first visit with Clarence on July 2 or 3, when he told Clarence that he would be speaking not to the fourteen senators who were members of the Judiciary Committee but to the American people. As Clarence walked past banks of cameras, Ken would say, "Give them a thumbs up," and Clarence would comply. When advising Clarence not to respond to press questions, Ken suggested, "Tell them, 'I wish I could answer that.'" Ken was aware of a Washington pilgrimage of Pinpoint residents to show their support of Clarence, clearly a media event designed to show that if Clarence lacked the support of the civil rights leadership, he had the support of the folks back home. He told Clarence that when he entered the Senate Caucus Room at the start of his first hearing, he should go up to the committee table and shake hands with each member. He insisted that Clarence, against his will, conclude the first hearing by complimenting the committee for being fair.

Ken never confused advice on matters of style with coaching on matters of substance, however. He made no effort to change Clarence's views to please the Senate or the public. In late August and early September, when Clarence was grilled in a mock committee setting and critiqued for his answers (a series referred to as the "murder board" proceedings), Ken began each session laying out the ground rules for the meeting. They were that those of us in attendance—Ken, Mike Luttig, White House lobbyist Fred McClure, myself, and a few lawyers—were not to try to change Clarence's mind on matters of substance. We were there to critique the form, not the content, of Clarence's answers and to make sure he did not hear questions for the first time when he appeared before the Judiciary Committee.

From the date of the president's announcement, I believed that the committee hearing would resemble a very long bar examination administered on nationwide television by fourteen senators over a period of about three days. In fact, Clarence testified for almost twenty-five hours over five days.[20] Mark Paoletta thinks that his September appearance alone was the longest testimony in the history of Supreme Court confirmations.

Unlike many other Supreme Court nominees, Clarence had not served long on a lower court. He had been on the court of appeals for slightly more than a year, and for nearly a decade before that he had not practiced law at all. It seemed to me that because of his brief history as a lawyer and judge, Clarence's first challenge was to get a "qualified" rating by the American Bar Association.[21] I thought as well that senators seeking to defeat him would keep him before the committee for a prolonged period of time, peppering him with difficult questions in an effort to show that he did not know enough law to serve on the highest court in the land.

I was particularly concerned that Clarence would not have enough time to study in preparation for the hearing and expressed this concern forcefully and repeatedly to Ken Duberstein. The hearing would begin soon after Labor Day, and July was consumed by courtesy calls on individual senators, responding to accusations made against him, and trying to persuade civil rights groups that he should be acceptable to them. As Clarence expressed it, trying to study that summer was like trying to concentrate "with bullets going over your head."

Mike Luttig, who was responsible for Clarence's preparation for the hearing, became alarmed that the politicking of the confirmation process was eating into study time. Three or four weeks had passed, and preparation for the hearing had not begun. Then the committee's request for documents arrived. In Luttig's words, "When we got the document requests, it was just staggering. No human being within a relatively short period of time could have complied with it." According to Luttig, one request "called for basically every document at the EEOC" for the period of Clarence's chairmanship.[22]

Study for the hearing did not begin in earnest until after Congress recessed in early August. Seven days a week, the routine was the same. Mike Luttig gave Clarence large notebooks, each covering an area of the law. For example, there were two notebooks on the right to privacy, which includes the abortion issue. Each notebook contained the text of important cases and law review articles on the subject. The material was voluminous. Clarence got up between four and six o'clock every morning to begin reading the notebook of the day. Every afternoon, Clarence and Mike met for two to five hours, usually at Clarence's house. Mike, who had done his own preparation in the morning, asked Clarence questions—about court opinions, about dissents, even about footnotes to cases. To Mike, the process resembled a study group at law school. They discussed cases and clarified points of law.

In addition, Clarence had videotapes of the Souter confirmation hearings. If he could not sleep at night, he got out of bed and watched Souter tapes, taking extensive notes.

Mike was impressed both by Clarence's discipline in applying himself to the work and by the quality of his mind. "It is not a photographic mind, but it is a very good mind," he said later. When the murder board meetings commenced in late August, I too was impressed by Clarence's mastery of the subject matter. My concerns about his ability to handle legal questions at the confirmation hearing disappeared.

Having watched videotapes of the Souter hearing, Clarence understood the distinction between a general discussion on a point of law and a specific commitment to decide a case in a particular way. Souter had done a masterful job of discussing his views on matters of jurisprudence while refusing to prejudge cases he might have to decide on the Supreme Court. This distinction is not a matter of cowardice on the part of the nominee. It is not the prudent avoidance of sensitive issues that could lose the votes of senators should the nominee's true position be stated in a forthright manner. Instead, it is a distinction that is crucial to the independence of the judiciary. A nominee who has stated a position in advance of sitting on a case, in advance of reading the briefs and listening to the arguments of counsel, cannot be an independent jurist. His or her ruling on a case would have been promised in advance as part of the political bargain to win the support of those who have the power to vote on confirmation. In his tutorial sessions with Clarence, Mike Luttig understood what a nominee could not promise. Luttig believed that a nominee should be as forthcoming as possible in telling the committee how he or she felt as a person but refuse to take the further step of saying how he or she would rule as a judge.

In fact, Luttig himself did not know how Clarence would rule as a judge. In Mike's eyes, Clarence had been "much more of a political person than he was a judicial or a lawyer person" prior to going to the court of appeals. Civil rights was the only area in which Clarence had a clearly defined position.

A nominee has two risks in telling the Judiciary Committee that he or she does not have a position on an issue. The first is appearing ignorant of the law. A critic might say, "What do you mean you have no opinion on that issue? Everyone who has gone to law school has an opinion on that. If you have no opinion, then you must lack either the knowledge or the intellectual curiosity to serve on the Supreme Court. I will oppose you on the ground of incompetence." The second risk is that the nominee might appear to be dishonest. In this case, the critic would say, "I am sure that you have an opinion, because everyone has an opinion on this subject. Therefore, I conclude that you are being dishonest in not telling me your thoughts in a straightforward manner."

This was precisely the problem for Clarence with respect to *Roe* v. *Wade*. It did not seem credible for him to say that he had no position and that he had never debated the issue, but it was true. I agree with Ken Duberstein that Clarence's response to the committee on the *Roe* v. *Wade* issue is the best evidence that, contrary to the assertions of various critics, Clarence was not overmanaged. At a murder board meeting, Ken pressed Clarence on his answer that he had not even discussed the subject with Ginni. As Ken remembers the meeting: "I asked him directly about his views on abortion and *Roe* v. *Wade*. And he essentially gave us the same answer that he gave to the committee.

He didn't have a position on that. Yes, he had been at places where it was discussed, but, no, he had never stated a personal view. He said to the murder board that he had not even discussed it with his wife, and I remember several of us saying, 'Oh, come on!' And he said, 'No, I'm telling the truth.' If you and I had managed or overmanaged Clarence, we would have worked on that answer, but that would be wrong. And that wasn't the purpose of the murder board, and that wasn't the purpose of our work with Clarence. That was Clarence Thomas's answer, not skewed by Jack Danforth or Ken Duberstein."

Mike Luttig also wrestled with the inadequacy of Clarence's answer on *Roe* v. *Wade* while they were preparing for the hearing: "The truth was, as Clarence told us, he had never debated or discussed the issue. He just hadn't. Now just pause for a second and ask yourself, 'Okay. What did you do with that fact?' which doesn't sound great, but is the truth. What could you say to him? We couldn't say to him, 'Clarence, that is not credible. You've got to go in there and tell people you have discussed it.' "

Mike Luttig thinks that it is "curious" that people think that Clarence was coached too much for the hearing. Mike found Clarence "very headstrong." Although Clarence did not have a well-formed jurisprudence, Luttig has said that "he had his own views, and nobody tells Clarence anything."

Mike questioned Clarence for hours on the various areas of the law and pressed relentlessly on the implications of his answers. For example, when discussing the establishment clause,[23] Luttig believed that it was his job to see that whatever Clarence said was factually and legally correct and that he understood how the committee would interpret his answers and what follow-up questions might be asked. Mike would make sure that Clarence knew what the Supreme Court had said about the separation of church and state, and then he would press Clarence on whether his answer on the law was in any way contradicted by past statements he had made about his family and his upbringing in religious schools. In Mike's mind, there was a big difference between the appropriate pressing of Clarence to think about the implications of his answers and the inappropriate coaching of Clarence as to what positions he should take before the committee.

Mike's questioning of Clarence encompassed more than legal issues. Much more challenging was preparing Clarence to defend strong political statements he had made while at the Department of Education and EEOC. Immediately after the announcement of Clarence's nomination, Mike's office began a review of several boxes of speeches and soon realized that the speeches posed a serious threat to confirmation. Every day Luttig's staff came to him with a new statement that could be turned against Clarence at the hearing. In addition to the references to Louis Farrakhan, Mike remembers "speech after speech attacking Congress and mocking them . . . praising Ollie North and exposing Congress for what it is. . . . It was inconceivable to me that someone would have put in public speeches as much as he had. I have never seen that. I was amazed at everything he had in his speeches."

Ginni attributes the outspoken nature of the speeches Clarence made during his second term at EEOC to the view he had at that time of his own future. According to Ginni, Clarence believed that his period of public service would soon end and that he would reenter private life. With a forum from which to speak and with no ambition for future government service, Clarence was uninhibited in speaking his mind.

Mike Luttig used the same question-and-answer method with respect to the speeches that he used with respect to issues of law. "Now, Judge Thomas, you said that Congress is a bunch of buffoons and clowns. What do you mean by that? . . . So from this statement it is clear that Congress has no role in a democratic society. Right? . . . Well, what role do you think Congress plays?" Through this sort of questioning, Luttig would lead Clarence to restate the rhetorical excesses of the speeches in more moderate terms: "Yes, from time to time, I share the commonly expressed exasperation with the way Congress conducts itself. Yes, I have a profound respect for Congress as an institution. Of course, I do not mean that Congress has no role to play in a democratic society. Congress is the people. That's what democracy is."

As his mentor, Mike Luttig was concerned that Clarence not over-react to accusations made against him. Mike recalls that almost without exception, Clarence's initial reaction to a charge was to want to issue a responsive statement; Mike's counsel was to let others re-spond for him. Especially because Clarence was given to making strong statements, Luttig did not want him to be involved in verbal combat in public. Luttig the lawyer had a second reason for being cautious: any oversight or factual misstatement Clarence might make in a response, however slight, could later be challenged and used in an attack on his integrity. Mistakes could be made in rushed re-sponses, issued under pressure, to outrageous charges. It would be better to have someone else answer for the nominee. I was tapped to do this job.

Luttig explained to Clarence the perils of giving public voice to his anger at attacks. If Clarence were to say what he thought, the next criticism would be that he lacked judicial temperament. It would be better to say nothing at all in public and to be content taking out any hostility on Luttig himself. Luttig told Clarence, "Voice your anger to me, not to the public. Hit me with it. Just let me have it. Just take it all out on me."

Throughout the confirmation process, Luttig worried that Clarence's strong feelings and passion to speak out would hurt him. Always, Clarence's first reaction to a charge was shock and outrage. While Mike thought that an element of disbelief was good, he explained to Clarence the importance of internalizing his anger and appearing to take attacks in stride. In Mike's words, "I would occasionally hit him with something that at first blush would sound completely outrageous to get his reaction to it, because in law practice that is what we would do with one of our witnesses who was about to go on. You would hit them with something that was completely off the wall, and the idea would be that they would have to be able to internalize their own re-actions, because, if they lash out, that will cost them."

Reflecting on his weeks with Clarence, Mike has said: "From day one I did not think he should be as rough and aggressive as his in-stincts might otherwise lead him to be. You know, Clarence would love to take shots at Congress . . . and the committee . . . I understand that. It is lots of fun, but I did not think from a strategic matter that that was wise. So throughout the preparations, I was trying to smooth the edges of what in front of national television could be perceived as a rougher personality."

Clarence recalls that Luttig was not alone in urging him to restrain his instincts to make strong responses when under attack. He remembers advice given to him in one of the murder board meetings: "If they go after you, just remember to let your friends defend you. You try to keep your cool."

Clarence insists that he did not back away from his positions when he appeared before the Judiciary Committee for his first hearing. Instead, he believes that he stated his views but in a calm way. In a phrase similar to Luttig's, he speaks of "rounding off the edges," by which he means not being combative. In Clarence's words:

"I think the process forces the nominee to jump through hoops. It forces the nominee to play by a certain set of rules and so you've got to be bland. . . . You've got to round the edges out. It zaps you not of core honesty, but it zaps you of the fire in the belly. It says you can't have fire in the belly. If you do, you wind up getting skewered the way Bork did and you wind up being attacked for not having judicial temperament. It forces you to dilute the edges you've had on prior statements, the zeal with which you've pushed prior ideas. You have to take their pounding. You have to play sort of rope-a-dope. . . . You have to lay back and you have to take more than you normally would take. You have to avoid being confrontational. You have to avoid showing passion. You have to be thoughtful or you have to appear to be thoughtful. You can't have any ideas or you're being seen as again lacking judicial temperament, not being open-minded. But if you're open-minded, then you're too soft, you're too wishy-washy, you're maneuvering. In the hearing I played by the rules. And playing by those rules, the country had never seen the real person. There is an inherent dishonesty in the system. It says, don't be yourself. If you are yourself, like Bob Bork was, you're dead."

Larry Thompson, an old friend, watched the September hearing on television in Atlanta as Clarence played by the rules. Larry believed that his friend seemed too restrained, too reticent, and not forthright enough with some of his answers. Remembering their time in St. Louis and their long discussions then about the world and their lives, Larry reached his own conclusion about the proceedings. After the problems of Judge Bork and the success of Judge Souter, perhaps this is appropriately politic behavior in order to survive the hearing. But that's not Clarence, concluded Larry Thompson.

Death and Life

Wednesday, September 25

Deputy to the White House counsel Lee Liberman received a forewarning of the Anita Hill accusation nine days before her September 25 telephone call to Clarence Thomas. On September 16, Melissa Riley of Senator Strom Thurmond's staff had reported overhearing a conversation between Senator Biden and Judiciary Committee chief counsel Ron Klain. According to Liberman, the substance of the reported conversation was:

Klain: "She could testify behind a screen."

Biden: "That's ridiculous. You can't do that. This isn't the Soviet Union."

From this snippet of a reported conversation, Liberman believed that there was some kind of allegation floating around about Clarence but that it was not a big problem because Biden was not willing to turn it into something.

At midafternoon on September 23, Ken Duberstein took a call from Steve Hart, deputy assistant to the president for legislative affairs. Hart was on his way to the Capitol for a meeting with Jeff Peck of Senator Biden's staff and Duke Short of Senator Thurmond's staff. The subject of the meeting was a written allegation about Clarence Thomas that had been submitted to the Judiciary Committee. A short time later, Hart called Duberstein to report that he was returning from Jeff Peck's office and wanted to stop in. When he arrived at Duberstein's office, he had with him a four-page typewritten statement of Anita Hill. In it, Hill alleged that when she worked at the Department of Education and at EEOC, Clarence Thomas had made attempts to date her, which she rejected, and that he had made explicitly sexual remarks to her that included descriptions of pornographic material. Duberstein encouraged Hart to show the statement to Boyden Gray and others in the White House counsel's office immediately, and then he called me. My immediate reaction was that this charge was no more than the latest in a series of attempts to defeat the nomination and that it was wholly inconsistent with the character of Clarence Thomas.

Ken understood from Hart that the Judiciary Committee wanted an FBI investigation of the Hill allegation, and he expressed his confidence that Boyden Gray would want an FBI investigation as well. Ken's own view was that it was important for the investigation to be immediate and thorough, that all relevant questions be asked, and that the FBI report its findings to both the administration and the Judiciary Committee. The integrity of the FBI process required that when the FBI interviewed Clarence it tell him of the allegation without advance notice and that it would be inappropriate for anyone to contact Clarence before the FBI did. In accordance with this understanding, the first contact made with Clarence was Lee Liberman's telephone call two days later, and he did not know the nature of the charge until the FBI visited his home on September 25.

Lee Liberman returned from a meeting to her office in the Old Executive Office Building between three and four o'clock on Monday, September 23, to find a message from acting attorney general William Barr asking her to call him as soon as possible. When she returned the call, Barr asked her whether she had talked to the deputy counsel to the president, John Schmitz; when she answered in the negative, he advised her to go to Schmitz's office in the West Wing of the White House immediately. When she arrived, Schmitz showed her Anita Hill's written statement and then called Barr. In that phone call, it was agreed that the White House would transmit the Hill statement to the FBI with the request to do whatever investigation they believed necessary as soon as possible on a highest priority basis.

The White House counsel's office was not impressed with the Hill statement. Gray and Liberman, who examined it with lawyers' eyes for detail, viewed it as a last-minute political attempt to derail the nomination—the end of a long effort that Clarence's opponents commenced on July 1. In Liberman's phrase, the statement "just seemed cooked" and not something to be terribly concerned about, and this conclusion was shared by Boyden Gray. At the same time, they realized that politics was a different matter from the merits. The Hill statement, if leaked, could cause a significant problem.

Liberman dismissed the credibility of Hill's statement for a number of reasons:

- The statement surfaced ten years after the alleged occurrence and at the last minute in the confirmation process, when all efforts to defeat the nomination had failed.

- This was Clarence's third Senate confirmation hearing after the alleged events. Hill could have come forward at any of the previous hearings and did not do so.

- Hill claimed that she was harassed by Clarence at the Department of Education yet followed him to EEOC—a "very curious" reaction, thought Liberman. In her analysis, the opponents of Clarence Thomas "have not produced any example to this day of somebody who has brought a harassment claim where she says, 'I was harassed at Job A, and I nevertheless followed the guy who harassed me to Job B.' "

- According to Liberman, there was evidence of motive in that Hill described differences of opinion with Clarence on appropriate remedies in civil rights cases.

- Liberman was suspicious about the role of Hill's corroborating witness, Susan Hoerchner. On reading the FBI file, she believed that Hill's account of what happened was somewhat different from Hoerchner's. To Liberman, "It rather looked like what was happening was that Hoerchner had been pushing Hill to come forward about this thing in a way that suggested, to me at least, that Hoerchner was motivated by something other than friendship for Anita Hill. And so that made it look cooked up."

Liberman's appraisal was bolstered by her interpretation of the FBI's preliminary report to the White House after its interviews with Hill, Hoerchner, and other witnesses listed by Hill as being able to corroborate her story. While the FBI does not state conclusions about its investigations of presidential nominees, it does, according to Liberman, convey messages by what she calls "body language" and "intimation language." The intimation Liberman drew from the FBI's call before they interviewed Clarence was that they saw nothing new or surprising and that there was no reason to worry. In Liberman's words, "They do have ways of letting you know when they think you have got a problem. And they were not treating this as, 'You've got a problem.' They were treating this as, 'You have got a last-minute allegation.'"

At 9:45 A.M. on Wednesday, September 25, Lee Liberman phoned Clarence at his home to tell him that the White House had received another allegation about him and to give him a number to call to arrange for an FBI interview.

Clarence, who was alone at home, asked Liberman to tell him about the allegation, and she responded that she could not. He would have to find out about it from the FBI. On the basis of the "intimation language" of the FBI, Liberman tried to reassure Clarence. "Don't worry about it. Just answer it honestly and we will talk about it afterward," she recalls saying over the phone. Clarence describes his reaction to the call as "panic."

Clarence compares his feelings before Liberman's call to waiting for a
jury's verdict. He had finished his own testimony on Monday of the
previous week, September 16. On Friday, September 20, the day all
testimony of the remaining witnesses was completed, Clarence and
Ginni set off for a long weekend away from Washington. They drove
first to Annapolis, where Jamal played in a high school football game
at the Naval Academy. They stayed a night at a hotel on the Eastern
Shore of Maryland before taking a ferry to Cape May, New Jersey. After the long ordeal of the summer—grueling preparation, five days of
testimony, various charges made by the interest groups and media—
this was a welcome getaway. There was nothing more to do but wait.
Yet it was impossible to relax.

Within five minutes of Lee Liberman's call, Clarence phoned Mark
Paoletta, also in the White House counsel's office. Like Liberman,
Mark had discounted Hill's allegation when he learned of it on September 23, but he could not mention the story to Clarence. As he
described it to me later, "Here is a last-minute, eleventh-hour allegation. You could have expected something like this. . . . they were
getting desperate."

Clarence knew that Mark could not disclose the substance of the allegation, and Clarence did not ask. Mark describes the call in these words:
"I think he was calling because I was a friend of his that was working on
this thing. . . . There's only so many people you can call when this is
happening because nobody else knows about it—so we just talked. . . .
I could tell he was really upset, and I felt terrible that I couldn't tell him
what the allegation was. He seemed just at the end of his rope. He
seemed like he had been punched in the stomach in the solar plexus and
just didn't know what to do. He had made it this far and to have something like this. . . . You know, we saw victory. We saw the end line . . .
and to have something like this and not know what it was. . . . I couldn't
imagine going through that. He just seemed destroyed."

Next, Clarence called to arrange his interview with the FBI. Clarence describes his feelings while waiting: "I'm panicking. . . . Every fiber in my body is on edge. I don't know what it is. What are they going to accuse me of? Can I defend myself? Do I know who it is? The nature of the charge? I know nothing. I was just sick. I felt like throwing up."

At about 1:00 P.M. two agents, one male and one female, arrived at his home. Clarence opened the front door, and they identified themselves. Between the front door and the dining area table where the interview was conducted, the FBI agents informed Clarence that they had an allegation from Anita Hill. Anita? The name had only positive meanings in Clarence's mind. When they got to the table, the male agent explained, "There's an allegation of sexual harassment."[24] Clarence recalls responding, "You've got to be kidding me." He thought someone was trying to play "a terrible, terrible joke" on him. He describes himself as being in shock as the male agent began going through Anita Hill's statement. The statement spoke of pornography and animals but was not as graphic or detailed as her testimony before the Judiciary Committee would be. Clarence recalls telling the agents, "You've got to be kidding me. I never had any such conversation with Anita." Then the male agent reported that Hill said that Clarence had tried to date her. Clarence responded that he never tried to date her.

In Clarence's words, "This was sort of like my own child accusing me of something. I was hurt. . . . I could have cried, I was so hurt. Then I felt this was the kind of charge . . . she said–he said kind of charge . . . that I can't clear myself of."

As Clarence recalls the interview, the FBI led him through Hill's allegations, and he refuted each one. He told them that he was dating another woman at the time of the alleged incidents; that he had helped Hill get a job at Oral Roberts University; that Hill had maintained telephone contact with him after she left EEOC and that she provided transportation for him in her Peugeot when he visited Oral Roberts University. He told them that he had never dated any member of his staff, that he "preached against that, not only because of potential for sexual harassment but because it . . . could confuse relationships in the office." He said, "I also preached against any kind of conduct that would be suggestive of sexual harassment." He suggested that the FBI interview other people who had worked for him in order to confirm his attitude toward women in the workplace.

Clarence's sense that Hill's accusation was "like my own child accusing me" stems from the circumstances under which he employed her when he was assistant secretary for civil rights. Until he died in a tragic accident in 1989, Gil Hardy had been one of Clarence's closest friends. Also a black lawyer, Hardy was a partner of the Washington law firm of Wald, Harkrader and Ross. In 1981, Hardy asked Clarence to hire Anita Hill, who had been a young lawyer in the firm for less than a year. As Clarence remembers the substance of Hardy's request, Hill was not getting good work assignments because she was having personal problems with a partner in the firm. Clarence's memory of the matter, which he says is vague, is that Hardy told him, and Hill confirmed, that the partner wanted to have a personal relationship with her outside the office, that she refused, and that the partner responded by withholding good work assignments and giving her work bad reviews. Diane Holt, Clarence's secretary at both the Department of Education and EEOC, has a similarly vague recollection that at the time Hill came to work at the Department of Education either Clarence or Hill herself had said Hill had to leave the law firm because her boss was sexually harassing her.

Clarence has told me, "Gil Hardy must be rolling in his grave. Because, Jack, without his death, this would be impossible." Clarence remains convinced that if Anita Hill was sexually harassed, it was prior to her employment at the Department of Education or EEOC and that Hardy would have made this clear if he had lived. He believes that the initial story of Susan Hoerchner is significant because it places the time of Hill's claimed harassment as being before she went to work at the Department of Education in August 1981, when she was employed by Wald, Harkrader and Ross.

When Clarence hired Anita Hill, he thought that the account of her problem was a sympathetic story, but the story did not matter to him.

What was important was that his friend vouched for her, that she was a graduate of Yale Law School, and that he needed good people in his office.

Political appointments, so-called Schedule C appointments, are made on the basis of the political contacts of the applicant and are subject to termination with changes of administrations. Schedule A appointments are not made on the basis of partisanship. Schedule A employees are career people whose jobs do not come and go with the changing tides of politics. Clarence Thomas hired Anita Hill as a Schedule A attorney.

Clarence reasoned that, because Hill was not a conservative, he could not place her in a political job within the conservative Bush administration. Her liberal ideology was not cause for him to deny her employment, but it did mean that she should be hired for a professional rather than a partisan position. Thus, the Schedule A designation.

Hill was outspoken and argumentative. In Clarence's words, "She was certainly not a Republican. She was not part of the Reagan team. She was very critical of the president, critical of the administration, critical of me, critical of the people I hired. . . . Her problem essentially was that she could never get over her ideology. In a nutshell, that was her problem, that she saw everything through an ideological glass as opposed to analytical framework."

Clarence describes Hill as "an intelligent black woman" and "a decent person." He says, "She was a charge that Gil Hardy had asked me to look out for," and "I felt a special obligation to Gil to look out for her." However, her work "wasn't spectacular," and "she was immature and very ideological."

Since his ordeal, Clarence has been restrained in making statements about Anita Hill and has not shown hostility toward her. During interviews, I asked people who know him well whether they heard him make hateful comments about her. No one has, including his wife, Ginni. In his discussions about Anita Hill with me, I detected no meanness whatever in his words or in his tone of voice. In his description of her political views and her immaturity, he did not seem hostile but rather was objective in discussing the characteristics of a person who had been a young lawyer on his staff and a "charge" given him by a friend.

I asked Clarence whether he found Anita Hill attractive. He said that he had no attraction to her and viewed her simply as a colleague. In conversations with his close friend on the court of appeals, Judge Larry Silberman, Clarence was more specific in describing his lack of attraction to Hill. On two occasions, first in late September 1991 and second on October 8, Clarence told Silberman that his first reaction on hearing that Anita Hill had charged him with sexual harassment was that "she wasn't attractive at all, and she had bad breath."

Diane Holt, Clarence's secretary at both the Department of Education and EEOC, observed Hill's behavior in both offices and described it as liberal and "pro-woman." Holt describes Hill as "always like a spoiled brat," "pouting. . . . Always wanting to have her own way. Always wanting to have the last say." Holt recalls that Hill "would argue and when she felt that her point of view wasn't going to be accepted . . . she just walked away."

Clarence has a similar recollection: "She would disagree with everybody. . . . When she didn't get her way, when she was arguing and somebody was getting the better of it, then she would just sort of almost explode. I wouldn't say totally explode. And then she would closet herself in her office."

When testifying before the Judiciary Committee, Hill addressed the issue of why she went with Clarence from the Department of Education to EEOC if she had been sexually harassed by him in the first job. Her testimony was to the effect that it was a reluctant move on her part, but that she was concerned that if she remained at Education, the department might be terminated and that her job would not be secure.[25] Clarence disputes her testimony. He recalls that after he returned to his office from the White House, having been told by

director of personnel Pendleton James that the president would nominate him for chairman of the EEOC, he broke the news to his staff at
Education. Both Anita Hill and Diane Holt asked him if he would
take them with him to his new office. Holt remembers that both she
and Hill were very pleased at going to EEOC and Holt describes Hill
as "pretty excited" about the new job.

Clarence describes Hill's pleading ignorance about her security at
Education as "nonsense." He says that he told her that "it was her option to stay at Education; even if the Department of Education were
eliminated, the Office of Civil Rights in which Hill worked had its
own budget, which was in surplus, and that the Office of Civil Rights
was going to remain intact.[26]

When Clarence arrived at EEOC, it became clear to him that Hill's
work was not of as high a quality as the work of other employees. In
Clarence's opinion, Hill was not knowledgeable about the law relating
to Title VII of the Civil Rights Act of 1964, the basic federal statute
on employment discrimination. Moreover, Hill "didn't try to take her
time and learn from the bottom up. She wanted to start at the top and
stay at the top, and I had other people at the top." Clarence's work at
EEOC was more demanding than that at Education, and as he had
competent and experienced people to rely on, he saw much less of
Anita Hill than he had seen in his previous position.

When Clarence arrived at EEOC, his first executive assistant was
Chris Roggerson, and it was to him that Hill reported directly. When
Roggerson left the office for San Francisco, Clarence appointed a
black woman, Allyson Duncan, as his new executive assistant. Clarence recalls that Hill was upset at this appointment; she complained
to Clarence that he dated a woman with a light complexion and that
Allyson Duncan had a light complexion. Diane Holt says that Hill
complained to her that Clarence "likes light women. Or, you never see
him with a dark complexioned woman."

Clarence was able to accept Hill's differences with his views on
various issues; it was all right with him that she was "way on the other
side" of affirmative action from him. But Armstrong Williams, of the
EEOC staff, saw her as a threat and tried to warn Clarence that "this

woman is your mortal enemy, and will do anything to destroy you."
Clarence dismissed the warning.

Clarence recalls that Hill was "very bitter" when he criticized her
work as not being sufficiently analytical and that she responded to the
criticism by keeping a log on her work. But despite the warning of
Armstrong Williams, despite the pouting and the bitterness she
showed over criticism, Clarence viewed Hill as his special responsibility, given to him by Gil Hardy, a young person whom he had helped
along the way, a person who he recalls phoned him at various times after leaving his employment, and a totally shocking source of a complaint of sexual harassment.

When the FBI left, Clarence phoned Lee Liberman at the White
House describing the FBI's visit. Liberman recalls that Clarence was
"really miserable," that he told her he felt "dirty all over," and that
the allegation was nonsense. Liberman told Clarence that in her opinion the story "looked pretty clearly ginned up," that that would be the
view of the Judiciary Committee, that the whole thing was going to be
a nonissue, and that he should not worry.

Clarence was not reassured. He was worried that the story would
become public. He had worked hard to build his good name, his most
prized possession. He had little money, few material goods. What he
had was his reputation. If this story were to become public, he worried, his good name would be taken from him.

That afternoon, on reviewing the completed FBI report, Lee
Liberman and the White House counsel's office concluded that the
Anita Hill story was not credible, but they did recognize the vast
difference between the substance of the story and the damage that
would result if the story became public. They were reassured when at
8:00 P.M. Senator Biden phoned Fred McClure at the White House
and said that the Judiciary Committee would meet at 10:00 A.M. Friday to vote on the Thomas nomination. To them, that meant that Biden
read the FBI report the same way they did, as not providing the
grounds for defeating the nomination. Nevertheless, a leak would be

damaging, more damaging than the substance of the allegation, and so on Wednesday night, Boyden Gray, John Schmitz, and Lee Liberman met with Steve Hart of the White House legislative affairs office to draft the White House response to any leak.

After the FBI left his house and after calling Lee Liberman, Clarence called Mark Paoletta again. As Mark recalls the conversation, Clarence appeared stunned by the allegation. He told Mark that he had helped Anita Hill in the past; he had been a friend to her and still considered her a friend. He appeared bewildered that she would make such a charge. Even so, Mark detected a measure of relief in Clarence's words. He now knew the substance of the charge, and he knew it was completely false.

When I heard that the FBI had completed its interview, I phoned Clarence to get his response to the allegation. As he remembers that call, I told him that I did not want to get into his personal life, and that whether or not the charge was true, I would support him to the end. Clarence's response to me that afternoon was the same response he has made ever since: there was no truth to Hill's accusation.

Here was the position I was in after hearing Clarence's story: I knew that the Judiciary Committee had received a statement charging Clarence with sexual harassment but discounted it as the latest in a line of accusations made against Clarence beginning the first week of July. I had been told directly and strongly by my friend of seventeen years that the charge was false. My mission was to build momentum for the confirmation vote by asking fellow senators to make statements on the floor of the Senate announcing their support for the nomination. This was especially my mission after the committee voted to report the nomination to the floor on September 27. I was asking fellow senators to make public statements of support without disclosing to them that the Hill allegation was in the possession of the Judiciary Committee. I remember particularly my pursuit of Pat Moynihan, repeatedly calling him in the days before the leak occurred and urging him to make a public statement of his support for Clarence. Pat and I were both freshman senators in 1977, and we have worked together on the Finance Committee. I respect him greatly and have a real affection for him. I recall wondering whether it was right to ask him to commit himself knowing that I was withholding pertinent information.

I think that if I have any standing in the Senate, it is because my colleagues trust me. I have tried to win that trust by telling them the truth and not being devious. Now I was urging them to act without telling them about a charge that could cause them to act differently.

Still, the strategy of trying to get senators to commit to Clarence was clearly correct. The sooner we could show that his victory was assured, the less fight would be left in his opponents. The less fight in them, the less likely they would be to continue dumping accusations on him. The question in my mind was whether candor required me to disseminate a story I believed to be scurrilous. My answer was no. If the Anita Hill story was to spread through the Senate and beyond, I was not going to be the person to do it.

From Mark Paoletta's standpoint, the confidential nature of the allegation meant that he was foreclosed from taking any actions that could be helpful to Clarence's defense. He could make no inquiries about Anita Hill or about her relationship to Clarence, because the mere process of asking questions would divulge information that was contained in an FBI report and in a confidential statement of Hill to the Judiciary Committee. The normal inquiries that would be made to test her accusation and to develop a defense for Clarence could not be made without disseminating the story.

During the afternoon of September 25, the male FBI agent who had interviewed Clarence phoned him with the information that the FBI had completed its report and concluded that the Hill story was baseless. They viewed it, said Clarence to his friend Butch Faddis who was visiting, as a "he said–she said" situation; there was nothing of substance to it and nothing for Clarence to worry about. Clarence recalls that after the call he relaxed slightly, hoping that the story would end there, but now worried that the story would not remain confidential, that it would delay the Senate's vote on his confirmation, and that he did not have the strength to go on.

Clarence's immediate reaction on learning of Hill's accusation is

best told by Butch Faddis, who had arrived at Clarence's home just after the FBI agents left.

Clifford "Butch" Faddis and Clarence Thomas had become friends
in the summer of 1974 while they took a law review course in St.
Louis in preparation for the bar exam. They had both moved to Jefferson City after the exam, Butch working as a lawyer in the Missouri
Department of Revenue and Clarence working in the attorney general's office. They went jogging together and enjoyed long discussions
after work. Now, with Clarence in Washington and Butch in St. Louis,
they maintained their friendship. After seventeen years, Butch Faddis
concludes that the more he knows Clarence Thomas, the more respect
he has for him.

As Butch recalls, the first words Clarence said when he arrived
were, "Butch, I'm as low as a hog's belly." He divulged that someone
who had worked for him had made a claim of sexual harassment. In
Butch's words, Clarence was "like in shock." Clarence told Butch,
"This is a person I tried to help to the best of my ability." Repeatedly,
Clarence asked, "Do you believe this?" He said that he could not believe that such a charge would be made by this person.

Butch inquired about the details of the charge. Did Hill claim that
she was going to be fired if she did not do something? Clarence said,
"No, no, none of that." If not, Butch asked, what is there to worry
about? Clarence said, "You don't understand; this is sexual harassment. . . . You don't understand what these people will do to me. . . .
For a black man, a single black man, this is the ultimate way to destroy. . . . It's a smear that you can't get off."

In recounting his visit with Clarence, Butch told me: "I think what
the concern was, [was] that it was going to go public and that he had
to be prepared to refute it. And then he kept saying, 'I don't know how
I can refute [it] because it's not true. How do you refute something
that is not true?' And there was never a waver, never even, 'Well, I
might have said' or 'I could have' or 'she could have interpreted it.'
There was never any of that. And, believe me, Senator, I have been
with this guy for many, many years through many, many experiences,
and I can tell you that if there was ever, if any of this had even slightly
been true, he would have told me."

Butch's visit with Clarence was not an uninterrupted dialogue. It was punctuated by calls between Clarence and the White House, Clarence's telephone denial to me, and the slight relief Clarence felt when the FBI agent assured him that he should not worry about it. And he also recalls that during that twenty-four hours there were some conversations not about the Hill allegation. Butch and Clarence sat on the patio, reminiscing. They barbecued hamburgers, and they took a long drive down to the Potomac and sat on its banks talking about their families and their lives and where they were heading. But always the talk returned to Anita Hill's charge of sexual harassment.

Butch was undergoing hardships of his own, including financial setbacks, and he shared his problems with Clarence. According to Butch, Clarence spent as much time listening to his problems as Butch spent listening to Clarence. Clarence told Butch that he knew he had the motivation and recuperative powers to overcome adversity and that he had confidence that Butch would be back. He gave Butch a book, *When Bad Things Happen to Good People* by Rabbi Harold Kushner, and said that he thought it would help Butch and give him strength. He got the Bible and showed Butch a psalm he had been reading that day, and they read it and talked about how much strength they found in God.

Butch says it is characteristic of Clarence to be concerned about the problems of his friend and to try to bolster his spirits. I asked Butch whether he found it remarkable that at a time when Clarence was in such despair about the charge made against him, he spent as much time supporting Butch in his troubles as he did discussing his own problems. Butch replied: "I guess it doesn't strike me as remarkable in the sense that I have known him so long and so well. That's why I was attracted to him as a human being. . . . That's the kind of guy he is, and he is very committed, and there is no vacillation on his part. You know, you don't ever sit around thinking, is he my friend? You know he is your friend."

Two other aspects of that visit stand out in the mind of Butch Faddis. The first is that Clarence never said anything negative about Anita Hill. He had attempted to the best of his ability to be her friend, and he was offended by what she was doing to him. But he said nothing derogatory about her. The second is a remark Clarence made: "If Gil Hardy was here, this wouldn't be happening right now."

With Lee Liberman's telephone call, a process began within Clarence Thomas. As he puts it, "I started destroying myself." For nearly three months, other people had been sifting through the details of his life, looking not for a full picture of a human being but for the worst aspects they could find. Now Clarence began the same process on himself. By his account, he had always been a perfectionist. He recalls a reference in his high school yearbook where he complains that he only got a 98 on an exam. In his words, "I was always upset about the two percent."

With Lee's phone call, Clarence started to sift through his life. He had not been a perfect person. After he left the seminary in 1968, he let his religious life slip for a period of time. He felt guilty that he had gone through a divorce. To him it was wrong; he had broken a vow. He had watched pornographic movies while a law student. He had "dated quite a bit" in the mid-1980s, before meeting Ginni. He had not been perfect, but he had done nothing wrong to Anita Hill. Perhaps this episode was a punishment that was being visited on him for past shortcomings. Perhaps if he had never "dated around" or watched an X-rated movie, this would not have happened. On September 25 and for the next two weeks, Clarence Thomas, ridden by guilt for past sins, became his own worst enemy.

At about six or seven o'clock, Ginni Thomas returned home from work and learned for the first time of the FBI visit and the Anita Hill allegation. Her reaction was that the story was "laughable" and "absurd" and that it would soon pass as all the other charges passed. Ginni and Clarence developed their own name for this, the most recent charge. To them it would be known as "the scum story."

Friday, September 27

The Judiciary Committee was to begin its executive session for the purpose of voting on the Thomas nomination at ten o'clock Friday morning. I knew that Joe Biden was going to announce his position in a Senate floor speech immediately before the committee meeting, and I was on the floor shortly after the Senate convened in order to respond to Biden's speech and to engage him in a brief colloquy.

My concern at that time was less the Anita Hill allegation than a delay in bringing the nomination to a vote in the Senate. Senator Howell Heflin had announced his opposition the previous day, and Biden's announcement meant that the committee would send the nomination to the floor after a seven–seven tie vote. I believed a tie vote would embolden the interest groups to redouble their efforts, and any delay would give them more time to organize their activities. The Senate was scheduled to begin its one-week Columbus Day recess at the close of business the following Friday, and I was determined to do what I could to encourage a vote before the recess. I had two purposes in going to the floor: to warn of the possibility of increased interest group activity, and to urge that the nomination be brought to the Senate expeditiously.

In fact, Senator Biden's speech was an effort to direct attention away from attacks on Clarence's character to concerns about judicial philosophy.[27] In the first minute of the speech, Biden said: "For this senator, there is no question that the nominee we are about to vote on is a man of high character, competence, and has sufficient legal credentials and credibility. . . . For me, the question that concerns me most, [is] Judge Thomas' judicial philosophy."

At the White House, watching the speech on television, Lee Liberman concluded that Biden and the Judiciary Committee shared her view that Hill's allegation was not sufficient to impede confirmation and that Biden was anticipating the possibility that Hill's story would be leaked to the media.

Ken Duberstein spoke with Biden both before and after the Judiciary Committee voted on the nomination. Throughout the week,

Duberstein and I had been impressed by Biden's fairness in handling the Hill matter. Ken especially thought that Biden was fair in not acting on Hill's charges until she was willing to be identified by name as the complainant. Duberstein recalls that both before and after the committee meeting, Biden told him that all members of the Judiciary Committee had been briefed on the allegations; they had access to Hill's statement and to the FBI report, and by committee rules, any member had the right to ask for a one-week delay in the committee vote. No one had asked for a delay.

In fact, the majority staff of the committee informed all Democratic members of the Hill charges. On the Republican side, Senator Thurmond, the ranking minority member of the committee, had access to the information, and Senator Specter, who had visited with Biden in the Senate dining room the night before the committee meeting, was told of the charges by Biden and then briefed by the majority staff. The remaining Republicans on the committee were not informed about Hill's charges prior to the committee vote.

Biden reiterated his confidence in Clarence's character in his remarks to the Judiciary Committee immediately before the committee's vote.[28] He told the committee of a telephone conversation he had just had with Clarence in which he called Clarence "a man of honor." He continued, "I also indicated in my discussion with Judge Thomas that I believe there are certain things that are not at issue at all, and that is his character or characterizations of his character.

"I have not heard anyone say anything to the contrary of what I am about to say, but if this does occur I assure Judge Thomas and I will assure my colleagues I will be an advocate for Thomas' position, and that is that this is about what he believes, not about what he is. And I know my colleagues will refrain, and I urge everyone else to refrain from personalizing this battle, to the extent it is one, on the floor of the Senate. I don't expect that to happen on the floor of the Senate. I don't expect it to happen off the floor, but I hope it won't happen off the floor of the Senate."

In a meeting in his office with Duberstein after the committee vote, Biden discussed the reasons for his positive remarks about Clarence's character. According to Duberstein, Biden wanted his colleagues in the Senate to know how strongly he felt about Clarence's integrity and that this was not open season on the nominee's character. Whether the Anita Hill story would surface or charges would be made concerning another story then circulating about Clarence (the alleged delay of a supposedly controversial court of appeals decision), Biden wanted the nomination decided on the basis of policy, not integrity. At this time, Duberstein says, Biden either said or led him to think that he believed Clarence Thomas.[29]

Duberstein also recalls that Biden believed he had followed the correct procedures: he had asked for an FBI report, had briefed Senators George Mitchell and Robert Dole, the party leaders of the Senate; and had made the FBI report available to the members of the committee. Nevertheless, Biden said, following the correct process would not suffice to protect him from attack should the Hill story become public. In that case, reports Duberstein, Biden believed he would be as much a target as Clarence Thomas. The media and liberal interest groups would attack him for not stopping the nomination in its tracks and holding hearings on the charges.

On September 26, the night before the committee vote, Arlen Specter was enjoying a martini at home when I reached him at about 10:45 to check if there had been any change in his position on the nomination. Specter had read the Hill statement and the FBI report before leaving the Capitol that night and had decided to continue to support the nomination. About 7:10 the next morning, the day of the committee vote, Specter called me from the Senate gym and asked if I could arrange for him to meet Clarence in my office prior to the committee meeting. He had become concerned about both the Hill story and about the report that Clarence had delayed a court of appeals decision until his nomination was decided.

Contemporaneously with the Anita Hill controversy, the publication *Legal Times* had reported that leaks from the court of appeals suggested that Clarence had improperly withheld a court opinion in

order to avoid controversy prior to his confirmation.[30] Because the
Code of Judicial Conduct restricts a judge from discussing a case before his court even in his own defense, Clarence could not defend
himself from this charge.[31] However, in general terms, he described to
me the impossibility of doing the work of the court during the confirmation process: "Writing opinions during the confirmation process
was like brain surgery while you are in a car race."

Clarence and Specter met while I was on the Senate floor for the
Biden speech. Specter remembers that although Clarence stated that
he was reluctant to discuss court practices, he did assure Specter that
there was no intentional withholding of a court decision. Specter characterizes Clarence's reply to his question about the Anita Hill story as
"a flat, unequivocal, categorical, emphatic denial."

Clarence then returned home. At about 11:30, he received calls
from his secretary and then from Ken Duberstein saying that Senator
Biden wanted to speak with him on the telephone. The committee
meeting on the nomination was in progress, but Biden would step out
to talk to Clarence.

According to Clarence, Biden explained that he was going to vote
against the nomination because of the composition of the Supreme
Court. He thought that Clarence was very bright and would probably
be a great justice, but he could not take the chance of putting another
conservative on the Court. He said that Clarence was of the highest
integrity and character and that if Clarence was attacked about the
supposed delay of the court of appeals decision or about the substance of the FBI report, Biden would be his "most adamant and
vigorous defender."[32]

At the time of this conversation, Ginni Thomas was standing beside
Clarence. She had returned after a short day of work, and they were
preparing to drive to Fork Union to watch Jamal play in a high school
football game. She recalls that Clarence held the telephone
so that she was able to hear both ends of the conversation, and that
Biden told Clarence that the Hill charge had "no merit," and that
"if it ever comes up, Clarence, I promise you I'll be your biggest
defender."

What Clarence and Ginni heard Biden say was in the same vein as the chairman's statement on the Senate floor, his statement to the committee, and his remarks to Ken Duberstein: he had read the Hill statement and the FBI report; he had briefed the Democrats on his committee along with Senators Mitchell and Dole; he had concluded that Clarence Thomas's character should not be at issue before the Senate, and if someone else tried to make it an issue, he, Joe Biden, would be an advocate in Thomas's defense.

Clarence Thomas, Ken Duberstein, Arlen Specter, and Lee Liberman all report the same feeling on the afternoon of September 27: they had not heard the end of the Anita Hill story. It had not altered a single vote on the Judiciary Committee, but that was not the end of the matter because the story would be leaked.

Lee Liberman took consolation in the Judiciary Committee's action. She believed that even if the story became widely known, the leaker would be taking on not just Clarence Thomas but also chairman Biden and the Judiciary Committee. The goal now was to line up the votes of senators.

Saturday, October 5

It had all the markings of a perfect weekend: blue sky, ideal temperature, no work to do, and time with Sally at our house in Washington. I had left the office on Friday afternoon feeling that victory was at hand. Only four days remained until Tuesday's scheduled vote, and fifty-four senators had announced publicly their intention to vote for Clarence. In addition, I was confident of Pat Moynihan's vote, and I thought we would end up with between sixty and sixty-five votes for Clarence. After the long struggle, confirmation was virtually assured, and I was prepared to enjoy the weekend thoroughly.

Since early July, Clarence had heeded the advice of Ken Duberstein and had kept his pride and joy, a black Corvette, hidden from public view in his garage. Perhaps it too would have been the basis of an attack on the nominee's life-style. Now Duberstein told Clarence that it was safe to drive the Corvette again. "We have the votes," he said. Clarence did not take out his Corvette that weekend, but Ginni remembers that she, too, was in a good mood that Friday, knowing that the Senate's vote was imminent, doubting that the Anita Hill story would become public knowledge at that late date, and thinking that even if it did, people would not believe it.

But the feeling of relief was not unmixed with concern. Allen Moore, my former staff director, recalls calling Clarence the Thursday before the weekend and being surprised at how "down" Clarence sounded. Allen remembers Clarence saying, "Man, there are some people out there who are trying to destroy me." When Allen replied, "Yeah, but that's past," Clarence said, "Man, but they are not giving up. They are still there." Ginni also recalls that even with the end in sight, Clarence continually brought up the subject of Anita Hill's allegations, repeatedly asking why she was doing this and what he could have said that led her to the conclusions she had reached. And when Duberstein told Clarence that he could take out his Corvette and enjoy the weekend because the battle was over, Clarence recalls disagreeing: "Ken, it's not over. I don't trust these people. These people are going to try to kill me. I don't like waiting over this weekend because I think they are going to do something to me over the weekend."

Clarence was not alone in his concern. His supporter, Senator Orrin Hatch, believes that leaks in Congress tend to occur over weekends when people are out of town. We hoped that the Senate would vote on the nomination on Friday, October 4. If that could be arranged, the majority leader's plan was to get an early start on the Columbus Day recess, which was to begin Wednesday, October 9. From my point of view, the worst scheduling possibility would be to postpone the vote until after October 4 and then begin the recess at the close of business that day and hold the vote until after the Senate reconvened on October 14. That would give the opponents an additional week and a half, including two weekends, to generate whatever opposition they could find. If the votes are in hand, if the opposition is relentless, and if a major story is in the making, the sooner the vote is taken, the better.

Democratic senators objected to a vote before the October 5 weekend, but I did not want ten or more days to elapse before the vote, so

I pushed for a delay in the recess until after October 8 so we could vote on that day. That plan was resisted, especially by Senators Mark Hatfield of Oregon and Ted Stevens and Frank Murkowski of Alaska, who had plans to be in their states and did not want to make a special trip back to Washington to cast a single vote, however important. After much discussion in Senator Dole's office and after several phone calls I made to Senator Hatfield, they graciously agreed to rearrange their schedules and to fly back to Washington for an October 8 vote.

As he left his office on Friday, October 4, Ken Duberstein believed that Clarence had at least fifty-seven votes with a possibility of reaching sixty-two. He did not think that a weekend surprise would necessarily occur but was concerned that the weekend would give the groups that opposed Clarence additional time to cause mischief.

Until early Saturday evening, October 5, the weekend had been as glorious as I had anticipated. I went jogging in my neighborhood that afternoon and I recall thinking: only three days and a few hours until the vote; Clarence will be confirmed for the Court, and this ordeal will be over.

When the phone rang, Sally and I were getting ready to go to dinner at Germaine's, a Vietnamese restaurant on Wisconsin Avenue, and then watch a thriller movie we had rented at the local video store, *Sleeping with the Enemy*. It was a measure of the equanimity with which I received the news in Ken Duberstein's call that Sally and I proceeded with our plans and thoroughly enjoyed our evening.

Ken's message was that National Public Radio (NPR) and *Newsday* had the story of alleged sexual harassment and they were going to run it. My relaxed reaction to the call was that the story was too late in coming; it seemed so much like a last-minute smear in a political campaign that the public would give it no credence. Clarence had all but won the confirmation vote; I thought.

Later that night, as we were watching the terrifying conclusion of the movie, Orrin Hatch phoned. I was mildly annoyed at the interruption and pressed the pause button on the VCR. Then I was shaken from my relaxed state. Orrin was mad. He was especially mad at Senator Howard Metzenbaum. He said that he had been interviewed by the media about the Hill story and that he had put the blame on Metzenbaum. When I told him that this was not a serious matter and that the public would dismiss it as last-minute politics, Orrin strongly disagreed. To him, the leak was an enormously important development. Shaken as I was by the strength of Orrin's concern, I pushed the play button, and we resumed watching the movie.

Saturday, October 5, was Mark Paoletta's birthday. Although he was anxious about some new development in the last days of the struggle, he was feeling good. His wife had recently told him that she was pregnant with their first child. After the pressure of the Thomas nomination, this was to be a night out. Mark put on the jacket and turtleneck shirt his wife had given him for his birthday, and they were preparing to go out to dinner together for the first time since July to indulge his fondness for Mexican food. Their dinner reservation was for 8:00 P.M. At 7:30 the phone rang. The caller, Lee Liberman. The message, "They have the Hill story." Nina Totenberg of NPR had called the White House Press Office saying that she had the Hill story. Although Mark canceled his dinner plans, he was not completely convinced that the story would run. He reasoned that the media would not necessarily publish such a serious and damaging allegation on the basis of an unsworn statement by one person.

At 6:00 P.M. Ken Duberstein was also preparing to go out with his wife, Sydney, to a dinner party honoring the birthday of Eli Jacobs, owner of the Baltimore Orioles. Ken's call came from Fred McClure at the White House, who said that NPR and *Newsday* were about to run stories on Anita Hill's allegation. Sydney went ahead to the party, and Ken followed about two hours later after making calls to Boyden Gray, me, and back to Fred McClure. He wanted to make sure that all of us were aware of the development, to determine whether the statement drafted at the White House in anticipation of a leak was still appropriate, and to make sure that the statement was available in response to media inquiries.

Ken remembers speaking on the telephone with Senator Biden both before and after the dinner party. Biden had heard from his staff that the story was in the hands of the media, and according to Ken was quite concerned. Ken recalls that Biden believed he would be criticized for not delving further into the Hill charges before the committee vote. Duberstein encouraged him to put out a statement that members of the committee had been briefed, that they had seen Anita Hill's statement, and that they had agreed that the process should move forward. Ken recalls urging Biden to do more than defend the procedures followed in bringing the nomination to a vote in the Judiciary Committee; as well he should put out a statement defending the character of Clarence Thomas. Biden said that he had directed his staff to refer the media to the statements he made on the floor of the Senate and in committee on September 27 to the effect that he had no question about Clarence's character. Ken responded that a reference to the prior statement was not enough; Biden should issue a fresh statement. To this request, Ken recalls Biden responding, "I'll do it, I'll do it."[33]

Clarence does not believe that any statement that Joe Biden subsequently made fulfilled the promise he had made over the telephone on the morning of the Judiciary Committee vote. In Clarence's mind, Biden had promised to be his strongest defender should the Hill story become public. Now the story was public, and Clarence wanted Biden to keep his commitment. Ken describes the substance of what Clarence said during a telephone conversation they had on Saturday night or Sunday morning: "Joe Biden told me he was going to be my biggest champ. Why isn't Biden out there defending me? Why aren't people speaking out? How can we let these liberal groups do this to me? Anita Hill is lying. Can't we just state that?"

Ricky and Larry Silberman had been friends of Clarence's for years. Ricky had served with him on the EEOC, first as a member and then as vice chairman of the commission. Her husband, Larry, was a colleague of Clarence's on the court of appeals. They were at the birthday party for Eli Jacobs, and when Ken arrived, he confided to Ricky that the Hill story was in the media's hands.

For the past two months, it had seemed to Larry Silberman that Clarence, after holding himself together, was running out of energy. Larry had experienced a queasy feeling when the vote on the senate floor was delayed until October 8, but when the Judiciary Committee proceeded with its vote without delay because of the Hill charges, Larry concluded that the committee felt that the charges were without merit. When he learned of the leak to the press, he was surprised, having thought that the issue had ended with the committee vote. And even with the leak, Larry reassured Clarence that weekend not to worry. Clarence had told Silberman of Biden's telephone call and of his promise to be Clarence's biggest defender. Larry assumed that Biden would say on the floor of the Senate that he did not think the complaint was meritorious. When the chairman of the Judiciary Committee defended the nominee's character, the Hill story would fade.

Early in the evening of October 5, Clarence and Ginni drove to the Potomac to look out over the water and talk. Clarence had just spoken with Mark Paoletta, who had assured him that if his opponents were to mount an attack, it would not be on Saturday night, when reporters were hard to find. When they returned home at about 7:30, Clarence found a message on his answering machine from Lee Liberman. He returned the call, and she told him that *Newsday* had the story. Ginni, who watched Clarence talking on the kitchen phone, said he appeared devastated. While still on the phone, he turned to Ginni and said, "It's the scum story."

By Clarence's account, he panicked. He tried to reach Ken Duberstein on the phone, but Ken had left his home for the party. He spoke again with Lee Liberman and then Mark Paoletta, and he believes he spoke with Boyden Gray. He recalls that they tried to calm him, but he was convinced that he could not defend himself against the charge. He felt that his one hope was that Joe Biden would issue a strong statement: that the Judiciary Committee had seen the story, that the FBI had investigated it and found it baseless, that the committee deplored the leak, and that was the end of the matter.

While Clarence waited for Biden to speak out in defense of his character, another member of the Judiciary Committee had stepped forward. In the *Newsday* article, Senator Paul Simon is reported to have said that "he and most other members of the Senate Judiciary Committee were not aware of the allegations when they voted on the nomination, though he has since read the FBI report."[34]

The report of independent counsel Peter Fleming, who was commissioned by the Senate to investigate the leak, flatly contradicts this statement. He found that all Democratic members of the Judiciary Committee had been notified of Hill's allegations before the committee vote and that Senator Simon had read the FBI file before the committee vote.[35] Simon's statement angered Senator Biden, who saw it as an untrue criticism of his handling of the matter. From the standpoint of the friends of Clarence Thomas, Simon's statement weakened our first line of defense: that the committee knew of the charges before it met and apparently thought that they were insufficient to justify further action.

Although Clarence describes his response to Lee Liberman's phone call as "panicked," his thought process was remarkably clear. Clarence told either Lee Liberman or Mark Paoletta that he wanted the White House to release a list of women who had worked for him and could be interviewed by the media. He was confident that they would say that Anita Hill's story did not correspond with anything they had experienced in his office. According to Lee, Clarence drew up a list of female employees, and, at his suggestion, she saw that it was turned over to Judy Smith of the White House Press Office. Judy Smith declined to release the list; she believed Clarence was doing well with the media at that point and that responding with the list would make the story unnecessarily bigger. She said that the list should not be given out except to specific reporters in answer to specific needs for it.

Sunday, October 6

Sally and I were getting ready for the 9:15 church service, but Ken Duberstein had asked the previous night that I call him before leaving home. What he told me destroyed my Saturday night pipe dream that this story would be dismissed by the media. Hill's allegation was already on NPR and in *Newsday*; soon it was going to be everywhere. So much for our plans to go to church.

Steve Hilton, my news secretary, had reached the same conclusion as Ken. Because I had held my knowledge of the Hill story in strict confidence, the first Steve heard of it was shortly after midnight, when he received a call at home from Ruth Marcus, a reporter for the *Washington Post*. The next morning, he turned on CBS radio news, which featured the Hill accusation as its lead story. Steve recalls that CBS used "a lot of color words" and concluded that this would be a major news item.

Throughout the course of Sunday morning, Steve and I talked on the phone four or five times. I told him this was a story that had to be met head-on and not deflected, and then dictated a statement to him that he used in response to calls from ten or twelve news organizations that morning. I also told him, pursuant to Ken Duberstein's recommendation, to schedule a news conference as early as possible. That afternoon at the conference on my front lawn, I responded quickly and directly to the charges against Clarence, consistent with the method we used to meet the almost daily attacks that occurred in July.

Clarence was not content to be represented by a spokesman, and he was certainly not satisfied with Biden's failure to defend his character. He wanted to speak for himself, especially after he got word that an unnamed person at the White House had claimed, erroneously, that Clarence had told the FBI that he had tried to date Anita Hill. For Clarence, this story was the last straw, especially if its source was the White House. Ginni told him that he should make his own statement, and issue a categorical denial. This is exactly what Clarence wanted to do, and he so told Ken Duberstein on the phone. Duberstein convinced Clarence that he should not issue a statement of denial, that to do so would only "give the story legs."

Ginni describes Clarence's state of mind the week that began October 6:

"He was having a lot of trouble sleeping. . . . He had stopped eating. I don't remember when he stopped eating, but I started noticing after a couple of days that he hadn't anything but like an apple the whole day. . . . I'd say, 'Just try because you're not emotionally up to it, you just need to keep sustaining yourself.' The nature of his anxiety . . . was the humiliation factor. That seemed to be his major concern. Here was this charge that was so against everything he had done in his public life and everything he believes in his private and personal thoughts, a charge that was being exposed and discussed by what looked like rational people, and it was killing him. Somebody was trying to destroy him and that was the major concern. He kept saying why are they trying to destroy me? He kept asking that question over and over again."

Trying to provide some comfort or at least some distraction for her husband, Ginni phoned Mark Paoletta around noon on Sunday and asked him to come to their house to watch football games on television. When Mark arrived at about 12:30 or 1:00 P.M., he was astonished by the media stakeout outside the Thomas house: four television vans with satellite dishes and approximately ten people, presumably reporters or members of camera crews, sitting in the vans or in cars parked on the street or sitting on beach chairs. At one point during his visit, Mark looked out the window to see a photographer peering in.

In order to avoid the scurrying for cameras and shouting of questions that he thought would result from arriving at the front door in a car, Mark asked Lee Liberman to drop him off a block away so that he could saunter down the sidewalk to the Thomas house, then suddenly veer toward the door. The contrast between the Clarence Thomas whom he had known and the man who now stood before him was striking. As Mark puts it: "I have seen him a lot, and he is a great guy, and he has always got this big, booming laugh, and he is always a giver. He is always, you know, you do right and things will work out, and you proceed ahead. . . . And he was a great inspiration, . . . a motivator and all of that for me. When I went over there, he was just totally very sad, like he had lost all hope." Mark remembers that Clarence "was completely destroyed," "depressed," "really tired," and "as if all of the energy had been zapped out of him." He speaks of "listlessness/hopelessness," of Clarence sitting silently, then pacing, then dozing off for perhaps fifteen minutes in front of the television set.

Ginni had prepared a big crock of chili. Mark recalls feeling guilty because he ate two bowls of it; Clarence ate nothing. The two friends did little talking, and Mark recalls no discussion of the Hill allegation. As Mark says, "We had become close enough where we could just kind of sit there and not have to talk." So they sat, mostly in silence, until Mark's wife picked him up at about eight o'clock.

That night, Mark Paoletta could not sleep. He could not stop thinking about how depressed Clarence was that day, and in the days ahead he repeatedly thought, "This is impossible. It can't be that this is happening. This is a terrible day for America."

Reflecting on October 6, Mark says: "It was a terrible day. It was a very terrible day . . . just sitting there, feeling terrible that I couldn't do more for him. . . . This guy who had lived his life, there couldn't be a better person that you could nominate. Even if they wanted to blow somebody out with personal attacks, you couldn't find a better person than Clarence Thomas, who was cleaner. . . . God knows what that means for the rest of us. Everything about this guy was just kind of moral fiber and all of that and source of strength, and to have it happen to him was just the ultimate, the ultimate disillusionment."

At about the time Mark Paoletta arrived at the Thomas home, I had reached Joe Biden by phone at his home in Delaware. Ken Duberstein and I had spoken, and as we agreed, I added whatever weight I had to Ken's request: that Biden issue a strong and favorable statement about Clarence. Biden responded by expressing concern that he was being criticized for how the Judiciary Committee had handled the Hill nomination. He spoke with anger of the erroneous statement Senator Simon had made that committee members had not been briefed on the Hill story before the committee vote. To my request that he make a statement about Clarence's good moral character, he responded by defending the committee's process. In strong terms, I told Joe that his response was not sufficient.

Just before three o'clock, before the media arrived on my front lawn for a news conference, I had a second conversation with Joe Biden. I told him that I was about to meet with the media and asked him to review the committee process with me. He said that it would be accurate to say that all Democrats on the committee had been briefed before the vote, that Senator Specter had also been briefed, that the FBI report was available at those briefings but that he did not know whether each senator had read the report, that any senator could have asked for a one-week delay in the committee vote as a matter of right, that no one asked for a delay, and that no one who read the FBI report or was briefed on it believed that there was any basis for further action by the committee, for further investigation, or for any delay.

Ken Duberstein spoke with Biden shortly after I did. According to Ken, Biden was concerned about what I would say at the news conference. Ken recalls that Biden thought I was about to strike out at my colleagues in the Senate for their handling of the Thomas nomination. Ken responded that the Hill story was a last-minute attempt to defeat Clarence, that Biden previously had expressed full confidence in Clarence's integrity, and that he should speak out now on behalf of Clarence. To Biden's claim that he was speaking out, Ken said that he was only speaking of the process and that he should be explicit in stating his faith in the nominee. If he did not have faith in Clarence, he should have said so on the day the committee met.

Ken characterizes the statement Biden issued that day as "a chronology of all the things that Joe did." "Some of it I interpreted as refuting what Paul Simon had said to *Newsday*."

Despite Ken's disappointment in Biden's demurral to issuing a strong defense of Clarence's character and despite his perception that "the press was in a feeding frenzy," Ken remained optimistic about the eventual outcome of the nomination. He had bumped into two Democratic senators at the ballpark in Baltimore, and they did not appear to him to be overly concerned about the Hill story. But beyond that visible sign that he thought he received, there was a more basic reason for optimism: "I believed, as I do today, Clarence Thomas. I looked him in the eye. I believed what he said and I felt that it would be a tough course, but we would wind up prevailing."

By the time for the front lawn news conference, various members of my office staff had gathered at my house: Rob McDonald, my administrative assistant; Steve Hilton, my news secretary; and Kerry Garvin of my Commerce Committee staff among them. Rob recalls that even as the television cameras were assembling, I still did not recognize the full gravity of the Hill story. He noted that I was treating this as just one more bad story in a long list of bad stories that began in July; just as we had "batted down" the other stories, so we would deal with this one. Rob did not share my optimism.

That, in fact, was my view, and that is how I treated it when I met the media. As I envisioned my mission that afternoon, it was to make two points. First, this was a last-ditch attempt to defeat a nomination that we thought we had won. The Hill story was identical to the weekend-before-the-election attacks made by losing candidates against winning candidates. Just as last-minute political attacks should be dismissed by the voters, so this last-minute attack should be dismissed by the American people. Second, as I had just confirmed with Joe Biden, the Judiciary Committee had reviewed this accusation and did not feel that it merited further delay or action.

That evening, Sally and I went to a small dinner party where one of the guests was an associate justice of the Supreme Court. With the background of the day's events, I asked him whether he thought the job was worth the cost of getting it. He answered that if he were asked to go through the confirmation process as it stood, he would not do it.

Butch Faddis remembers a telephone call he placed from St. Louis. With tears rolling down his cheeks, he left an encouraging message on Clarence's answering machine and then was struck by an idea that is remarkably parallel to a comment Clarence later made to the Judiciary Committee. He thought of standing on the federal courthouse steps in St. Louis with a noose around his neck. He called another friend of Clarence's, Mark Mittleman, who had served in the state attorney general's office, and said, "Mark, they're hanging this guy. Let's go do something like they are doing to him." Butch did not act on the idea, but he recalls, "I felt like I was in a mob . . . where we are taking him out and trying to hang him, and don't worry about the facts."

Monday, October 7

By Monday morning, even I realized that the Anita Hill accusation was not just another charge, to be answered and disposed of like all the others. The evening news, the morning news, and the morning newspapers were all full of the story. This was no longer a countdown to the hour of expected victory; the scheduled vote was a little more than thirty hours away, and the wheels were coming off.

My early thought that morning was that Clarence's opponents would demand to postpone the vote. They would want a full-scale investigation, with plenty of time to explore not only Hill's charge but the most personal aspects of Clarence's life. As well, they would want as much media attention as they could get and as much time as possible to build further opposition to the nomination. But the time of the vote, Tuesday October 8, at 6:00 P.M., had been agreed to by unanimous consent of all senators, and, under Senate rules, what is agreed to by unanimous consent can be changed only by unanimous consent. In short, no matter how intense the pressure for a delay in the vote might be, a single senator could insist that the vote proceed as scheduled on Tuesday evening.

Of course, to hold a vote and to win a vote are two different matters. If senators who were supporters of the nomination called for a delay, ignoring their request could cause defeat. In such a case, the only good purpose that would be served by insisting on voting at the scheduled time would be to render the coup de grace, to put Clarence's suffering to an end. This thought—blessed relief for my suffering friend—was very much on my mind that day and the next as the dilemma of whether to vote now or ask for a delay drew closer.

I first raised the issue of a possible delay with Clarence on Monday morning. His response was immediate and emphatic: no delay. He wanted to get it over with, win or lose. He told me that he couldn't take it any longer. He had been undergoing tremendous personal agony since the Hill accusation was brought to his attention, and it was particularly mortifying to him that the story was now in the media.

Remembering that Monday and the next two days, Clarence says: "I was physically ill. I didn't throw up. I couldn't eat. I couldn't do anything. My stomach was sick. I felt like throwing up. . . . I forget which morning it was . . . that Virginia threw up. . . . Then my mother calls up and she saw it and she couldn't go back to work. . . . She was sick. My brother called up and my sister-in-law called. They were all in tears."

The previous week, in the hope of winning the vote of Senator Max Baucus, a Montana Democrat, I had scheduled a Monday morning meeting between Baucus and Clarence in Fred McClure's White House office. By Monday, that meeting was so overshadowed by the Hill story that it seemed beside the point. Nevertheless, we had agreed to a meeting, and both Baucus and Clarence arrived for it. To me, Clarence showed considerable discipline in proceeding with the meeting, answering the questions Baucus put to him. But to Clarence, questions on matters of legal philosophy no longer had any relevance. Clarence recalls, "I was worrying about what's going to happen to our life. What's going to happen to everything we've built?" After the meeting with Baucus, Fred McClure told Clarence that Anita Hill was beginning a news conference in Oklahoma. Clarence said, "Fred, you guys can have the thing," and left the White House for his house.

While Clarence was meeting with Senator Baucus, Ginni learned at her office that Anita Hill had scheduled a news conference. Her first instinct was to call Clarence on the telephone, and she reached him in Fred McClure's office as the Baucus meeting was ending. Clarence's comment to Ginni approximated what he said to McClure: "That's it, they can have it. This is not worth it."

Knowing of the Hill news conference, Ginni left the office for home, unable to focus on anything but her husband. She watched part of the news conference in their bedroom. Clarence, who had also returned home, did not. After the conference, Ginni told Clarence that it looked to her as if Anita Hill believed what she said. She appeared to be credible.

Ken Duberstein had a somewhat different view. He thought that Hill was cool and clever. On the surface, she appeared to be credible, but she lacked passion in her appearance. He recognized, though, that his own view did not coincide with that of many other people, including the media, which Ken describes as, "all ga-ga, all enthralled by her performance."

On hearing Ginni's report, Clarence thought that the Hill news conference had escalated the campaign against him. Now, he thought, nobody would believe him, and everybody would believe Anita Hill. Ginni determined that it was time for Clarence to speak for himself. Anita Hill had made a public statement, and Clarence should do the same. He should deny her charges in his own words, and the sooner the better.

The question of whether Clarence should issue a statement of denial was discussed at a late afternoon meeting in Fred McClure's White House office. Ken Duberstein, Fred McClure, and others present were aware that one school of thought held that Clarence should make a statement. They did not agree, and in an afternoon phone call, I concurred with their view. From the day his nomination had been announced, we believed that Clarence should not personally answer the charges made against him, so, in part, the decision not to respond resulted from our past policy. But now we had another concern: that if Clarence did make a statement, he could not stop there. Reporters would surely ask questions, and those questions might not be limited to the Anita Hill story. Clarence could be asked about any subject that entered a reporter's mind—matters dealt with in the confirmation hearing or about any other matter. It would be open season on Clarence. We believed that for Clarence to be peppered with endless questions on any subject would risk far more harm than it could do good.

As Clarence held his silence, Mark Paoletta had set off on a project of his own: an attempt to prove a negative. To Mark, proving a negative is virtually impossible. When one person makes a claim for which there are no witnesses, it is usually a matter of competing credibility. But Mark had heard that sexual harassment normally is not an isolated event. Where it exists, it is part of a pattern of behavior that is repeated with a number of women. If he could prove that there was no pattern of abusive behavior and that in fact Clarence had treated other women honorably, it would tend to follow that Clarence had behaved honorably toward Anita Hill.

Mark began by working his Rolodex, phoning women who had worked with or for Clarence over the years and asking them whether they had any knowledge of conduct by Clarence that was inappropriate toward women co-workers or employees.

Mark's telephone project, to prove a negative, had to be comprehensive. He realized that Clarence's staff at EEOC had consisted mainly of women, and he attempted to call all women who had worked closely with Clarence. He estimates that he spoke with twenty to twenty-five women. He is confident that if there had been any indication of improper conduct, he would have learned of it in those calls.

Instead, he said, every woman he spoke with was shocked by Anita Hill's story, and every one of them was willing to go to bat for Clarence by submitting an affidavit on his behalf or testifying. Mark concluded from his calls that it would be difficult to find a person with a better record of treating women in the workplace. Proving a negative may be nearly impossible, but Mark thought he had done so.

Late Monday afternoon, my concerns about a move to delay the scheduled vote took concrete form when Senator Jim Exon, a Nebraska Democrat and announced Thomas supporter, went to the Senate floor to suggest in a speech that the vote be postponed for further inquiry into the Hill story.[36] Exon had learned of the allegations as he was returning to Washington after a weekend at home, and he had met with me immediately before making the speech. Like all other senators with seniority, he had what is known as a "hideaway" in the Capitol Building—a room with a couch and other comfortable furniture where he could work without the frequent interruptions of his regular office or relax during the Senate's late evening sessions. His hideaway was perhaps a hundred feet from the Senate gallery, on the third floor of the Capitol. From its window, I could see the Supreme Court and the Library of Congress. On one wall was a framed photograph of Captain Harry S Truman on horseback in France during World War I. That room was the site of our meeting. I did my best to allay his concerns and did not expect him to ask for the delay. Clearly, his speech was a setback, and it turned out to be the harbinger of a trend that would be followed by pro-Thomas Democrats the next morning. But on Monday evening, Ken Duberstein and I still agreed we had enough votes of Democratic senators to proceed with the vote the following afternoon.

From the viewpoint of Clarence's defenders, by far the most dramatic turn of events on Monday was the discovery of telephone logs preserving the records of calls from Anita Hill to Clarence after she left

EEOC.[37] We believed that the calls—both their number and their content—were wholly inconsistent with the story of a woman who claimed that she had been sexually harassed by her former employer.

The big break occurred midafternoon on Monday. I do not recall whether the information came to me from Clarence or from Anita Hill's press conference or from some other source, but I understood that in the spring of 1991, Anita Hill had telephoned Clarence and asked him to make a speech at the University of Oklahoma Law School. I phoned Clarence in order to find out whether Anita Hill's call was merely formal—no more than the extension of an invitation—or whether there was any small talk that would tend to show a friendly relationship between them.

Clarence said the call was made not in the spring of 1991 but on November 1, 1990. He was certain of the exact date because he had checked his phone logs. In response to my question, he expressed certainty that the conversation was more than terse and businesslike and that he and Hill had discussed such subjects as how he liked being a judge and how she was doing at the University of Oklahoma. By his estimate, the conversation lasted ten or fifteen minutes. I asked whether there were any other times Anita Hill called him. Yes, he said, she had called probably five or six times over the years and I could check his phone logs with Diane Holt, who had been his secretary at EEOC. I then had at least two phone conversations with Diane Holt. She did remember calls from Anita Hill to Clarence—perhaps five or six of them—and when Anita Hill called, she seemed cordial.

Clarence's law clerks made the search of his phone logs that afternoon and evening and turned up records of eleven calls from Anita Hill to Clarence made from 1984 to 1990, after she left EEOC. The logs were not a complete record of all calls Anita Hill made, but only calls made when Clarence was out of the office or otherwise could not take them. They were copies of memo slips, informing him that she had called.[38] Some of the memo slips contained Diane Holt's notations of messages Anita Hill asked to be conveyed to Clarence. One congratulated him on his marriage; another left the number of the hotel room where she was staying during a trip to Washington.

Mark Paoletta was in his office in the Old Executive Office Building when the phone logs began arriving in piecemeal fashion by fax from Clarence's law clerks. In his mind "they were gold." He believed that the personal messages contained in the memos, and especially the fact that Hill left the number of her hotel room, showed that her claim of sexual harassment was absurd.

Ken Duberstein too concluded that they were devastating to Hill's case. In his mind, a sexually harassed woman would not follow the harasser from one job to the next, and she certainly would not initiate phone calls of a pleasantly social nature. But before he celebrated the new development, Ken wanted to find out more about Diane Holt and the logs she kept. The best way to make sure was to get Diane Holt on the phone and ask her himself:

Were the logs in her own handwriting?

Yes.

Were they made contemporaneously with the phone calls?

Yes.

Were they for real?

Yes.

Was she an enemy of Anita Hill?

No, she had been a friend.

Did she have political motives?

No. She was a career civil servant.

Confident in the reliability of the phone logs and convinced of their potency in destroying Anita Hill's story, Ken next considered how to put them into the public domain. Time was of the essence because the scheduled vote was now less than twenty hours away. The American people would be the ultimate judges of the credibility of Clarence Thomas and Anita Hill, and faxed phone logs that he believed were devastating to Hill's story were in his hands. What to do? Get them to the press. Where? The *Washington Post*.

The White House phoned the *Post* and offered the logs off the record. The *Post* said they would take the phone logs but only if the White House and supporters of Clarence Thomas could be attributed as the source. Ken Duberstein did not think this was fair. He suspected that the *Post* would write a phone log story that would try to show not the weakness of Hill's allegations but that the White House was trying to do a job on Anita Hill. To Ken, the source should be those who kept or discovered the logs. Important information should not be turned into a story about the White House.

Failing to get the phone log story to the *Washington Post* on what he considered to be fair terms, Ken next thought of Alan Simpson, the Senate's Republican whip, who was to be on the ABC television program "Nightline" at 11:30 that night opposite one of the reporters who broke the story, NPR's Nina Totenberg.

Al Simpson from Cody, Wyoming, is one of my favorite senators. Very tall, very skinny, very thoughtful, very funny, he has one characteristic that is not universally shared by politicians: he says exactly what he thinks with force and spirit and with no apparent concern for the consequences. Ken reasoned that if the *Washington Post* would not cover the full story of the phone logs in the morning paper, at least Al Simpson could alert the country to the outlines of the story on "Nightline."

Al and Ann Simpson and Sally and I were at a dinner at the Folger Library that night at an event that honors outstanding American writers, who give readings prior to a late dinner. Ken reached Al by phone at the dinner, told him of the phone logs, and read him some of the notations on the memo slips. After talking to Ken, Al found me at the dinner and whispered that he wanted to speak with me. We slipped into the hall next to the dining area, and Al, referring to notes he had taken of the phone call, told me of the results of the search of the phone logs. It was even better news than I had expected—not five or six calls, as both Clarence and Diane Holt had guessed, but eleven, and references to specific comments Anita Hill had asked to be passed on to Clarence. I was relieved and delighted by this development. Who would believe Anita Hill after this? So when Al asked whether I agreed that he should tell of the phone logs on "Nightline," I said, definitely yes.

Simpson left the library at about 10:45 for the ABC studios and was briefed further by Ken over his car phone. As he planned, he did raise the phone log story on the program, but what stands out in his mind about the program and its immediate aftermath was not the phone logs but his flareup with Nina Totenberg.

Washington participants on "Nightline" are in the same ABC building but not on the same set. Each guest is in a separate room; they can see each other on television monitors. On this program, the three guests were Nina Totenberg, Al Simpson, and Senator Paul Simon. Al recalls that he was physically tired; that he was reminded in the lead-in to the story that Totenberg had played a part in bringing down a previous Supreme Court nominee, Douglas Ginsberg; and that she looked completely satisfied on the television monitor. Al remembers erupting on the program and accusing Totenberg of biased journalism. He describes himself as "jabbering like a monkey, making an ass out of myself."

After the program, according to Al, he walked out of the studio onto the street where he found Totenberg talking to Senator and Mrs. Simon. He says that he walked up to Totenberg and said, "I want to tell you something, Nina. What I said in there, don't take it lightly. I meant every word of it." To which, he says, she replied in an obscene rage, hurling the now-popular four-letter epithet at him three times in a string of obscenities that went on for about three and a half minutes.

By Monday night, Clarence and Ginni had had enough of the media stakeout outside their home. At 9:30, after the reporters and crews had left for the day, they drove to Georgetown to spend the night and the next day in the home of friends, the Silbermans. Larry Silberman recalls that while Clarence was visibly fatigued, both he and Ginni seemed relieved that the end was hours away. Ricky Silberman remembers that when Clarence arrived that night, he seemed exhausted, that he kept shaking his head saying, "I don't understand it," and that he and Ginni soon went to their room on the fourth floor of the Silbermans' home. Ricky recalls one thing Clarence said to her that night: "He told me that he had decided he had done everything that he could do. That he had been as good a person as he could be and that if this was going to happen, it was just going to happen and he would be able to live with it."

Tuesday, October 8

Every Tuesday when I am in Washington, I begin the day by celebrating Holy Communion at St. Alban's Episcopal Church. The Tuesday communion service is one of my few ministerial responsibilities, and it is generally attended by ten to fifteen people. This Tuesday, there were a few more in attendance—old friends appearing to show support on what they knew would be a trying and important day. One of the members of the congregation that day was Jim Cannon, a delightful and highly able person I knew from his days as chief of staff to then Senate majority leader Howard Baker. After the service, Jim gave me a scrap of paper on which he had written what he claimed was the prayer of a medieval knight: "Lord, I shall be verie busie this day. I may forget Thee, but do not Thou forget me."[39] I carried it in my pocket the rest of the day.

By midmorning I received strong indications that the day would not be as decisive as I hoped. On my way to a 10:00 A.M. meeting in Senator Dole's Capitol office, I ran into Senator Pat Leahy, the Vermont Democrat and a member of the Judiciary Committee. He suggested that we should delay the vote and put both Clarence and Anita Hill under oath so that the matter could be cleared up. As he made this suggestion, I thought that it would clear nothing up to put the two under oath, for it would be simply his word against her word.

The Leahy suggestion became a refrain for the balance of the day as one senator after another suggested delay and one senator after another stated that another hearing would put the controversy at rest. I was of the view that another hearing would accomplish nothing; it would fuel the energy of the interest groups opposed to Thomas and extend the ordeal of my friend.

What occurred in Senator Dole's office was more a freeform happening than a formal meeting. In addition to staff offices, the minority leader has three large rooms on the west front of the Capitol with a splendid view of the Mall and the Washington Monument. The three major parts of the office are from north to south—a reception room, a conference room, and the leader's personal office—all quite spacious and elegant. I moved from room to room, person to person, place to place. The office served more as a nerve center than a conference site, and the atmosphere was both busy and nervous.

From my arrival at ten o'clock until midafternoon, much of the discussion was about the wisdom of agreeing to a delay of the scheduled vote. Arlen Specter had told a television reporter on a morning news program that he thought the vote should be postponed, and he repeated this opinion now. Arlen believed that delay was important for the sake of the Senate, the Supreme Court, and Clarence Thomas. Given the seriousness of the charge, he thought that all would lose face if there were not an inquiry into the Hill allegation. He held that the Court should not be under the cloud of an unexamined charge, and that to proceed that day would undermine public confidence in the Senate as well.

Ken Duberstein and Fred McClure, also in the office much of the day, disagreed. A delay was a mistake, they countered, and we would lose ground if the vote was postponed. The longer the delay, the more time the interest groups would have to attack Clarence and drum up opposition to his confirmation. I agreed with Ken and Fred, and I continued to believe that further investigation and further hearings would not settle the question given the he said–she said nature of the controversy. Also, Clarence did not want a delay, and we should not ask him to consider one unless we as his supporters strongly recommended that course.

During the morning, though, it became increasingly clear that Clarence would not be confirmed if the vote was taken on schedule. Richard Bryan, a Nevada Democrat who had previously announced his intention to vote for confirmation, told me in a phone conversation that it was necessary to postpone the vote and hold a hearing on the charges. He was prepared to vote against confirmation if the vote were held that afternoon. In another call, David Boren of Oklahoma suggested that he might vote present if the vote were held that day; he could not vote for confirmation absent a delay.

When I walked to the Senate floor, where Senator Joseph Lieberman was presiding, I asked his views. Joe still expected to vote for confirmation but thought the vote should be delayed.

As the day progressed, it became clear that most of the thirteen Democratic senators we counted on to vote for Clarence wanted a delay and that they would not vote for him if the vote were held that afternoon.

By early afternoon, Ken Duberstein had concluded that we would have forty-seven votes for confirmation that day but could not reach fifty. At the same time, Ken believed that further delay, especially one extending through another weekend, would give the rejuvenated opposition more time to find more ways to oppose confirmation.

Of those present in the minority leader's office, Bob Dole himself was the strongest in advocating a delay. If the vote were held that day, we would lose; therefore, in his opinion, delay was the only practical option. In the middle of the afternoon, at Bob Dole's conference table, Senator Thurmond asked for an assessment of the chance of winning if we voted that afternoon. The consensus, especially as expressed by Bob, was that we could not win. Strom brought the discussion to a close: "Well, that settles it."

That settled it in the minds of the Republican senators. We could not win unless we agreed to a delay, so we must agree to a delay. But the ultimate decision was not ours, and we recognized that. The decision belonged to Clarence. We could not force him to continue his ordeal if he was unwilling, and at that point, he was unwilling.

Clarence and Ginni were still at the home of their friends the Silbermans. By the accounts of all present, Clarence was tense, nervously pacing the patio and around the pool and smoking cigars. Ricky had gone off to work, and Larry and Ginni were busy answering the telephone.

Larry Silberman says that Tuesday was "one of the worst days of my life." As Clarence paced, Larry and Ginni tried to keep up with events on television. Larry recalls trying to cheer up Clarence with reports that none of the senators had changed his or her announced position, but by 2:20 P.M., Clarence looked tense, gray, and miserable.

During the morning, Ginni had talked to Clarence about whether the vote would occur as scheduled. He told her that, whether or not he had the votes, he did not want a postponement. He wanted his ordeal to end at a time certain, six o'clock that evening, so that, win or lose, he could get on with his life.

As we were meeting in the minority leader's office that morning, Duberstein and I decided with others that I should hold a news conference in the Senate news room and release two documents: the phone logs documenting Anita Hill's calls to Clarence and a sworn statement, signed by Clarence, denying Hill's charges. To that point, Clarence had not made public statements responding to any of the charges made against him during the entire confirmation process. Now, all of us in the minority leader's office agreed that the time had come for Clarence to depart from that rule and to speak through a written affidavit. The matter was too serious for the response to be in the form of my paraphrasing Clarence's denials to me. I should go to the media, but as a messenger carrying Clarence's own words, issued under oath.

According to Ken, the drafting of the affidavit involved Clarence and Larry Silberman on one end of the phone line, and himself, McClure, a half-dozen senators, and a few Senate staffers on the other end, and about ten drafts were produced before the final affidavit. Ken recalls that Clarence produced the first draft, which was quite specific, and that there was much discussion about whether Clarence should refute each detail of Hill's charges with specificity or simply issue a general denial. Finally the participants to the discussion agreed that a strong and clear general denial of the entirety of the Hill allegations would be more powerful than a point-by-point denial.

Now I had a concern that continued through the next two days and vanished only after Clarence persisted in his strong statement that there was no basis whatever to the charge against him: that Clarence would make statements overstating the case and thus provide grounds for a charge of perjury. In my mind there was one possibility that was infinitely worse than losing the confirmation: a subsequent impeachment proceeding based on the misstatement of a sworn fact. To me, any statement under oath was perilous.

This is not to say that I was doubting Clarence's veracity. I was not. Rather, I was trying to make some sense out of Hill's charges. Suppose, I thought, that Clarence had once made some comment to Anita Hill that he thought innocent. He may have forgotten that he made it. Suppose she thought he was being sexually suggestive, even if no such meaning was intended. It seemed possible to me that a case of mistaken meaning could first be the cause of our present predicament and then, worse, become the grounds for a charge of perjury.

I had previously served on a special Senate committee receiving evidence on the impeachment of U.S. district judge Walter Nixon and had witnessed the result of an exaggerated statement under oath. Judge Nixon had sworn that he had never discussed a certain case with any person, when, in fact, he had discussed the case but under circumstances that seemed innocent and trivial.[40]

As the week went on, several of Clarence's friends pressed him hard, not to test his veracity but to learn whether there might have been a misunderstanding between him and his accuser. Repeatedly, Clarence made the same response: there was no basis whatever for Anita Hill's story.

Larry Silberman questioned Clarence about any possible social interaction with Anita Hill before Clarence signed the affidavit. Clarence told Larry that once or twice he had taken Hill to her home from work and that, at her invitation, he had gone to her apartment for a Coke or a beer. At first, Larry was concerned that this might suggest to some that Clarence was pursuing Hill and that perhaps he had asked her for dates. In response, Clarence repeated what he had previously told Larry: he did not find Hill attractive, and she had bad breath. By the time of the hearing, when Clarence testified that he had visited Hill's apartment for a Coke or a beer, Larry concluded that this fact was not incriminating but exculpatory. In Larry's mind, a woman who had been sexually harassed would not invite the harasser into her apartment for a drink.

When the final draft of the affidavit was agreed to by Clarence, Ken and the others assembled in the minority leader's office; it was typed at the Justice Department and taken by a notary to the Silbermans' house for Clarence's signature. Finally, Clarence was going to speak for himself.

After Dole, Thurmond, Duberstein, McClure, and I concluded that we could not win a vote that evening, I went to the small desk in the reception room to phone Clarence. When Larry Silberman answered, he could tell from the tone of my voice that the news was not good. He called Clarence to the phone in the kitchen, and he and Ginni listened in on the discussion.

I told Clarence that I thought we would lose if the vote were held that day but that I could not assure him that we would win if we delayed. I reviewed my conversations with Senators Bryan and Boren and told him that it would be like pulling the plug to proceed with a vote that evening. Our recommendation was to seek a delay of two days before the vote, but it was a decision only he could make.

Clarence, very upset, asked, "What are they doing to me?" He said that he did not know if he could take it anymore, but that he wanted to think about it for a few minutes and speak to me later. During that conversation, it was my impression that Clarence was thinking about pushing forward with the vote that day in order to end the agony. As he put it weeks later, "It wasn't so much that I didn't want a delay. I didn't think physically I could take it."

After Clarence hung up, he talked with Ginni and Larry Silberman. According to Larry, Clarence was leaning heavily toward letting the vote go forward. Larry argued strongly in favor of delay, more out of concern for Clarence's honor than for winning the vote. He argued that if Clarence ended it, it would look as though he was afraid of further investigation and afraid of another hearing, and, therefore, not telling the truth. Larry added a second argument: "You have to dance with the girl that brought you. . . . Jack Danforth has run this thing this far. You ought to follow his advice." He thought that it would probably take more than an additional forty-eight hours, but that Clarence "should go through whatever time it takes."

Uncertain of whether Clarence could endure a delay, Ginni was far more tentative in her counsel than Larry. Perhaps it would be better to proceed with an immediate vote if that was what Clarence wanted. At least a vote would put an end to the suffering.

About fifteen minutes after the first call, I phoned Clarence again and put him on the phone with Senator Simpson. He recalls that after speaking with Senator Simpson, he spoke with Senators Dole and Hatch and then with Allen Moore, who had been my legislative director when Clarence worked on my Senate staff. I remember standing behind Dole's desk, looking down to the Mall at the Washington Monument, not listening to what was said. To me, the decision belonged entirely to Clarence. If others tried to persuade him, that was their business.

Clarence recalls that Senator Dole talked about the political reality: not enough votes for confirmation. The theme of the other callers, especially Allen Moore, was more personal. Clarence had to agree to delay the vote and endure a hearing in order to clear his name. He could not clear his name by walking away from the fight.

Al Simpson recalls that Clarence told him, "I am exhausted. I'm washed out," and "I can't understand why she would do it." In that call, and in a call the following Thursday night, Simpson adopted the style and the verbiage he learned from a football coach while he was in college. He recalls telling Clarence, "Buckle up your guts, pal, and get on the field and forget all the other stuff." Simpson's locker-room-style pep talk was borne out of his own experience, not only as a former football player but as a person who in his youth had spent a couple of nights in the Laramie jail and had been on federal probation for shooting mailboxes. In Simpson's words, he had "internalized the whole issue by then . . . they had been going through this guy's laundry for 103 days . . . they did it in the most contrived and ugly way every week. Every three days they would stick one in his ear." To Al's mind, this was no time for weakness and self-pity on the part of Clarence. He remembers saying, "Look, if somebody did this to me and it was all a lie, I'll tell you what I'd do, Clarence, and if you can't do that, I won't vote for you."

Orrin Hatch remembers taking a gentler approach. His purpose "was to try to buck [Clarence] up. . . . It wasn't a question of courage. He had that. He is a strong person. It was a question of helping him to realize he has friends and that we are going to bat for him." Clarence, he says, was very upset during the conversation; he wanted to end his ordeal as quickly as possible—but he also wanted to clear his name.

Allen Moore had reached the conclusion that if there was to be a delay, Clarence should seize the initiative by being the one to ask for it, stating that he wanted to clear his name. Allen went to the minority leader's office to press his view, and when he learned that Orrin Hatch was talking to Clarence, he stood next to Orrin so that he could talk to him. Allen remembers saying to Clarence, "You get on the phone with Jack. You ask Jack for a delay. You tell him you want to clear your name."

I then picked up the phone for a very short conversation with Clarence. I asked him what he wanted to do. He said, "I have to clear my name, Jack," and asked me to try to get the vote postponed. I assured him that I would try for a postponement of forty-eight hours.

Whether to agree to a delay in the scheduled vote, and if so for how long, was a strategic question for Clarence's supporters in the Senate, but it was a purely personal matter for Clarence. Ginni Thomas recalls the few minutes between the two calls and the conflicting emotions she observed in her husband. Clarence was at the outer limits of tolerable suffering, and that was a strong motive for seeking an immediate resolution to his torment—just end the suffering, whatever the result. Even a defeat could be seen as a merciful coup de grace. Ginni believes, on the other hand, that there were two reasons Clarence agreed to endure delay and the ordeal of a second hearing. First, Allen Moore's argument was persuasive. Clarence had worked a lifetime building his reputation; he could not allow it to be destroyed without a fight. He had to clear his name. Second, Ginni believes that Clarence did not want to let down the president, me, and all the others who had supported him. Permitting a vote that day would be inviting immediate defeat, tantamount to quitting—and thus not permissible for Clarence Thomas.

For me, the alternatives of delay and immediate defeat were almost equally tormenting. Certainly I did not want my friend to lose, especially when the loss would be more than a seat on the Supreme Court; it would be a stain on his character. But what would come of more investigation, more sensational stories in the media, the circus of a public hearing? How could Clarence vindicate himself under these circumstances? How could he prove a negative?

In an effort to avoid the dilemma of immediate defeat or prolonged agony, I had an idea; I doubted it would work but thought it was at least worth a try. Those of us who were gathered in Senator Dole's office understood that Senator George Mitchell was simultaneously holding a meeting with thirteen Democratic senators who had previously indicated their intent to vote for Clarence's confirmation. Of course, I knew all of them, and some of them were good friends. Maybe they would yield to a final appeal. Maybe if I could meet with them, I could persuade them that delay would accomplish nothing, that the nature of Anita Hill's allegation was unprovable one way or the other, and that they should do as they had intended: vote that afternoon to confirm the nominee.

It was an odd idea and unlikely to succeed; senators of one party do not attend strategy meetings of the other party. But I asked Sheila Burke, Senator Dole's chief of staff, to phone the majority leader's office and ask if the Democratic senators would see me. The response was instantaneous and expected: absolutely not.

With no possibility of a successful vote that day, the only alternative to certain defeat was postponement of the vote. The remaining questions were the duration of the delay and the ground rules for what was to follow.

Clarence's supporters—especially Ken Duberstein, Orrin Hatch, and I—believed that the period of postponement should be as short as possible. Ken recalls that during the afternoon, Clarence's Senate supporters made reference to the ill-fated nomination of John Tower for secretary of defense.[41] The longer a nomination was pending, the more time the opposition had to develop more stories.

Orrin Hatch was especially anxious that the vote occur before another weekend elapsed. Weekends, for Orrin, were the most likely times to expect sensational attacks. If there was a prolonged delay, anti-Thomas interest groups would have more time to develop attacks, and Clarence would lose. In his words, "There is no question that the groups would dredge up anything else they could find, factual or otherwise." Additionally, Orrin believed that day after day of pounding in the media would create a momentum against the nominee in the opinion polls. In Orrin's analysis, a nomination that was lost in the public opinion polls would be lost on the floor of the Senate. Finally, Orrin believed, as did I, that Clarence was so upset by events that he could not have endured many more days without a resolution.

During the next several hours, my effort was to get the vote rescheduled as soon as possible. I asked Senator Thurmond's top aide, Duke Short, to phone the Justice Department to find out how long it would take for the FBI to conduct any additional investigation. The word I got back was that it could be done in twenty-four hours. I had told Clarence that my goal was to get the entire matter concluded in forty-eight hours.

In retrospect, although a longer delay may have been unbearably agonizing for Clarence, it would have better served the cause of his defense. In effect, this was the trial of his life, but it was a trial with no procedures and almost no time to prepare a defense. Like any other defendant, Clarence should have retained legal counsel, and that counsel should have had the time and the power to examine Anita Hill's prior statements in advance of the proceeding, to interview Anita Hill in advance, under oath, and to interview other witnesses who might be helpful. None of this occurred. I should have insisted on it. I should have insisted that Clarence have the benefit of an adequately prepared attorney. Instead, I was so concerned about the activities of the interest groups and about the mental state of my friend and so convinced that a hearing would prove nothing that I demanded a rushed proceeding. A disorganized fire drill followed, and I was the one who had sounded the alarm.

After Clarence agreed to a delay of the vote, his Senate supporters left Senator Dole's office and proceeded to the Senate floor. I sought recognition and explained to the Senate that I had spoken with the nominee on the telephone and that he had asked me to seek a postponement of the scheduled vote so that he could clear his name.[42] After that speech, various interested senators, including Senators Mitchell and Biden, Senators Bob Graham, Wyche Fowler, Joe Lieberman, and Dennis DeConcini (the announced pro-Thomas Democrats), Simpson, Thurmond, Hatch, and myself met in the conference room of the majority leader's office to discuss what procedures would be followed with respect to a new hearing and a date for a vote in the Senate.

I was pressing for the shortest and most expeditious process possible. I suggested that only Clarence Thomas and Anita Hill should appear as live witnesses, that they should be questioned only by counsel, that senators should not make time-consuming opening statements, and that any other witnesses should submit testimony in the form of written affidavits.

Ken Duberstein recalls that at some point during the afternoon, a senator raised the possibility of holding the hearing in executive session, that is, behind closed doors. However, everyone else agreed that since the charges had been made public, the hearing would have to be public.[43]

While I was pushing for a speedy hearing and vote, Joe Biden stated that he did not want the proceedings to appear to be rushed and that that would be the appearance if he agreed to my demands. I was convinced that the leaders of the Thomas opposition wanted as long a delay as possible in order to continue their attack. But Joe's insistence that his committee proceed deliberately had nothing to do with aiding the opposition. At no time have I doubted Joe's motives; he had an extremely difficult challenge, and he was trying to be fair. Biden was more hopeful than I was that the hearing would produce useful information. Moreover, women's groups had mobilized, and they would severely criticize the Senate if the process appeared too rushed.

The meeting in Senator Mitchell's office was interrupted by a vote in the Senate on the Foreign Aid Conference Report. A reassuring comment Senator Moynihan made to me during the vote was further evidence that senators who had leaned toward voting for confirmation saw the delay more as a way to satisfy the opposition groups than as a threat to the nominee. Senator Moynihan expressed confidence that, while a reopening of the hearing was necessary, confirmation would follow. It was a comforting comment by a Senate friend, but it did not correctly foretell either the horror to follow or Pat Moynihan's own vote against confirmation.

It is said that the Senate is a club, a place of warmth and civility where political differences are contested with the gentleness of friends as if on the golf course or the tennis court. To a remarkable extent, that characterization is true. Senate rules are designed to promote civil debate. For example, during floor debate, a senator is not permitted to attack a colleague's motives and is supposed to direct all statements to the chair, not to a fellow senator. This indirect form of debate lessens the possibility of personal confrontation.

Off the Senate floor, relations are generally friendly. In the Senate gym or around the lunch table, we put aside legislative differences in good-humored exchanges. This is not to say that we all are civil to each other all the time. Tempers do flare, and sometimes dramatically, but in my years in the Senate, I had never witnessed an explosion of uncontrolled anger like mine in the late afternoon of October 8.

It started in the conference room of Senator Mitchell's office. I was sitting at the table with perhaps six or eight other senators, and I completely lost my temper in a table-pounding, shouting, red-in-the-face, profane rage. Senator Strom Thurmond, then a vigorous eighty-nine years old and a beloved institution in the Senate, was shocked by my behavior. He came up to me afterward and said, "You are a minister. You shouldn't take the Lord's name in vain."

I attribute my explosion to the extreme frustration of the moment. The confirmation of Clarence Thomas had consumed my time and energy for more than three months. Having warded off a series of attacks against my friend, I was prepared for certain victory. The votes were in hand; the months of tension were behind me. Then, as all was nearly won, all appeared lost. Clarence seemed close to ruin. Triumph became disaster, not through accident, but by the design of Clarence's opponents. Colleagues I had counted on to support my friend were withholding their support, insisting on another hearing, insisting on what I knew would be extreme torment for Clarence.

My outburst was threatening as well as shocking. I threatened my colleagues, and the threat was as deceitful as it was angry. Here was the threat: the same moderate Democrats who had announced their support for Clarence Thomas and were now withholding their votes were counting on me to take the lead in fashioning a compromise on civil rights legislation that was then before the Senate. Southern Democrats, in particular, were in a difficult political position. Their black constituents wanted civil rights legislation passed that would overturn several unfavorable cases that had been decided recently by the Supreme Court. Their conservative constituents and their business supporters were fearful that Congress would pass a "quota" bill, that is, legislation that would require the hiring of blacks on the basis of their numerical representation in the workforce. I was their best hope, for I offered the possibility of a Republican-endorsed civil rights bill that they could claim would not entail quotas. During the weeks immediately before the scheduled vote on the Thomas nomination, many of the same Democrats who had threatened to withhold their votes had asked me how I was doing in my efforts to produce a civil rights compromise. My counter-threat was that if they would not support my friend, they could forget about a civil rights bill.

It was a threat I did not mean, and for that reason, it was deceitful. After working nearly two years on the civil rights legislation, I was not about to walk away from it.[44] Perhaps my threat can be explained as the rhetorical excess of an enraged person. Whatever the explanation, it was wrong. I am ashamed of my outburst that day and of much else that I did and said in the week that followed. I will do my best to give the flavor of it by quoting from notes I made a few weeks after the event:

"I said that this makes me really mad, and that this is the kind of treatment I get for my friend. The leaks, the delays, this is a problem that was created by the Senate and by the Senate staff. Now you want to keep torturing this guy for an indefinite period of time. Senators threatening not to vote or vote no unless we have the delay are the ones who say to me every time I come on the floor of the Senate, How's the civil rights bill coming, Jack? What are you doing for us on the civil rights bill? You guys rely on me to save you on the civil rights bill and to work out something that is acceptable to you and then you treat me like this. I'm getting sick of it. I'm getting tired of it. Forget about it."

I think that for some people temper tantrums are a negotiating technique. Certainly at the time of my flareup, I was trying to work out the timing and rules for what would follow in the confirmation process, and it occurred to me that a show of temper could do no harm. But this was not a contrivance. It was real rage together with a sense that there was nothing to be lost in letting it escape.

Later, however, when the agreement for scheduling the hearing and the vote had been reached and no useful purpose could be served by a further display of passion, I could not regain control of my furor. Early that evening, I again took the Senate floor and let loose an un-restrained tirade against the foes of Clarence Thomas.[45] Shaking with anger, I attacked the leak of Anita Hill's statement, and, with a stare fixed on staffers of Senator Metzenbaum seated on a bench at the back of the Senate chamber, I attacked those I believed to be the leakers.

Allen Moore watched that speech on television at his kitchen table. He had known me very well for a long time and had worked closely with me on a daily basis for more than a decade, first as legislative director in my Senate office and then as chief of staff when I was chairman of the Commerce Committee. Few other people know me better. Months later, Allen said of that speech, "You scared me. I thought, 'He's way out there on the edge.' It was weird."

But it was not relentless, uninterrupted rage. There was work to be done—work in arranging the details of the second round of confirmation hearings, and this was done first in Senator Mitchell's office and then in a meeting in Senator Dole's office between Biden and me, later joined by Duberstein, Hatch, and Mitchell.

We asked for the earliest possible date for a vote in the Senate and stated that we thought the hearing should be on Thursday and the vote on Friday, October 11. Senator DeConcini said that he had a personal conflict on that date. We settled on Tuesday, October 15, for the vote.

We asked that the hearing be limited in scope to Anita Hill's charges and that it not include general issues of sexual conduct such as whether Clarence had ever seen an X-rated movie or extraneous matters such as his travel schedule while at EEOC. Biden said that the hearing would be limited to sexual harassment, whether of Anita Hill or anyone else.

We asked that Clarence be given the choice whether he or Anita Hill would testify first. Biden agreed. We asked that the hearing not be expanded to include character witnesses. Again, Biden agreed.

Speaking of Joe Biden's procedural decisions controlling the second round of hearings, Orrin Hatch has said, "I think he knew that this was an unfair process, and I think he was bending over to make it fair, and so was Mitchell at that point." That was true.

Ricky Silberman returned to her Georgetown home about six o'clock to find Clarence and Ginni still there and her husband, Larry, nearly as morose as the nominee.

Larry was Clarence's colleague on the court of appeals and that day had served as Clarence's adviser and companion in distress. He had advised Clarence to agree to delay the vote but now was having second thoughts. Larry remembers: "I couldn't cheer him up because I felt so terrible. . . . I was worried that the advice I gave him was wrong; that he might be better off forcing it to a vote."

That same fear dogged Larry throughout the week that followed. Watching the broadcast of Anita Hill's testimony he thought that "it was so awful maybe I had been wrong the week before. Maybe it would have been better just to go through with the vote, and whatever way it happened, it was over."

Again and again that Tuesday as Clarence paced the Silberman house, he told Larry that he loved being a judge on the court of appeals; losing the vote and returning to his job would not be a terrible result. Again and again, Larry agonized over whether it was a mistake to urge his friend to endure what was to come.

Having served as Clarence's vice chair on the EEOC, Ricky Silberman knew Clarence at least as well as her husband did. An admitted optimist, Ricky saw a potential silver lining in a second hearing, and in a heart-to-heart talk with Clarence that evening, that is what she told him. At one point, Clarence looked at her and said, "Boy, you sure can find a pony anywhere."

Ricky explains that she was heartsick at the first hearing. She was convinced that the public had not seen the real Clarence Thomas. In her mind, there was no question that Clarence had been overly managed. She says, "He looked like he was being handled.

"I had felt that in the packaging of Clarence Thomas that they really took something away from Clarence. Because Clarence values, above everything, courage.

"I think he was scared over the summer, and he didn't like being scared." Now he had a second chance—a chance to show the real Clarence Thomas to the American people.

In Ricky's view, during the first hearing, the public "felt that he hadn't been straight, and he had been evasive and he had not come across with the strong character he had. If he sat there this time and was himself, that would be more important than anything. The American people had to see Clarence for what he was."

To Ricky, sexual harassment "was the worst possible charge that could have been leveled against Clarence. You could have said he had stolen and it would not have been as important as somebody saying that he took advantage of someone who worked for him—of a woman." But in a strong fight talk, Ricky told Clarence that this "worst possible charge" gave him a chance to be himself again.

Ricky recalls that there was some discussion about whether to send out for Chinese food, but that Clarence said that he wanted to go home. Then she recalls that I phoned Clarence and that I, apparently, turned the phone over to Ken Duberstein. Ken has no recollection of the ensuing discussion and concludes that someone else must have been on the phone. In any event, Ricky could hear only Clarence's end of the conversation, which had to do with his preparation for the upcoming hearing. What Ricky heard Clarence say was just what she wanted to hear, although his new strength was momentary. In her words:

"He said, 'Now wait a minute.' He said, 'We'll talk tomorrow.' He said, 'But I want you all to understand one thing. I did it your way last time; I'm doing it my way this time.' Those are his exact words. 'They're going to see me, the unvarnished me, and if that's not good enough, so be it.' At that point, he was really mad. He had gone from despair, despondency, 'I should have gotten out,' to, 'Yeah, I'm going to fight.' . . . Clarence said, 'I will write the statement. I'm going to go home and write the statement, nobody's going to have anything to do with that.' "

When Clarence hung up, he and Ginni packed and left the Silberman's house. As Ricky recalls, "He looked awful."

Wednesday, October 9

Ginni Thomas describes Wednesday as "a roller coaster of a day." It certainly was, as were the two days that followed. For three days, Clarence was on an emotional and deeply spiritual journey. The journey was not a steady progression from one point to the next. It had ups and downs, much despondency and some exuberation, panic and hope, weakness and strength, despair and faith, all changing by the hour, all accompanied by the one constant of fatigue, all leading from the death of this proud and strong man to the resurrection of Clarence Thomas.

When Clarence returned home Tuesday night, the surge of determination observed by Ricky Silberman had vanished. They went to bed, and Ginni was drifting off to sleep, when Clarence broke down. "That was the night, in my opinion, Clarence was really destroyed," says Ginni. She held him and tried to comfort him as he cried, and as they talked, Clarence said he needed Kay James and Elizabeth Law and their husbands to come to him and to pray with him.

Clarence describes his feelings as he lay in bed with Ginni: "It was so clear to me when I told Virginia to call them that there was no way out—that I was in a canyon with no way out."

Clarence was accustomed to prayer, but his prayers had been private. He had never asked people to come to pray with him. At 12:25 A.M., he asked Ginni to call the Laws and the Jameses.

Steven Law, Senator Mitch McConnell's administrative assistant, answered the phone at 12:45 A.M. It was Ginni asking for Elizabeth. Elizabeth works for the Family Research Council and had known Ginni a number of years; at one point she and Ginni had been in the same early morning Bible study group. Ginni asked if Elizabeth and Steven could be at the Thomases' house at 8:30 that morning.

Kay James remembers that her phone rang at about 1:00 A.M. She had known Clarence through what she calls "the conservative black network," and she knew Ginni through a Bible study group. After speaking with Ginni, Kay and her husband, Charles, speculated on what could have prompted the call. Two possibilities occurred to them: either Clarence was making the decision to withdraw and needed friends to stand with him, or there was some element of truth in the Anita Hill story and Clarence needed to share it with someone. Whatever the reason, Kay and Charles were determined to be with Clarence.

When the Laws and the Jameses arrived at 8:30, the sidewalk outside the Thomas house was crowded with television camera crews. The shades were down and the curtains pulled tight to preserve privacy. It seemed to Kay that the Thomases were prisoners in their own home. She recalls an urge to open the curtains and the windows and let the captives out.

Clarence was sitting in the family room when they arrived. It was immediately obvious to Kay that he had had no sleep. She describes him as "a broken human being." Ginni told her that the previous

night he lay in bed in the fetal position. Steven Law remembers that
Ginni opened the front door "looking tired and stressed." Clarence
was sitting in the family room "looking very worn-out and tense, but
controlled."

Charles and Kay tried to be upbeat. To cheer him up, they gave him
T-shirts and buttons that Clarence's supporters had provided. One
said, "Clarence can, so I can too." Another, "Dreams can come true."
Another, "Taking a stand so Clarence can take a seat." Clarence took
these and put them aside. "He really wasn't interested," says Kay.

For the next three hours, the six friends prayed and read the Bible
and talked about the spiritual implications of what was happening.
Steven Law noticed that Clarence was not teary and thought, "This
guy doesn't have anything left in him to cry."

Over and over again, Clarence looked down, shook his head, and
said, "I just don't understand what's going on. Why are they doing this
to me?" Kay remembers him saying, "I have not been a Christian all
my life, and none of us are perfect. And there are things that maybe
they could have said or maybe there are things they could have dug
up, but this isn't one of them."

In the course of the visit, Kay told the group that the week before,
she discovered that she had a tumor. While she was waiting in a
Houston hotel room to learn the results of the tests, she asked, "Why
me?" She told her friends that she concluded, "Either you believe in
God or you don't."

Clarence responded to Kay's story saying simply, "I do."

Kay countered with, "Well, then, if you do, you have to figure out
what this means for your life. Those are the kinds of things we need
to be thinking about and not despairing."

Clarence remembers that they read Scripture, held hands, and
prayed. He says, "There was a lot of anguish and outpouring of pain.
A lot of turning it over to God. A lot of recognizing our own fallibility,
our own weaknesses. . . . Someone said to me that we have to lean on
God. I said, no, no, no. You don't understand. I've been leaning on
God all summer—this time God has to lift me up. There was only one
set of prints in the sand."

The friends talked about the biblical story of David hiding in a cave and how wretched he felt,[46] and they began calling themselves "cave dwellers."

In trying to make sense of Clarence's suffering, Elizabeth Law suggested that perhaps God wanted to strip away any notion that Clarence was being put on the Supreme Court by the president or the Senate or political handlers. She suggested that if Clarence is on the Court, it must be clear that God puts him there. There is nothing more that Clarence can do to get it; it is in God's hands.

To this, Clarence replied, "I don't even care if I get it anymore. I am happy with the job I have got."

The Laws gave Clarence and Ginni "praise tapes," soon supplemented by other religious tapes that Ginni bought. The Laws' idea was that the Thomases' home should be permeated by religious music.

Both Clarence and Ginni clearly recall that one of the subjects discussed in the meeting was the reality of evil. Evil was discussed as a cosmic force with earthly manifestations. Spiritual warfare was fought between good and evil, and a theater of that war at that moment was the fight over the confirmation of Clarence Thomas.

According to Kay, Clarence seemed "indignant and resolved" that Wednesday morning but not bitter. She had no sense that Clarence was desperately asking God to help him get out of his situation. Rather, he was trying to make sense out of events, to see God's hand in what was happening. Kay remembers Clarence saying, "I can see that this is bigger than me. This is about where the country is going. This is about the course of America."

The group met at least once more in the following days, although the participants are unsure of the time. There were several phone calls, especially by Elizabeth Law who repeatedly left the same message on the Thomases' answering machine, "Stand firm." Kay remembers that amid the solemnity there were moments of laughter. Kay and Clarence spoke of their black forebears who held to their faith despite their tribulations. Someone laughed and said, "I guess when they prayed for rain, they carried umbrellas." That developed into a code question for the group. They would say to one another, "Do you have your umbrella today?"

Clarence's friends made a promise to him that they kept during the hearing: whenever he testified, they would pray for him.

As Clarence was receiving the spiritual support of his friends, the consequences of my insistence that we rush ahead with the hearing were dawning on his supporters, especially those with legal training. Lee Liberman knew "it was an incredibly tight timetable, and here we were, preparing the case of the century with no time and no investigative resources."

Not only did we have these limitations to overcome, we also risked the dispersal of our Senate team. The Senate had reconvened for the votes scheduled on the preceding day but was now in recess until the following Tuesday. Members of the Judiciary Committee would be present for Friday's hearing, but there was nothing to keep them in town in the interim, and when the Senate is in recess, senators leave town.

Republican senators had to get organized quickly, before they left town. This was the frantic thought that hit me as I drove to the office that morning, so I called Bob Dole on the car phone with a request: put out a call to all Republicans on the Judiciary Committee and ask them to meet in his office that morning, before leaving town. Bob Dole followed through on that request.

As I made that call, I had one idea in mind, and I knew it would be hard to sell my fellow senators. I thought that under conventional Senate hearing practices, it would be impossible for Clarence to have an adequate defense, and that it was essential that he be represented by an experienced trial lawyer who could question Anita Hill for an extensive period of time.

In a normal Senate hearing, each senator is recognized in turn for a fixed period of time, usually five minutes. I saw such a format as a disaster for Clarence, whether the time segments were short or up to a half-hour each. Even if each Republican senator had been a skillful litigator, the proceedings would be herky-jerky at best, with little time to pursue a line of questioning and ask probing follow-on questions. And not all Republican senators had trial experience; indeed, Senator Chuck Grassley was not a lawyer. Even those who had tried cases were rusty with inexperience. No private party would willingly put his future at stake in a trial held under these circumstances. Although I anticipated that senators would not want to yield to an outsider in such a high-profile responsibility as questioning Anita Hill, I became convinced that such would be in the best interest of Clarence. If the allotted time of all Republican senators could be aggregated and placed in the hands of a trial lawyer, then Clarence would receive a more adequate defense.

On the slim chance that senators would agree to retaining outside counsel, I knew that I must have the name of a first-rate person who could begin preparation for the hearing immediately. As soon as I reached my office, I phoned Larry Silberman to express my concern and to get his suggestions.

Larry had been thinking along the same lines and had already expressed the same concern to White House counsel Boyden Gray. His idea was to retain a first-rate litigator, if not to examine the witnesses, at least to advise Clarence, the Republican senators, and the White House. Boyden referred me to two lawyers who were experts on sexual harassment litigation, Zachary Fasman and Barbara Berish Brown, and they were kind enough to meet with Orrin Hatch and me in my office that afternoon. But the suggestion of retaining an experienced trial lawyer to examine the witnesses was, as expected, rejected by the Republican senators.

Later, Larry Silberman said, "In hindsight, it was really astonishing to me that Republican senators were criticized for their tough questioning. . . . A little more sophistication in terms of cross-examining witnesses would have been helpful. . . . A good trial lawyer would not necessarily have been meaner or tougher. He, or she, would have been more probing."

We met in Senator Dole's conference room at nine o'clock Wednesday morning. In addition to Senator Dole and myself, Senators Hatch

Resurrection

and Brown were present. Duke Short, Senator Thurmond's chief assistant, was there too, and Senator Thurmond arrived later. I began by expressing my concern that the normal format for a Senate hearing would be disastrous, even if each senator were allowed as much as thirty minutes for a round of questioning. I suggested that an experienced trial lawyer should be retained who could conduct all the questioning. We should propose to the Democrats on the committee that both sides should retain outside counsel; if the Democrats refused, we should do so regardless.

No one agreed with me. In particular, Senator Hatch argued that to retain outside counsel would appear to the public as though we had brought in a hired gun to attack Anita Hill. But although there was no support for the idea of outside counsel, all believed that it would be wise to designate one senator to question Anita Hill so that the questioning could be systematic.

Senator Hatch recalls that Senator Warren Rudman, not a member of the Judiciary Committee but highly regarded for his judgment, happened into Senator Dole's office and suggested that Hank Brown be the designated questioner. Hank is very able and has an appealingly gentle demeanor, but we rejected this idea because Hank did not have significant courtroom experience.

Orrin Hatch thought that the best person to question Anita Hill would be Arlen Specter. Orrin respected Arlen as a good lawyer with a great deal of courtroom experience. Arlen had been U.S. attorney in Philadelphia. In Orrin's mind, Arlen was both low key and tenacious, with the ability to burrow in as a questioner and persist without raising his voice. Orrin reasoned that Arlen was the most liberal Republican on the committee, and he had excellent credentials with women's groups as a supporter of choice in abortion. In addition, Orrin said that Arlen would not risk yet more wrath from Pennsylvania conservatives by turning against Clarence Thomas, having enraged them by opposing the Supreme Court nomination of Robert Bork.

Arlen Specter is a very independent senator who, in October 1991, was facing reelection in thirteen months. Clearly in the moderate camp of Senate Republicans, he succeeds in Pennsylvania by appealing to constituents beyond the reach of more staunchly conservative Republicans. It is normal for senators to anticipate the next election, and we considered whether we could expect Arlen to be aggressive in questioning Anita Hill. And if he was aggressive, would he demonstrate his independence by being equally tough on Clarence Thomas? Clarence needed an advocate. He needed what any party to a lawsuit is entitled to as a matter of right: a lawyer who would give full allegiance to him. Those present in Senator Dole's office were concerned that Arlen Specter would see himself not as an advocate but as an independent seeker of truth, and for that reason we decided that the designated Republican questioner of Clarence Thomas would not be Arlen Specter. Rather, we chose Clarence's strong supporter, Orrin Hatch.

We decided that I should phone Arlen and ask him to question Anita Hill and any other witnesses except Clarence Thomas. At Senator Hatch's suggestion, the basic message we gave him was, "We are really counting on you, Arlen."

It was not the ideal way to discuss an important matter; Arlen was on a car phone, on his way to New York for a meeting with the consultant for his forthcoming reelection campaign, David Garth. At least twice the conversation was interrupted as Arlen's car went through tunnels. I began by telling him of my concern about the disjointed nature of Senate hearings and my belief that we should retain outside counsel. Arlen too rejected this suggestion. I then said that it was my request and that of his colleagues on the committee that he be the one to question Anita Hill and the other witnesses, except Clarence Thomas, who would be questioned by Orrin Hatch. Orrin then got on the phone and repeated the message, "We are counting on you."

Arlen recalls that I wanted him to be an advocate for Clarence Thomas and that he said, "I can't do that, Jack. I can't do that." Even in that initial discussion, even before Arlen had accepted the responsibility I had asked him to take, there was a clear distinction in his mind between the role of a lawyer who owes undivided loyalty to the client and the role of a U.S. senator. Here is how Senator Specter explains the distinction: "I actually did not conduct myself the way a lawyer representing Clarence Thomas would conduct himself. Absolutely not. I said at the outset that I was not an advocate. . . . I have only constituency. . . . I don't have clients—constituency, the people of Pennsylvania."

Arlen Specter was acting as a senator, not as an advocate. He was representing a constituency, not a client. And he would face that constituency the following year. The political consequences of what he was about to do were in his mind.

A highly visible role in the hearing might help Arlen mend fences with conservative Republicans after Arlen's vote against Robert Bork, but Arlen was not concerned about a challenge he faced in the Republican primary from a candidate from the Far Right. He thought that his Republican challenger was so extreme as not to present a serious problem. More damaging by far would be the loss of support from women. Indeed, as it later turned out, his general election opponent was a woman, and the principal cause in her campaign was Arlen's support for Clarence Thomas.

In retrospect, Arlen has no doubt that his role in the Thomas hearing hurt him with women, but that was not clear to him at the time. What was clear was that "the smart thing to do politically is to keep your head down." With an election a year away, the wisest political approach was, he thought, to do nothing. Why take risks in such a highly visible and uncertain way? Arlen answers: "I said to myself, this is really an important matter, and I think I can make a contribution. . . . I wasn't going to be in the Senate and on the committee and shy away from something because it was risky."

Strom Thurmond arrived in Senator Dole's office after we had settled on Arlen Specter to question all witnesses except Clarence and on Orrin Hatch to question Clarence. As the ranking Republican on the committee, Strom understandably felt that decisions on how Republicans conduct a hearing should be his, and he expressed his anger that we were acting without his consent. Orrin put his hands on Strom's shoulders and said how much he respected him. Strom snapped, "Get your hands off me." Strom is as thoughtful and considerate as any member of the Senate. As I demonstrated the day before, tense times produce short tempers.

On Wednesday afternoon, Larry Thompson was in his office in a large Atlanta law firm when he received a phone call from his friend Clarence Thomas. An accomplished trial lawyer and a fellow black Republican, Larry had served as U.S. attorney in Atlanta. Clarence asked for help. He explained that he was getting legal advice from well-meaning people in the White House and the Justice Department who had no courtroom experience. Referring to his opponents, he said, "These people are after me and I need you, buddy." Larry said he would be in Washington the next day.

I drove to Clarence's house early that Wednesday afternoon, arriving at about one o'clock. I had not seen him for two days, not since before the Hill press conference, not since before the decision to delay the vote, and not since it had become clear that Clarence Thomas, the person, not just the nominee, was to go on trial before the nation.

I have a dread of pain, not so much of feeling it as of seeing it. Since I was a little boy, I have dreaded seeing accidents. When I see an ambulance stopped on a street, lights flashing, I cannot look. I dread visiting a family where there has been a death. It is not a quality in myself that I am proud of. And now I dreaded seeing Clarence Thomas, dreaded talking to him, dreaded seeing a human wreck who was my friend.

Dread and self-doubt. What do I say? What do I do when I am with him? What words, looks, touches are any good at all? Yet I had to go, just as one has to visit places of sickness and death, not knowing what to say or do, just to be there, praying and hoping that God will speak through you.

It was easy to locate the Thomases' home in its neighborhood of densely packed small houses by the large contingent of reporters and cameramen gathered on the sidewalk out front. One had a motorcycle so he could follow the Thomases if they left the house. Cameramen shouldered their cameras and reporters shouted questions as I walked to the door.

Ginni remembers that I arrived fifteen or twenty minutes after the Laws and the Jameses left. As she opened the door, she remembers saying to me, "There's nothing left of Clarence. He's been destroyed." And she recalls my saying, "It's my fault." I do not remember why I said that or what I meant by it. Perhaps I thought that this would not have happened had I not asked Clarence to leave St. Louis for Washington years earlier. Or perhaps I was beginning to doubt, as Larry Silberman was doubting, the previous day's decision to delay the vote and hold another round of hearings. Perhaps it was only an inane remark at an uncomfortable moment before a difficult visit with a friend. Whatever the meaning, Ginni pointed me to Clarence and then left us alone.

Clarence was in the family room, dressed in a white shirt, suit pants, and suspenders because he and Ginni had been invited to visit President and Mrs. Bush at the White House that afternoon.

Clarence hugged me, not with the happy embrace of friends but the desperate clinging of a lost soul. He sat on a couch, I on a chair next to him, and he put his head in his hands and sobbed. It was not constrained tearfulness but the sobbing of a man beside himself with pain. What came from his mouth was not reasoned discussion but outbursts of emotion. He repeatedly said, "I don't know what to do." He said that he could not survive this, that all the strength was sapped out of him, and that he did not know how he could go any further. I reached over and held his hand until he could regain some measure of composure.

To Clarence's refrain, "I don't know what to do," I responded, "Clarence, what do you want to do? What do you see as your options?"

Clarence answered by listing four options, the first of which was to have forced the question to a vote the previous day, lose, and put the matter behind him. The second option was to quit, to withdraw his name from consideration. I asked him if that was what he wanted to do, and he answered no. The third option was to appear before the Judiciary Committee on the committee's terms, to answer the questions they asked, to be defensive, and to be further humiliated. The fourth option was to be very direct with the committee, to take the offensive, to take the issue to the American people, to fight back. To my question, "What do you want to do?" he answered, "That's what I want to do." Clarence believed that what was happening to him was unfair. He would consent to it no longer. The time had come to take his stand.

Then I took Clarence's hand in mine and prayed with him as we did many times over the next three days, a prayer that remained essentially the same. I prayed that in our weakness we call out to God, and that God has assured us that our prayers are heard and answered. I prayed that we had no strength of our own, that Clarence had nothing left within him, and that any strength he had would have to be supplied by God. I asked that God be with Clarence and empower him as he prepared for the fight that was before him.

The days that followed had their ups and downs, but that afternoon marked the beginning of new hope for Clarence Thomas. Since Sunday he had complained that he had no strength, that he was too weak to continue the struggle. Now there was the hope of power to be supplied by a source outside himself. Not that he was instantly rejuvenated as we sat in his living room. He was visibly weak, red eyed, and haggard. New life was beginning not in a flash but in flickers. Yet there was the beginning of a sense of freedom and of purpose. He was free of the burden of having to win confirmation. Clarence stated with conviction what he had said to Larry Silberman: he did not need to be on the Supreme Court; he was perfectly satisfied with his job on the court of appeals. His words were from a popular country and western song, "Take this job and shove it."

Reflecting on that afternoon, Clarence distinguishes between wanting to serve on the Supreme Court and wanting to win the vote in the Senate. In his words, "Not that I ever wanted to be confirmed. I know this sounds odd, but I wanted to win the process of being confirmed. I never said that I wanted to be on the Supreme Court, but I didn't want to lose the game. It was that I had to relinquish."

And he had a new purpose, a purpose beyond his own ambition, beyond even the need to clear his own name: the cause of standing up
to the Senate and the interest groups, of standing up to what in his
mind was manifest injustice. If one is off to battle, there can be no
room for self-pity. Now the challenge for Clarence would be to keep
his attention directed toward his cause and away from himself. In the
days ahead, the strength of Clarence Thomas was in direct proportion
to his capacity to look beyond himself and the need for confirmation
by the Senate to the cause of justice he thought he was serving.

With new freedom from self-concern, Clarence started warming to
the fight before him with abandon. He would no longer be on the defensive. He would not be mincing his words, concerned about how
each of them might invite criticism. He would be on the offensive, attacking a wrong with gusto, attacking a wrong to himself and a wrong
to the country.

Contrary to what Ken Duberstein had persuaded Clarence to say at
the conclusion of his first round of hearings, Clarence did not think
that the confirmation process was fair, and it was time to say so. It was
wrong for the interest groups to scour the country for dirt on a nominee. It was wrong for the Senate to leak confidential reports. It was
time to go public and attack a process that had become grotesque.

Ginni joined us and agreed with Clarence's decision to take the offensive. At last, she thought, the American people would see the real
Clarence Thomas. I encouraged Clarence to take this approach. I told
him that whether he won or lost the vote on confirmation, he would be
making a major contribution to the country because he would be
standing for an important principle: that government cannot be mis-
used as it was against him, that the system is wrong when ideologues
destroy an individual for the sake of a political agenda. I told him that
even if defeated, he would become famous for standing for principle.

On that afternoon and for the three days that followed, I also told
Clarence that in taking the offensive, he would have a phenomenon
going for him that was not of his making: the contempt Americans
have—misplaced, I think—for Congress. I said that many people
thought that members of Congress are check kiters, deadbeats on res-

taurant bills, and people who keep raising their own pay. I said that the American people are in the mood for a champion to tell off a self-serving Congress.

Larry Silberman gave Clarence much the same message before the second round of hearings. Larry recalls telling Clarence, "The senators are bullies, and if you stand up to them, don't back down. But people don't stand up to them because they are worried about confirmation. Forget the confirmation. Just care about your honor."

I was encouraging Clarence to take the offensive but told him that this had to be his own decision. I said that I felt that I was encouraging someone else to charge the enemy guns, and that while I thought that the offensive approach was right, it might not be.

My caveat meant nothing to Clarence. Enthusiasm for the task at hand swept over him. It was a spike of exhilaration that followed a trough of despair, and within hours it would be followed by the deepest trough of all. Then more ups and downs would follow, but from that afternoon there was always the vision of a battle greater than his own confirmation, greater even than the purpose held out to him by Larry Silberman, that of upholding his own honor. Clarence explains: "After I spoke to you, I didn't think much about the name thing. . . . I didn't focus as much on my name. Sure, I was worried about it. But even that became kind of a selfish thing. . . . Speaking to the American people and bringing to their attention what was happening to me and how this could happen to them and what was going on with Congress and the country became more important."

I had agreed to drive Clarence and Ginni to the White House for their visit with President and Mrs. Bush. I moved my car into the Thomas's driveway so they would not have to run the gauntlet of reporters and cameramen, but there was a flurry of media activity as the Thomases walked the few steps from their front door to my car. As we pulled out of their driveway, the motorcyclist assigned to pursue them wherever they went mounted his machine. Caught up in the high spirits of the moment, I decided to have some fun. A few blocks from the house, I slowed my car to a crawl, so that the motorcyclist had to pass us. When he stopped his motorcycle to wait for us, I resumed normal speed. When he again pursued us, I again slowed the car. At that point, he abandoned the pursuit. Ginni and Clarence roared with laughter.

Ginni describes the mood of the moment: "He didn't care whether he got it [Supreme Court confirmation] or not . . . this was a kamikaze mission, which was fine with me. . . . We were all laughing. The two of you started acting like you were kids going off into the sunset. . . . It was uplifting and it was positive and it felt like we were on a different mission."

During the drive to the White House, Clarence warmed to the fight ahead. He was especially excited by the prospect of an open confrontation with the interest groups that had been working against him. I recall him saying, "Just think of all the groups in the country that we're going to be breaking up over this." Ginni remembers my saying that the most aggressive liberal opponent of the nomination, People for the American Way, might sue me for attacking them. She quotes me as saying, "This is great, Clarence. They'll sue me and take all my money and they'll take your name, but we will have had our day."

After more than three months of silence, more than three months of passivity, more than three months of taking one low blow after another, Clarence Thomas was about to fight back, and with the abandon of a person who had nothing more to lose. This was going to be fun, we thought, for a fleeting moment on a sunny Wednesday afternoon as we drove to the White House.

Ken Duberstein attributes the idea of inviting the Thomases to the White House to President Bush and believes that the meeting was significant for two reasons. First, it was an important signal to the country that the president had confidence in his nominee and was standing behind him. Second, Ken thought that it was psychologically important to Clarence. As Ken puts it, Clarence "had been through the meat grinder." Knowing that the president had faith in him would boost Clarence's morale.

The visit to the White House had the hoped-for effect on Clarence's morale. Clarence calls it "wonderful." Ginni says it was "very up-lifting." The president and Mrs. Bush met the Thomases in the Oval Office for pictures. Then the president and Clarence and Mrs. Bush and Ginni left the office for separate walks around the White House grounds. The president was apologetic for Clarence's ordeal. Clarence says, "He took it as his personal responsibility." The president expressed concern about what was happening to Virginia and Clarence's family. He expressed anger at Congress and inquired about who Anita Hill was and why she was doing this. Clarence said that he did not know.

Mrs. Bush was similarly sympathetic with Ginni. She spoke of how politicians and their families experience personal attacks. After the visit a deputy marshal drove Clarence and Ginni back to their house.

Late Wednesday afternoon, I met in my office with the two lawyers recommended by Boyden Gray as experts in the law of sexual harassment, Zachary Fasman and Barbara Berish Brown. Also present were Orrin Hatch and John Mackey of the Justice Department. Two aspects of that meeting stand out in my memory.

First, the legal experts explained to me the reasoning behind the exceptionally short statute of limitations in sexual harassment and other employment discrimination cases. A sexual harassment charge must be filed with EEOC within 180 days of the alleged event.[47] The reason, according to the experts, is the peculiar unreliability of memory in those cases. Because the law recognizes that memories change in highly emotional cases, an unusually short statute of limitations is necessary to protect defendants from charges that have no basis in reality. Therefore, according to the experts, Anita Hill's charge was not reliable because it was made more than ten years after the alleged events.

Second, the two lawyers expressed their opinions about the sequence in which witnesses should testify before the committee. This was a question that Clarence's supporters continued to debate until its resolution on Thursday night. The lawyers believed strongly that Anita Hill should testify first, that she should make whatever charges she had, and that Clarence would then be in a position to refute her testimony. They thought it would be dangerous for Clarence to testify first, to try to anticipate what his accuser might say, and to speak in generalities, leaving open the possibility of later and more specific testimony by Anita Hill that would go unchallenged. John Mackey and I expressed our view that it would be better for Clarence to go first and seize the initiative, especially since, with the exception of Clarence's affidavit, her charges had dominated public attention since the previous weekend.

At 7:30 on Wednesday morning, before the arrival of the Laws and the Jameses, Clarence had phoned Janet Brown, whom he had known since she was my news secretary and he was a legislative assistant in my Senate office in the late 1970s.

Since I have been in public life, I have enjoyed going to work each day. What makes the job enjoyable is not simply the challenging subject matter but also the daily interaction with very good people. Those who have worked with me through the years have been my joy. They are bright—a requirement of employment—and in every way, highly motivated, with good values, wonderful company. To those who constantly complain about the shortcomings of government, I say meet the people who have worked with me these past twenty-five years. To a great extent the story of the days leading up to the Anita Hill hearing is a story of those who have known Clarence Thomas, in my office and elsewhere, and who came to his side at his time of need. Janet Brown, an alumna of my office, now executive director of the Commission on Presidential Debates, and a first-rate person, got the call from Clarence Thomas.

Janet remembers the beginning of the call: "I answered the phone. He said, 'Hi, J.B.' And I said, 'I just don't believe this.' And there was silence, and he was crying." Janet asked if it would help if she came out to see him that day and later told Ginni that she would bring dinner that evening along with friends of Clarence's from his days in my Senate office.

The old friends who gathered at the Thomases' home that evening were Janet Brown, her husband, Mike Brewer, Allen Moore, and another former legislative assistant in my office, Chris Brewster. Allen recalls that when he arrived, Chris was already there. Janet and Mike arrived later. Clarence was wearing a polo shirt, old pants, heavy socks, and no shoes—a mess by Allen's description. "He is disheveled. His eyes are red. It is as though his spirit has been broken. There was a severely crippled person."

For more than ten years in my office, first as my legislative director, than as staff director of the Senate Commerce Committee, Allen Moore had been a student of the U.S. Senate. His job was to understand the Senate, to develop legislative strategy, to know how senators would react to one strategy or another. He saw this evening as a chance to bring his legislative skills to bear in the service of his friend and fellow staff associate. In Allen's mind, this was to be a working session designed to identify the best approach to help win Senate confirmation.

Allen thought that there must have been some misunderstanding between Clarence and Anita Hill, some word or action that she took in an unintended way. Because this was to be a working session, Allen though it best to get to business quickly. He could be of no help without knowing exactly what happened, so he began asking questions, questions to which he expected answers that would allow him to piece together an explanation of how two people could come to opposite conclusions about the same set of facts. Allen was surprised at the categorical nature of Clarence's answers, answers that left no room for concluding that this could be a reasonable difference of interpretation. Question: Did you ever ask her out? Answer: Never. Question: How good-looking was she? Answer: Not that attractive.

Allen realized that the easiest defense—that this was a case of mistaken meaning—was not available. He also realized that Clarence was not listening to him. Clarence buried his head in his hands, then shook his head, then buried his head in his hands again, and said, "I can't talk about it. I don't want to talk about it." "So much for the working session," thought Allen. "He is not focused. He is not ready. . . . He has got one day, tomorrow, to get his act together, and he is in no condition to get his act together."

Later in the evening, Allen remembers that Clarence told him, "For the first time in my life, I have given up on the truth. The truth is not helping me here." Later still, Clarence said, "I feel like someone has reached up inside me and ripped out my insides."

Allen also recalls a conversation he had with Ginni that evening. Ginni said that always before when Clarence was down, anger was the emotion that would give him the strength to do what had to be done. This time, she said, "His anger is gone."

When Janet Brown arrived with her husband, after a few minutes of attempted good-humored small talk, she and Clarence went to the living room so they could talk alone. Janet says, "I don't ever want to see anybody the rest of my life in as bad shape as Clarence was in. The one thing that was marked, he couldn't stop moving. He was constantly rubbing his head, dropping his hands, twitching. . . . He would be switching his feet, knees. He would constantly be rubbing his head, rubbing his eyes. He didn't stop moving. He was in absolute, complete distress."

Janet began their private conversation the same way Allen had: she wanted to know the truth. She herself had once been the victim of sexual harassment, and she knew there was the possibility that innocent intentions had been misinterpreted. She asked, "Did you ever ask her out?" "No." "Did you ever discuss porn flicks?" "No." "Did you use locker room language, tell any kind of off-color jokes, do anything that she may have thought just wasn't funny and made her feel uncomfortable?" "No."

Knowing that there was no possible defense of mistaken intentions, Janet realized that if Clarence was to deny the charge effectively, he would have to believe in himself. She thought that the best way to encourage that belief was to try to make him angry. Here too there was no passion. Then Clarence repeated the concern he had laid aside that afternoon. He said, "I have lost my name. It's the only thing

I wanted out of this, and I have lost my name. I can't get that back."

Clarence cried in the living room, and Janet tried to console him, holding his hand and putting her arm around him. Several times, Clarence said, "I just don't know that I can do this." Janet said, "It's going to be all right." Clarence said, "Is it?" Janet said, "Yeah, it is."

Four or five times, Clarence asked, "Is it going to be all right?" Each time, Janet's answer was "Yes." She thought, "I've got to infuse this person with some strength. All reserves are gone. It's not sea level; it's minus sixty feet. And he has got an enormous task in front of him."

Janet and Clarence returned to the family room where the others had started dinner. They tried to change the subject, to divert Clarence's attention to lighter matters. They talked of Chris and his wife Jane's new baby. Chris tried to say something funny. His son, Will, had seen him being interviewed on television, and said, "I would like to be on television someday, but would I have to talk about Clarence Thomas?" They all laughed, except Clarence, who, said Allen, "never reacted. He was never a part of it. He was just a slug in the corner, who looked lost and totally distressed."

Clarence and Ginni have similar explanations for Clarence's despondency that evening. Except for the warmth of Janet's reassurances in the living room, the help his friends were offering was not what Clarence needed. Clarence says, "When they came over they were talking strategy again. It just wore me down. They were trying to be helpful. You should do this, you should do that. It had me focusing on my plight. Then I was worn down. . . . I could go in there and sit down with Janet. She understood the hurt and wasn't talking you need to do this and you need to do that. They were all trying to be helpful, but it was refocusing on this and I just got really despondent."

Ginni agrees. "People started strategizing about what he should do or what he should say." Referring to the morning visit of the Laws and the Jameses, she said, "It felt so different to have our prayer partners in our home. How uplifting and wonderful the feeling was versus people strategizing and not thinking about God and that element of it."

On Wednesday night, Clarence did not sleep at all. Ginni started to sleep, but was soon awake with her husband's tossing and turning at her side. He got out of bed and was on the floor. Ginni describes it as "like something was inside of him, physically, like there was this battle going on inside of him. Like it's not over yet. Like those prayers aren't enough. There's something else. . . . What it felt like is that Clarence still had some sin in his life and he had to get that out in order to be open to the Holy Spirit and that he had a vestige of sin, that he was in this furnace and God wasn't going to let him keep going without eliminating this vestige of sin."

Ginni told me no details about what happened that night. She did say that Clarence's agony lasted until 5:30 or 6:00 A.M. There are matters that should remain private between a husband and a wife— certainly matters that are hard to include in a book about a good man who is a friend. That a future justice of the Supreme Court was writhing on the floor is awful enough to tell. But it must be told, for this is the result when there are those who believe a cause justifies the destruction of a person. With Clarence in agony on the floor, the groups that sought to destroy him had reached the pinnacle of their success.

We all ask of any misfortune, "What have I done to deserve this?" It is a question from biblical times. "God exacts of you less than your guilt deserves," said one of Job's would-be comforters.[48] "Who has sinned, this man or his parents, that he should be born blind?" the disciples asked Jesus.[49] "Mea culpa, Mea culpa, Mea maxima culpa," Clarence recited as an altar boy in Georgia.

Since the arrival of the FBI disclosing Anita Hill's charges, Clarence had reviewed his life. "Maybe in life, I did do something wrong. I don't know what it is. But I know it wasn't this," he said. Surely there must be some reason, something in his life, something he could point to that caused this punishment. "I don't think that I had truly repented for the way I had conducted myself since 1968," he said. "In some sense, I felt that this punishment was being visited upon me."

Tormented by guilt for past sins, Clarence fought his own spiritual battle that night. He describes the process as a purging. "I thought that in a sense that going through this, total accountability, and then having to directly confront any indiscretion that I might have made or engaged in my life required me to become a better person . . . than I was before, to be more accountable to not only myself—it's hard because I'm really hard on myself—but to God. . . . And it was the first time, I think, since the sixties that I have just opened up and not just asking God for help, but opened up and asked Him to take charge of my life, and also to connect myself to following His will. And it was in that sense that I became a better person and purged myself of what I had done before and refined myself and became closer to what Jesus was."

Thursday, October 10

Elizabeth and Steven Law recall that they arrived at the Thomases' house at eight o'clock on Thursday morning, that the Jameses were not present, and that their visit was brief because Clarence had to leave for a meeting. They describe him as being more animated than he had been the previous day, although Steven Law says, "I don't know that it was necessarily a happy animation." Steven describes Clarence as "uptight" about attending strategy meetings. Clarence told the Laws that people were trying to tell him what to do and how to answer questions. He said, "I know these people mean well, but this is draining . . . I don't want to talk strategy." They also remember him confessing that he had been too concerned about his own reputation and about clearing his own name. Clarence told the Laws that he kept hearing himself say, "*My* reputation. I have got to clear *my* name . . . *my, my, my,*" with far too much emphasis on himself.

Mike Luttig, lawyer and soon to be federal circuit judge, felt that he had a substantially reduced role to play after the Antia Hill phase began. The days of bar review tutorials on constitutional questions were over. In his mind, the next stage was congressional and political—and beyond his expertise. Still, there was lawyers' work to be done. As lawyers always prepare witnesses for trial, so a lawyer had to sit down with Clarence Thomas, go through the charges in detail, and make certain that he would be prepared for any question the Judiciary Committee might ask. On Wednesday afternoon, the White House asked Mike to prepare Clarence. Mike went to Clarence's chambers on Thursday morning for a meeting that lasted two or three hours.

Mike arrived at about nine o'clock and was sitting at the conference table when Clarence came in. He stood as Clarence closed the door. Clarence broke down immediately. He headed toward the conference table in what Mike describes as "loud tears." He began to stagger and seemed about to collapse. Mike caught him halfway between the door and the table and "almost carried him over to the conference table. Clarence was crying and hyperventilating." Now he was seated, Mike standing over him with his arm around him, saying, "It will be okay. It will be okay. You are going to be fine." For about fifteen minutes, Clarence was "just wailing."

Mike remembers Clarence's words: "These people have destroyed my life. They have destroyed everything I have ever had. They have destroyed my family. They have ruined me. I have nothing left anymore." He added that Ginni had been physically sick.

When Clarence regained his composure, Mike began the painstaking process of questioning Clarence, not only about Anita Hill's charges but about the intimate details of his life. In Mike's words: "I asked extremely direct and extremely clear questions about every conceivable aspect of the allegation. . . . I grilled him on every question to be sure that there was nothing, no stone unturned. . . . We went over each fact and explored around it to be sure that there was nothing that could have given rise to even that kind of suggestion. . . . I would explore with him whether he could have made any or some of these comments in a joking way, not intending to mean anything by them at all." To each question, Clarence's denial was categorical.

I interrupted the meeting with a phone call to Mike, which he took in another room. Several points had occurred to me that I thought Mike should raise with Clarence, the most important of which was the danger of perjury. I was still concerned that Clarence might overstate the truth, as Judge Walter Nixon had. My worry was that Clarence, in his insistence that he had said nothing intentionally offensive, would wrongly state that he had said nothing at all. I asked Mike to warn Clarence of this and to tell him that there was one thing far worse than failure to be confirmed for the Supreme Court: impeachment from the circuit court.

Mike returned to the conference room and pressed this point with Clarence, insisting that he be absolutely accurate before the committee. There could be no misstatement of fact. He said, "Clarence, you cannot lie to the nation for the next two days."

Mike also raised the possibility that Clarence might consider withdrawing. This was not meant as a recommendation but as an option for Clarence's consideration. He told Clarence that withdrawal would be relatively easy. All Clarence would have to say would be, "There is nothing to these allegations at all, but I am not going to put myself and my family through the kind of charade that it would take to establish that."

Clarence would have none of it. He replied, "Mike, this has all been made up. I don't know what she is talking about. And if I were to leave at this point, I could never live with myself."

The direct and adamant way in which Clarence answered every question left no doubt in Mike's mind that he was telling the truth. Equally persuasive was Clarence's candor on other matters. Mike went beyond Anita Hill's charges and, in his words, "asked him about every sensitive and potentially embarrassing aspect of his personal life throughout his whole history. Clarence was completely open, confessing his past, doing nothing to avoid embarrassment." Later, Mike said, "When someone goes to that length to talk about things that are obviously uncomfortable, it causes you to believe the other things. So that when he said, 'I have done all these things, but I have never done what she says,' then it was credible."

Clarence was open with Mike in discussing the intimate aspects of his life, but he made it clear that he would not do this before the committee and before the world. He would not tell the world about his relationship with his wife or with any other woman. He would not discuss in public what happened in the privacy of his home. As Mike recalls, "He had to come out of the process with something intact of his personhood. . . . If being on the Supreme Court required him to talk about the intimacies of his private life, he didn't want it."

Mike recalls that during that meeting, he and Clarence disagreed about how confrontational Clarence should be with the committee. Clarence said that members of the committee and committee staff were in concert with interest groups in an effort to destroy him. Mike, thinking that it would be a mistake to attack the committee, said that he had no reason to believe that the committee was trying to get Clarence. Clarence summarily rejected Mike's point.

When Ginni saw Clarence early that afternoon, Clarence told her that the meeting with Mike went very well, that he told Mike everything, and that he felt better. Mike believes that it may have been important for Clarence to discuss the details of his personal life, even though the details were not related to Anita Hill. It was as though Clarence was unburdening his soul, as though it was a confessional.

Supporters of Clarence Thomas feared that the plight of an individual we knew and loved was being swept away by the urgency of a cause. To us, the message of the Hill supporters seemed to be: "Whatever the facts, this case calls attention to the problem of sexual harassment, and that is good." We thought that this message was frightening—that a person was made expendable in the service of a greater good that had nothing to do with him. We thought that the specifics of the case were essential; the people involved were real, and they were suffering real pain. They were more than symbols of their sexes. Nancy Altman, an ardent feminist and long-time friend of Clarence, was most aware of the distinction between the generality of a cause and the reality of a known individual.

Nancy is a graduate of the University of Pennsylvania Law School and has taught at the Kennedy School of Harvard University and at Harvard Law School. She got to know Clarence when they served together as legislative assistants on my staff and shared an office. Nancy considers herself "radical" on "feminist" issues. She says, "I care very, very deeply about women's issues. I do not take sexual harassment lightly. In some ways I am radical on a lot of women's issues. I really believe women are oppressed in our society in many, many ways, and I am very concerned about it. And probably, if I didn't know Clarence and I read all of this in the paper, I would be with everybody else on this issue, but I know him. And I don't believe that every single man oppresses women. Here was someone who was really the victim in this, not the victimizer."

On leaving my office, both Nancy and Clarence had gone to the Department of Education. In Nancy's words, "We became good friends . . . we followed each other's careers and kept in touch and shared weddings and joys and all kinds of things together."

Nancy had "overwhelming good feelings" about Clarence's nomination to the Supreme Court. She says, "I think he has the kind of character and the kind of intellect we should have in our judges." She describes him as conservative but not rigid, as "fair minded," as someone who "will listen to the claim put before him and not have an ideology or an agenda." She calls Clarence "one of the most decent people that I know, just [one of] the warmest hearted, [most] generous people I know."

Since July, Nancy had watched her friend's struggle from a distance, and what she saw infuriated her. She was especially angered by the suggestion that Clarence's reference to Louis Farrakhan in a speech was a sign that he was antisemitic. On this subject, she had first-hand knowledge. She recalled their discussions of the Holocaust when they served on my staff. Given what she calls "strained relations between Jews and blacks," she found his understanding of the Jewish experience "especially unusual." When she heard the suggestion that Clarence was antisemitic, she was "furious because it was just a complete flip of who he is."

That Clarence could commit sexual harassment was just as unthinkable for Nancy. In her view, sexual harassment is not an isolated event; rather, it is a manifestation of a general attitude. In her words,

"It has the quality of not respecting the other person. It is either there or it is not there. And if it is there, then it is not there just with one person. . . . My view is that it is repetitive. . . . People in the workforce know who has that because it doesn't happen to one person."

When Nancy heard that the Senate's vote on confirmation had been delayed, she thought that the matter was over. Clarence would never sit on the Supreme Court. Nothing Nancy could do would save Clarence's nomination. Still, she had to act, not to win the vote but to vindicate what she believed was the cause of justice. Nancy Altman had to take a stand.

She placed a call to Clarence on Tuesday night and left a message on his answering machine. He returned the call on Wednesday morning and told her, "Nancy, I need your help," and gave her a name at the White House to call. She remembers that the White House asked her if she could be on the scene during the hearing, acting as a "spin doctor," and she consented to that request while thinking that it was not enough.

Nancy was convinced that if anyone was to vindicate the cause of justice, women must do it. Women must be in the front lines of this battle—women who knew Clarence Thomas, who could speak from their own experiences, who could tell the world that the Clarence Thomas they knew could not be guilty of sexual harassment.

In addition to thinking that women could demonstrate that sexual harassment was inconsistent with Clarence's behavior toward women, Nancy had a second reason for wanting women to defend Clarence: she thought that the public would dismiss whatever any man might say in his defense. Women following the news would assert that men do not understand, but this could not be said if women were doing the talking.

Nancy's attention to this role of women in the defense of Clarence began Monday or Tuesday with calls she made to other women who had worked with Clarence. The initial reason for the calls was to commiserate. Janet Brown and Sherry Jackson, who worked with Nancy and Clarence in my office, were two of the people she remembers calling.

By Wednesday night, Nancy formed a clear idea of what must be done, and she pressed that idea with diligence for the next four days. In the first of what would be a number of calls she made to me, she reached me at home that night and insisted that women must testify for Clarence at the hearing.

I told Nancy that the Judiciary Committee would not allow the women to testify. At my own insistence to Joe Biden, the hearing would be limited in scope; there would be no character witnesses. It seemed at the time that Nancy's idea was out of the question. Nevertheless, if the women could not testify before the committee, they were not precluded from taking their message to the public. The ultimate jury in this case was not the Judiciary Committee but the American people. Nancy and the other women could have a news conference and tell the country about the Clarence Thomas they knew. I told Nancy that I had too many things to do to organize a news conference and asked if she could do it. She said she would. I gave her the phone numbers of my news secretary, Steven Hilton, and of Ricky Silberman, who proved helpful in producing the names of a number of people who attended.

Janet Brown left the Thomases' home on Wednesday night, after the stakeout of reporters and cameramen had gone home. She remembers standing on the sidewalk in a light drizzle with Mike, Allen, and Chris, doubting whether they had been of any help to Clarence and wondering what to do next. She went home and called Nancy Altman, who told her to call me.

The phone rang in our bedroom at 11:30 P.M. It was Janet, in tears, telling me of her experience at the Thomases' house. We talked about the idea of a news conference, and Janet remembers calling Steve Hilton at 5:30 Thursday morning.

Janet shared Nancy's view that women should come forward to say that they know Clarence Thomas and that he would not engage in sexual harassment. In addition, she had a special message of her own, a painful message but one she felt had to be told: Janet had been a victim of sexual harassment in a job she held after leaving my office. When that happened, the person she sought out for counseling was her friend, Clarence Thomas. Now, Janet Brown wanted to tell the world how it feels to be sexually harassed and how a victim treats a harasser: a victim has contempt for the harasser and would never follow the harasser from one job to the next, call him repeatedly on the phone, or leave a message about the room number of the hotel where she was staying.

I had no part in organizing the news conference. Steve Hilton notified the media, and my office arranged for the hearing room, but Nancy Altman, Ricky Silberman, and Janet Brown called the women. My role was to go to the news conference for the purpose of drawing media coverage.

Nancy remembers that before the news conference the women met in my office and I told them, "Be yourself. Show your emotion. If you feel like crying, cry." It became clear that I did not have to say that. The women had prepared their own statements with almost no advance notice. They had their own messages. What followed was one of the most emotional events I have ever seen.

The news conference was held at noon in the hearing room of the Senate Commerce Committee, down the hall from my office. Seventeen women attended to speak about Clarence Thomas. In a period of twelve hours, beginning midnight the night before, seventeen women had volunteered to appear before a bank of microphones and television cameras, to speak about Clarence Thomas and the charge against him. They were black and white. They had worked with him in my office and at the Department of Education and at the EEOC. Some knew Anita Hill, having worked with both of them at close quarters. One by one they walked to the microphones. One by one they spoke, many with tears streaming down their faces. One by one they testified to the decency of Clarence Thomas and the unthinkable nature of the charge against him.

After the news conference, Allen Moore, my former staff director, asked to speak with me for two minutes. He had seen Clarence, "a broken man," the previous night, and he was worried about Clarence's

ability to figure out what he was going to say the next morning. I was
going to see him that afternoon with Orrin Hatch, but Allen said that
he thought it would be better if I went alone. "He doesn't need a committee. He needs one person to help him through." I called Clarence
and told him that I was coming out to his house, not to get in his hair
but to be available if he needed me. I arrived at his house at about
3:30.

Larry Thompson, Clarence's lawyer friend, was already there. I had
never met him before, but I was instantly comfortable with him. Clarence says, "When Larry came, I had both a friend and a lawyer."
Clarence remembers saying, "Larry, I need your help," and Larry re-
plying, "I'm here, and I'll be here until this is over."

Larry and Clarence had been close friends since they had worked
together in 1977 and 1978—both lawyers, both blacks, both about the
same age. In their St. Louis days, they had enjoyed going to a Chinese
restaurant together, talking about the problems of the world and their
shared view that America's black leaders do not represent the interests of their own people.

Larry too thought that Anita Hill's charges were inconsistent with
the person he knew: "Based upon my knowledge as Clarence Thomas's friend, unless it was just the most unbelievable lapse in his character and the way I know him, he wouldn't have run his office in a way
that would allow him to have done the things that she said he did. He
is not an angel. He is a human being, and he is not perfect, but he
wouldn't have done those kinds of things."

When Larry arrived that afternoon, he recalls, he and Clarence
talked about the lack of black organizations coming to Clarence's aid.
Clarence was a sitting federal judge. In Larry's mind, the black organizations would have arrived at the Senate with pickets had the same
charges been made against a Democrat or a liberal black. In Larry's
words, Clarence was being "hung out to dry because he was thinking
for himself."

Larry describes his arrival at the Thomases' house, still surrounded
by television cameras, as "an amazing scene." Clarence seemed very
happy to see his friend but "obviously disturbed, confused and dis-

traught." Larry, the trial lawyer, was shocked that Clarence had made little progress in preparing for the hearing the next morning. Especially shocking to Larry was that Clarence seemed emotionally unprepared to be a witness. Clarence had called Larry as a litigator, but Larry had no experience in this kind of litigation, no knowledge of what was expected of him or of Clarence. He concluded that it was more important for him to be not a lawyer but a friend and that the most important gift he could make was not legal advice but moral support.

When I arrived, Clarence and Larry were alone. Clarence may have seemed distraught to Larry, but to me he seemed in better condition than the day before. He was dressed in a long-sleeved pullover sport shirt, shorts, and jogging shoes without socks.

After Clarence, Larry, and I sat down, Clarence handed me several pages of a very rough draft of a statement he had written. It was a start, but it was too defensive and lacked punch. I made one specific suggestion to him: to delete a direct attack on Joe Biden. The statement said that he believed Biden when he said he was going to be fair and when he said he was going to be Clarence's champion if he were attacked.

That afternoon, I had a strong feeling that Clarence had something smoldering inside him that had to escape. My role, as I saw it, was to encourage him to give voice to what he felt. The draft of his statement was too restrained, too negative, too lacking in feeling. If Clarence was to be vindicated, he must express to the country exactly what he believed.

I told Clarence that since July he had maintained his silence in the face of one charge after another. Now he would have his chance to speak, and he should say exactly what was on his mind. If he thought he was being treated unfairly, he should say so. If he thought the confirmation process was unfair, he should say that.

Larry Thompson recalls that I told Clarence not to worry about the senators but to speak over them to the American people. He recalls that I said, "These people are trying to take away the most precious thing that you have in life, and this is your reputation. Don't worry about the Supreme Court. You have a good job. The only thing this is all about is preserving your reputation. That's the most important thing you have, and they are trying to hurt you and they are trying to hurt your family, and you are not going to stand by and let them do it."

My repeated theme was, "Say what is in your heart. If a thought comes to you, let it out. Open yourself to God. When God gives you words to say, say them."

We prayed that God would do just that. Clarence, Larry, and I bowed our heads and I said a prayer. Again, I said that Clarence had no strength and that he turned to God to supply it. I asked that God be with Clarence as he prepared his statement for the hearing, that God put the thoughts in Clarence's mind and the words on his tongue so that God's will might be served the next day.

Then the work of preparing for the hearing began in earnest, with Clarence pacing, thinking out loud, occasionally scribbling a word or two on a small piece of paper he held in his hand. Ginni returned home and sat at a table, taking down the words that came from Clarence.

My role was limited. I was no more than a prompter. Clarence would speak of his ordeal, of his sense of its unfairness, of the wrong done to him and to the country. If there was a pause, I would suggest a word or a phrase, but I told him, "This has to be your statement, nobody else's statement. Nobody can speak for you. If some of the ideas that I have are incorporated in your thoughts, fine. If not, fine." I would ask, "What do you think, Clarence?" or "What do you want to say? If it's in there, say it. Let it out," or "How do you feel about what has happened?" or "How do you feel about the delay?" "How do you feel about the leaks?" "Say what you think. Let God speak through you." The point was to encourage Clarence to be Clarence—to encourage him to be absolutely open in speaking his mind. The result was that the statement he made on Friday morning before the committee was entirely his own.

I recall one specific suggestion I made to Clarence that indicates my combative state of mind. We discussed the importance of maintaining the parameters of the hearing, of not letting the committee

wander beyond the subject of sexual harassment into a general explo-
ration of Clarence's private life. If a senator asked him such a question, I suggested he reply, "I will not discuss my personal life unless
you put yours on display." The committee never asked such a question, and Clarence never gave such an answer.

I urged Clarence to be aggressive, to defend nothing. Ginni remembers coming home that afternoon. In her words, "The room was filled
with a lot of new hope and new expectation and new energy that this
was going to be a different kind of message and a different kind of battle than we had probably all thought about a few hours earlier."

Ginni and Clarence asked Larry to spend the night at their house,
but Larry thought it best to let them be by themselves the night before
the hearing. Ginni agreed. I told Clarence that I would be as close as
his phone and that he should feel free to call me at any hour. At seven
o'clock I drove Larry to his hotel and proceeded to a meeting of Judiciary Committee Republicans that had commenced an hour earlier in
Senator Thurmond's office.

Jon Chambers was my legislative director in 1991. As such, he was
my principal adviser on matters of public policy and my daily confi-
dant. A characteristic of Senate staff is to worry about senators, and
Jon was worried about me.

After Anita Hill's charges became public, my Senate staff had little
contact with me. I was preoccupied with a crisis that had little to do
with the normal course of Senate business, and I was dealing largely
with Clarence Thomas and Ken Duberstein. Jon was concerned that I
was saying things and doing things I would come to regret and that
I was putting my political career in jeopardy. During the week that
ended with the second round of hearings, Jon expressed his concern
to me. He remembers my saying, "It doesn't matter what happens to
me. The whole issue is Clarence Thomas, and I will do anything. I will
go on any show, and I will say anything, and I will go before any cameras and all the rest in order to make sure that things go all right."

From talking to the staff of Judiciary Committee Republicans, Jon knew that they had similar concerns about their senators. He found a "widespread concern amongst the staff for how far each of the Senators were being pushed and that there was sort of this whirlwind and they were all being spun out further and further, and that all of you were vulnerable and yet unwilling to either recognize the vulnerability or unwilling to back off on it."

Jon and other Republican staffers were in Senator Thurmond's office that Thursday evening. He recalls, "All of the senators were really sort of in a froth and pumping each other up. . . . If you looked at the staff and you looked at the senators, you would think people were having a different experience."

When I arrived in the middle of the meeting, the first thing I heard about was Angela Wright.

Earlier in the day, the staff of the Judiciary Committee had alerted Ken Duberstein that Angela Wright, "another woman," had come forward to charge that Clarence had made improper sexual comments to her. Within an hour after hearing of Angela Wright's allegation, Ken learned that she had been fired from a congressman's office, that she had been fired from the Agency for International Development and had charged her supervisor with racism, and that she had been fired by Clarence Thomas after referring to a homosexual as a "faggot." With this information, Ken phoned Jeff Peck, staff director of the Judiciary Committee, to warn him to be very careful about Angela Wright. Ken also alerted me of her charge and told me what he knew of her background.

Based on Ken's call, I was not concerned about Angela Wright; I saw her as no threat at all. This opinion was bolstered when I arrived at Senator Thurmond's office. The Judiciary Committee staff had conducted a telephone interview with Angela Wright that day, and copies of the transcript were available in Senator Thurmond's office. Those who were familiar with the interview, especially the staff present, said that they did not think she would be a credible witness. I was further reassured when I reached home that night and read the transcript for myself.[50] I concluded that she was not only not a threat to Clarence Thomas but that she might be of some benefit to him if she testified.

Her story seemed so weak and so open to attack on cross-examination that it might taint the whole case against Clarence.

Most of the discussion in Senator Thurmond's office concerned the sequencing of witnesses—that is, whether Anita Hill or Clarence Thomas should testify first. Joe Biden had given Clarence the choice. If Clarence testified first, he would be given the opportunity to follow Anita Hill with rebuttal testimony. In reality, the decision was whether Clarence should take an offensive or a defensive approach to the hearing.

The defensive approach, advocated by the White House counsel and relayed to us by Ken Duberstein on the phone, was that Clarence should follow Anita Hill. In that way, he would have everything she had to say before him as he made his reply. It was better to know all the charges when presenting the case than to be surprised by the unexpected. For a lawyer, this is the standard procedure: the plaintiff rests the case before the defendant responds.

Although the sequencing of witnesses might be viewed as a strategy to get live television coverage of Clarence's rebuttal during prime time, that result was purely fortuitous. Our discussion did not consider the possibility of live nighttime coverage but did touch on the "news cycle"—the need to have Clarence's testimony in time to be covered on the late afternoon network news. Ken Duberstein suggested that if Anita Hill testified first, she would conclude her testimony in time for Clarence to testify before network news time. The senators present were concerned that Anita Hill could be kept before the committee until Saturday and that the day's proceedings would be controlled entirely by her unless Clarence testified first.

All Republican senators at the meeting believed strongly that Clarence should go first. Orrin Hatch recalls the discussion: "He had not had a chance to tell his side. All we had had were days of Anita Hill. . . . We were afraid if she went first that the Democrats would drag out her testimony to the point where it would take all of Friday and she would be the Friday evening news and then most of the Saturday news."

Al Simpson had the same view, expressed in more colorful language: "She had gone on first three days in a row without one volley of criticism. She was the toast of America, the beleaguered one who had come forward, the martyred one, the aggrieved, and he was just the ogre of the piece. And all he had was a statement, which was about a paragraph and a half long, which just said, 'I categorically deny all of this!' "

I shared the opinion of the others that we could not take the risk that Anita Hill would have yet another spectacular day of dominating the news without a word from Clarence on his own behalf. Still, there were more compelling reasons for him to testify first. I thought that Clarence must take the offensive; he must say what was on his mind and not be in a position of rebutting point by point what Anita Hill would say. The time for rebuttal would come later. First, Clarence must speak to the country, from his heart, of the injustice that was being done to him. The issue was not Anita Hill and whatever she might say. The issue was the confirmation process: the groups, the lies, the leaks, what that process had done to Clarence Thomas, what the process was doing to America. That was Clarence's message, and it had little to do with the testimony of Anita Hill.

My additional concern was for Clarence's emotional state. Whenever he spoke, he must speak with strength. That afternoon, Clarence had warmed to the thought of speaking his mind to the committee, but over the past twenty-four hours, he had experienced every emotional extreme. I hoped that he could rise to the occasion of taking his cause to the committee, but I was afraid he would be shell-shocked if Anita Hill preceded him.

Ken Duberstein rightly believed that although the senators had strong opinions on the sequence of witnesses, the decision should be up to Clarence. I called Clarence and presented the choice to him. He asked for fifteen minutes to think about it and then called back to say that he would go first. During one of the two calls, Al Simpson took the phone and gave Clarence another locker room pep talk: "You've got to charge. You've got to be really strong."

Arlen Specter left the meeting in Thurmond's office at about 7:30, well before it ended. His job the next morning was to question Anita Hill, and he had had no time to prepare. Throughout the day, his phone had been ringing off the hook, and then Senator Thurmond had wanted him to attend the meeting. Now he had to do some preparation.

He arrived home at 8:30 and read materials until midnight. He had time only to sketch out a short outline of topics to cover. During the evening, he recalls, his aunt Rose from Wichita called to admonish him: questioning Anita Hill was not a smart thing for him to do.

On my way home from the Capitol after the meeting in Thurmond's office, I spoke to Ken Duberstein on the car phone. Ken was sensitive to criticism that during the first round of hearings, Clarence had been overly managed. The *Washington Post* had carried a front-page picture of Ken, Fred McClure, and me sitting behind Clarence signaling time-out to Chairman Biden. Ken suggested that it might be good symbolism if only Ginni were sitting behind Clarence the next morning. I thought about it and called him back. I agreed that Ken and Fred should not be there because they were truly the professional support team, but I thought Clarence needed someone he could turn to, and that I should be with him.

After Larry and I left the Thomases' home at seven o'clock that evening, Clarence had one critical responsibility, perhaps the most critical challenge of his life: preparation of the opening statement that he would read to the Judiciary Committee at ten o'clock the next morning. Clarence was determined that his statement would be entirely his own work. He sounded so independent about writing it that some of his advisers were concerned. I had spoken with Ken Duberstein the day before. Ken said, "Clarence is angry. He is angry at Duberstein. He is angry at everybody, and he doesn't want any input in preparing his statement." Ken seemed hurt but understood that Clarence was facing the biggest challenge of his life and that he wanted to prepare for it by himself.

Larry Thompson remembers that after he returned to his hotel room, he received at least two calls from Mike Luttig and another from either Lee Liberman or Mark Paoletta, all for the purpose of finding out what Clarence was planning to say. Larry did not know, but Clarence was in a very good emotional state. He told them what we had discussed at Clarence's home that afternoon and described the aggressive approach Clarence was taking. Larry quotes Luttig as saying, "I don't think that's the right approach."

The single part of Clarence's statement that was included on my advice and at the insistence of Ken Duberstein was that he had searched his mind to see if there was anything he could have said or done that could have caused Anita Hill to have concluded that he had sexual intentions toward her, and that if he had said or done anything, he was sorry. Ken believed, as did several of Clarence's friends, that this could have been a case of misunderstanding between Clarence and Anita Hill, that she might testify to something she misconstrued, and that that eventuality should be covered in Clarence's statement. I believed, on the basis of my meeting with lawyers on the previous day and of my concern about the possibility of perjury through overstatement, that such a disclaimer was important.

Together, Ken and I persuaded Clarence to include it, but this insertion was discordant with the indignation and strong denial that were the heart of Clarence's statement. If this disclaimer had any relationship to what was in his own mind, it was as a general confession of guilt for the unrelated sins that tormented him as he sought some personal reason for his punishment. But, in the mind of Clarence Thomas, there was no thought that there could have been a misunderstanding between him and his accuser. There was no basis—none whatsoever—for Anita Hill's allegation.

That night, I was reasonably optimistic about the hearing. I thought that even if Clarence were to lose, he would make a strong statement of principle about the confirmation process and that such a statement was important, perhaps more important than winning the vote. Whatever happened, Clarence could regain his dignity by speaking to the American people.

Mike Luttig did not share my optimism. When Mike had seen him that morning, Clarence was in no condition to collect his thoughts sufficiently to face the Judiciary Committee. Mike phoned Clarence several times on Thursday night to find out what Clarence planned to say in his statement. Each time, Clarence responded with a very general sketch of his thoughts but made it plain that he did not want to discuss the details. Initially, Clarence's refusal to talk was of little concern to Mike. He understood that this was a time when Clarence needed to speak from the heart, when advice about legal matters was unnecessary. But as he thought about it, Mike became increasingly concerned. Suppose Clarence was unable to sleep that night. Suppose he appeared before the committee with nothing at all to say. Suppose he froze.

Again Mike phoned Clarence. "No, I'm fine," insisted Clarence. "Call me back around ten o'clock and I will read to you what I have got." Mike did phone Clarence at ten o'clock. Here is his description of that call:

"So I called him back at ten o'clock, and he started to read me something that did not even resemble a statement. It was incoherent. It was disorganized, and in total it might have represented a single page of handwriting. . . . I said 'Is that it?' He said, 'Yes.' And I said, 'Okay.' And he said, 'And I'm going to go to bed.' I said, 'Okay. You need your rest, and that's good.' I said, 'Now maybe in the morning we can talk about some points you may want to make.' He said, 'Okay, okay,' but clearly just brushing me off."

Alarmed, Mike jotted down a couple of pages of notes as a safety precaution in case Clarence arrived at the Senate with nothing else. He then called Ginni with some ideas for Clarence if he woke up in the middle of the night, started to write, and froze.

Shortly after Larry Thompson and I left his house at seven o'clock, Clarence had attempted to write a statement, but the phone kept interrupting him, and he was exhausted. Clarence recalls that my call from Senator Thurmond's office was less a request for his decision than an announcement that he would testify first. With that, he recalls, he started to panic. The hearing was little more than twelve hours away, and he had prepared nothing. He felt that he was rushing forward to inevitable disgrace and destruction. So far, a powerful opening statement remained elusive.

Marie Flanagan, one of Clarence's neighbors, cuts hair and she arrived at about 9:30 to give him a haircut and a head massage. Ginni recalls that Clarence was exhausted. Clarence remembers that before he went to bed at 11:30, he put his hands to his head and told Ginni, "I'm tired, I'm exhausted, I'm scared." He still had nothing prepared. While Clarence dozed, Ginni stayed up to try to put together something from the various notes on the dining area table. At one o'clock Clarence was awake. Ginni told him that she had been working on his statement. Clarence went downstairs to find the table cluttered with notes, yellow pads, and drafts. He returned to the bedroom and said, "Virginia, it's all a mess down there and it's not all together and I don't have a statement." She put on her robe and went downstairs to try to help him. Both Ginni and Clarence described his condition as panic.

Clarence said, "Take all these things away," so Ginni calmly cleared the table and gave Clarence a blank pad and pen. It was 1:30 A.M.

Clarence recalls what happened next: "I said, well let me just think. Let me open up to the Holy Spirit. Then I just started from square one. Not with other people's ideas. I looked at the draft and I just started writing. I continued writing."

Clarence did not use an outline, and did not attempt a detailed response to Anita Hill's charge. He wanted to say what the confirmation process had done to him and why it was wrong.

Ginni went upstairs to turn on the computer. Clarence sat at the dinner table writing in longhand. As he finished a page or two, Ginni took his work upstairs and put it on the computer. By 4:45, they completed a second draft of the statement and went to bed until Clarence got up at six o'clock. He had slept for ten minutes at most.

Friday, October 11

At 6:30 Clarence called to read me his statement. It was pure Clarence Thomas, his feelings in his words—no "rounding of the edges," as he had described his appearance in the first hearing. I made only two minor suggestions: to delete a passing complimentary reference to the Senate because it was inconsistent with the adversarial stance he was taking with the committee and to add my name to his wife's as the only two people he had shared the statement with. With those two small exceptions, Clarence's statement was exactly as he wrote it a few hours earlier.

Before Clarence left for the Senate, Mike Luttig phoned to see if he had prepared a statement. "Yes," replied Clarence, and then he told Mike that he would not read it to him.

A deputy marshal picked up Clarence and Ginni and drove them to the Russell Senate Office Building, where they went to my office for an hour's wait for the start of the ten o'clock hearing. Clarence seemed strong to Ginni that morning. He was quiet at home and on the way to the Senate. As Ginni listened to religious music through ear phones, Clarence gazed out the car window. The deputy marshal took a slightly roundabout way to the Russell Building so the Thomases would not have to ride by protesters.

Mike Luttig was in my office when the Thomases arrived at nine o'clock. He met with Clarence to review the points Anita Hill had made in her allegation and gave Clarence a list of suggestions to consider including in his statement—the same fail-safe suggestions Mike had jotted down the previous night. Clarence said that he had a statement. Then Mike wished Clarence well and told him to do his best, and said that he just wanted to be there with him.

I entered my office as Mike left and gave Clarence one additional thought. At the previous hearing, Clarence had approached the committee table and warmly shook hands with the senators in what became a melee of photo opportunities. I told him not to repeat the handshakes. He would be there to confront the committee. He should not be rude, but he should not be genial either.

My office was a mob scene, and it remained so throughout the weekend. Across the hallway, Justice Department lawyers had commandeered the room used by my legislative correspondents, just as they had done during the first round of hearings. In the first hearings, their job was to be a ready source of legal research for any question of law that might be put to the nominee and to supply the complete texts of the many speeches and articles Clarence had written in the past. Their role in the Anita Hill phase of the process was unclear. Rob McDonald, my administrative assistant, tried to use his desk, but the rest of his office was occupied through most of the weekend by a dozen or so women who had worked with Clarence—the Nancy Altman group. The secretary's room between Rob's office and my own was a milling area for a variety of people who were officially or unofficially part of the Thomas team. The reception room was a din of ringing telephones and a television set and served as a campground for anyone who wandered in.

In the hallway outside my office, separated from me by a door and transom, a crowd had gathered, mostly black church people, who wanted to demonstrate their support for Clarence. There was no quiet, little privacy, and a constant sense that a horde of people might burst through the door at any time. Certain of the confusion we would find that morning, knowing that any loud sound from my room could be heard in the hallway and in the secretary's room, I had decided that the only truly private place in my office, the only place from which nothing could be overheard, was my office bathroom. With that in mind, I arranged in advance for a tape player to be set up on the washstand. I inserted the tape, adjusted the volume, and cued the tape to exactly the right place.

It was 9:45, fifteen minutes before the scheduled start of the hearing, fifteen minutes before Clarence spoke for himself. Clarence, Ginni, and I were alone in my room. It was time for prayer. They asked me to get Sally, who was in the next room. The four of us sat on two adjacent couches. We held hands, and I said the prayer. I acknowledged that we were calling to God in weakness. I asked God to give Clarence strength, for he had none. I prayed that God would give Clarence the words to say and the power to speak from his heart. Clarence remembers that I asked that he be free of the burden of wanting to be on the Supreme Court and that God's will be done. I was to offer similar prayers that evening and the next day as Clarence returned to continue his testimony.

Clarence remembers that, as we stood up, I said, "This is going to sound a little hokey." I asked them to follow me. Clarence, Ginni, Sally, and I crowded into the bathroom. There was barely room for the four of us to stand in a circle. I closed the door behind us and pressed the play button of the tape player. The Mormon Tabernacle Choir sang. We reached out to each other and held hands as we listened:

> *Onward Christian soldiers*
> *Marching as to war*
> *With the Cross of Jesus*
> *Going on before.*

I looked at Clarence. His eyes were closed, his head bowed; his foot beat time to the music.

The choir sang two verses of the old hymn. I pushed the stop button, put my hands on Clarence's shoulders, and spoke as a minister: "Go forth in the name of Christ, trusting in the power of the Holy Spirit."

Clarence says that by the morning of the hearing he "felt pure." He had asked God's forgiveness for past sins, and he "felt as though God had cleansed me." Now he was ready to give his testimony. As he left my office for the walk to the Senate Caucus Room, he said he "felt as though I was armed for battle then. I was still scared, but I felt that God was with us. That God was going to guide me. That God had given me these words. And that I was going to speak these words. And that if they ran me out of town, I had spoken what I thought God had put on my tongue. . . . I know that mentally I did not have the capacity to speak those words. I didn't have the capacity to make a speech or to develop a speech. I had to sit there at one in the morning and open up when I was dead tired. So I felt that God had given me those words and that God had opened me up. I felt that God was with me. That I was doing God's will as I went upstairs."

Ginni recalls that Clarence had a mission when he left my office—a purpose that was bigger than he was. Ken Duberstein noticed "how focused his eyes were, very intense—passion." Clarence reassured Ken, "I'm going to be okay. I'm going to be okay." He added, "I'm going to let them have it." Ken replied, "You should."

Allen Moore had never been more depressed than he was while standing in the secretary's room waiting for Clarence to go to the Caucus Room. He imagines that he must have looked as depressed as he felt. Clarence walked out of my room, saw Allen, took his hand, and said, "It's going to be all right." Allen thought, "Oh, my God! Now he is comforting me."

As Clarence, Ginni, and I walked into the hallway, cameramen rushed backward ahead of us. The hallway was lined with what seemed like hundreds of supporters, many of them black church people, shouting, "Thomas, Thomas."

Janet Brown, Ricky Silberman, and about a half-dozen other women who had been at Thursday's press conference left my office early and went to the hearing room so they would be present when Clarence entered. They wanted the press to know they were there. Larry Thompson arrived in the hearing room before Clarence began his statement. From the banter in the room, he concluded that most of the audience believed that Clarence was finished. Specifically, he recalls speaking with a woman from a union organization who boastfully said, "His goose is cooked."

As we climbed the marble stairway from the second to the third floor of the Russell Building, we saw Elizabeth and Steven Law standing just outside the door of the Senate Caucus Room. Elizabeth said to Clarence, "Just visualize Jesus standing behind you, Clarence, with his hands on your shoulders."

We entered the magnificent Senate Caucus Room, with its marble walls, red damask curtains, and massive Corinthian columns extending to an ornately painted ceiling two stories above. It was packed with media and spectators. Clarence walked directly to the witness table. Ginni and I took our seats behind him. Ginni whispered to me, "I may have to hold your hand from time to time." At one point that morning, I did reach over to take her hand.

As Clarence waited at the witness table for the hearing to begin, he was angry: "I felt abused. I felt that they had wronged me. I felt that they had hurt me. They had hurt my family. They'd hurt my friends for political ends. I felt that God wanted me to tell the whole country that this wasn't right. . . . I felt a disdain for the committee. They looked like petty little thieves sitting up there. . . . I felt as though the people in the press gallery were a cabal. They were evil people who conspired in my lynching and were going to destroy our country. I felt that I was charged by God to tell them and tell the world that this wasn't right. I felt hurt, but I felt that I had to be strong. Don't give in to self-pity. That I had to be firm, but not insulting. That I had to be tough in what I said, but not ill mannered."

Before we left my office, I had given Clarence a brown file folder in which to carry his statement. As he sat at the table, he wrote on the outside of the folder, "In the name of Christ," and repeatedly read those words—"In the name of Christ. In the name of Christ"—while Joe Biden made his opening remarks. "Then when he finally got around to me," Clarence said, "I read my statement in the name of Christ. A sort of a feeling overcame me to give me the peace, the firmness, to look them in their eyes, to not avert their faces and watch them looking down and avoiding me. To have the kind of delivery that wasn't wooden. That wasn't hurried. It was measured and firm."

At last, Clarence began to read from the sixteen pages Ginni had typed for him just hours earlier:

Mr. Chairman, Senator Thurmond, members of the committee: as excruciatingly difficult as the last 2 weeks have been, I welcome the opportunity to clear my name today. No one other than my wife and Senator Danforth, to whom I read this statement at 6:30 A.M., has seen or heard the statement, no handlers, no advisers.

The first I learned of the allegations by Prof. Anita Hill was on September 25, 1991, when the FBI came to my home to investigate her allegations. When informed by the FBI agent of the nature of the allegations and the person making them, I was shocked, surprised, hurt, and enormously saddened.

I have not been the same since that day. For almost a decade my responsibilities included enforcing the rights of victims of sexual harassment. As a boss, as a friend, and as a human being I was proud that I never had such an allegation leveled against me, even as I sought to promote women, and minorities into nontraditional jobs.

In addition, several of my friends, who are women, have confided in me about the horror of harassment on the job, or elsewhere. I thought I really understood the anguish, the fears, the doubts, the seriousness of the matter. But since September 25, I have suffered immensely as these very serious charges were leveled against me.

I have been wracking my brains, and eating my insides out trying to think of what I could have said or done to Anita Hill to lead her to allege that I was interested in her in more than a professional way, and that I talked with her about pornographic or X-rated films.

Contrary to some press reports, I categorically denied all of the allegations and denied that I ever attempted to date Anita Hill, when first interviewed by the FBI. I strongly reaffirm that denial.

Clarence then related to the committee the history of his relationship with Anita Hill. He had hired her on the recommendation of his friend Gil Hardy, and she had worked with him at the Department of Education and at EEOC in a "professional" and "cordial" relationship. Since leaving EEOC she had driven him to the Tulsa, Oklahoma, airport when he visited Oral Roberts University and had made telephone calls to him. At no time did she give any hint that she was uncomfortable with him.

After recounting his relationship with Anita Hill, Clarence continued:

> During my tenure in the executive branch as a manager, as a policymaker, and as a person, I have adamantly condemned sex harassment. There is no member of this committee or this Senate who feels stronger about sex harassment than I do. As a manager, I made every effort to take swift and decisive action when sex harassment raised or reared its ugly head.
>
> The fact that I feel so very strongly about sex harassment and spoke loudly about it at EEOC has made these allegations doubly hard on me. I cannot imagine anything that I said or did to Anita Hill that could have been mistaken for sexual harassment.
>
> But with that said, if there is anything that I have said that has been misconstrued by Anita Hill or anyone else, to be sexual harassment, then I can say that I am so very sorry and I wish I had known. If I did know I would have stopped immediately and I would not, as I have done over the past two weeks, have to tear away at myself trying to think of what I could possibly have done. But I have not said or done the things that Anita Hill has alleged. God has gotten me through the days since September 25 and He is my judge.
>
> Mr. Chairman, something has happened to me in the dark days that have followed since the FBI agents informed me about these allegations. And the days have grown darker, as this very serious, very explosive, and very sensitive allegation or these sensitive allegations were selectively leaked, in a distorted way to the media over the past weekend.
>
> As if the confidential allegations, themselves, were not enough, this apparently calculated public disclosure has caused me, my family, and my friends enormous pain and great harm.
>
> I have never, in all my life, felt such hurt, such pain, such agony. My family and I have been done a grave and irreparable injustice. During the past two weeks, I lost the belief that if I did my best all would work out. I called upon the strength that helped me get here

from Pinpoint, and it was all sapped out of me. It was sapped out of me because Anita Hill was a person I considered a friend, whom I admired and thought I had treated fairly and with the utmost respect. Perhaps I could have better weathered this if it were from someone else, but here was someone I truly felt I had done my best with.

Though I am, by no means, a perfect person, no means, I have not done what she has alleged, and I still do not know what I could possibly have done to cause her to make these allegations.

When I stood next to the President in Kennebunkport, being nominated to the Supreme Court of the United States, that was a high honor. But as I sit here, before you, 103 days later, that honor has been crushed. From the very beginning charges were leveled against me from the shadows—charges of drug abuse, antisemitism, wife-beating, drug use by family members, that I was a quota appointment, confirmation conversion and much, much more, and now, this.

I have complied with the rules. I responded to a document request that produced over 30,000 pages of documents. And I have testified for five full days, under oath. I have endured this ordeal for 103 days. Reporters sneaking into my garage to examine books I read. Reporters and interest groups swarming over divorce papers, looking for dirt. Unnamed people starting preposterous and damaging rumors. Calls all over the country specifically requesting dirt. This is not American. This is Kafka-esque. It has got to stop. It must stop for the benefit of future nominees, and our country. Enough is enough.

I am not going to allow myself to be further humiliated in order to be confirmed. I am here specifically to respond to allegations of sex harassment in the workplace. I am not here to be further humiliated by this committee, or anyone else, or to put my private life on display for a prurient interest or other reasons. I will not allow this committee or anyone else to probe into my private life. This is not what America is all about.

To ask me to do that would be to ask me to go beyond fundamental fairness. Yesterday, I called my mother. She was confined to her bed, unable to work and unable to stop crying. Enough is enough.

Mr. Chairman, in my forty-three years on this Earth, I have been able, with the help of others and with the help of God, to defy poverty, avoid prison, overcome segregation, bigotry, racism, and obtain one of the finest educations available in this country. But I have not been able to overcome this process. This is worse than any obstacle or anything that I have ever faced. Throughout my life I have been energized by the expectation and the hope that in this country I would be treated fairly in all endeavors. When there was segregation I hoped there would be fairness one day or someday. When there was bigotry and prejudice I hoped that there would be tolerance and understanding someday.

Mr. Chairman, I am proud of my life, proud of what I have done, and what I have accomplished, proud of my family, and this process, this process is trying to destroy it all. No job is worth what I have been through, no job. No horror in my life has been so debilitating. Confirm me if you want, don't confirm me if you are so led, but let this process end. Let me and my family regain our lives. I never asked to be nominated. It was an honor. Little did I know the price, but it is too high.

I enjoy and appreciate my current position, and I am comfortable with the prospect of returning to my work as a judge on the U.S. Court of Appeals for the D.C. Circuit and to my friends there.

Each of these positions is public service, and I have given at the office. I want my life and my family's life back and I want them returned expeditiously.

I have experienced the exhilaration of new heights from the moment I was called to Kennebunkport by the President to have lunch and he nominated me. That was the high point. At that time I was told eye-to-eye that, Clarence, you made it this far on merit, the rest is going to be politics and it surely has been. There have been other highs. The outpouring of support from my friends of long-standing, a bonding like I have never experienced with my old boss, Senator Danforth, the wonderful support of those who have worked with me.

There have been prayers said for my family, and me, by people I know and people I will never meet, prayers that were heard and that sustained not only me, but also my wife and my entire family. Instead of understanding and appreciating the great honor bestowed upon me, I find myself, here today defending my name, my integrity, because somehow select portions of confidential documents, dealing with this matter were leaked to the public.

Mr. Chairman, I am a victim of this process and my name has been harmed, my integrity has been harmed, my character has been harmed, my family has been harmed, my friends have been harmed. There is nothing this committee, this body or this country can do to give me my good name back, nothing.

I will not provide the rope for my own lynching or for further humiliation. I am not going to engage in discussions, nor will I submit to roving questions of what goes on in the most intimate parts of my private life or the sanctity of my bedroom. These are the most intimate parts of my privacy, and they will remain just that, private.[51]

Ken Duberstein, watching from the back of the room, remembers, "I thought he was coming across with such emotion and such heat, that there was silence in the room. You could have heard that proverbial pin drop."

Allen Moore, a long-time Senate staffer, describes Clarence's testimony both Friday morning and Friday night: "[I] had never seen in all my years up here a hearing that had such a shocking effect on senators. I have always been struck by the power, the ability of senators to gain the upper hand on any witness. . . . I felt like it was a shock wave in the room. . . . They were stunned."

When Clarence completed his statement, the committee was uncertain how to proceed. The normal course would be to begin questioning the witness, but on what? The committee had an FBI report, but, under Senate rules, its content was confidential. All the committee had that could be the subject of public interrogation was an unsworn statement by Anita Hill. Unsure of what course to follow, the committee retired to Senator Kennedy's nearby office to discuss matters. I left Clarence and Ginni to attend the meeting.

Senator Biden decided that the committee should not question Clarence until Anita Hill made her statement. Focusing on our concern about the evening news cycle, I then made an unreasonable request: that Anita Hill testify but that any unfinished testimony be interrupted at four o'clock so that Clarence could rebut it. Of course, Joe Biden denied that request. He said that Anita Hill would testify and after questioning of her was completed, Clarence could return. This result was not what I asked for, but it was what Ken Duberstein thought was the best scenario: Clarence would speak, Anita Hill would testify, and Clarence would return to answer questions.

As far as Clarence was concerned, he was prepared to start answering questions then and there. As he puts it, "After I delivered that statement, I was loaded for bear." Clarence assumed that the committee was allowing Anita Hill to control its agenda by refusing to allow her statements to be released until she testified. He recalls, "I was kind of ticked."

While the committee was meeting in Ted Kennedy's office and Ginni and Clarence were standing near the witness table, Janet Brown and Ricky Silberman crossed the rope barrier that separated Clarence from the press and audience. Janet's eyes welled with tears as she gave Clarence a hug. Clarence said, "J.B., don't cry. It's going to be okay."

As the committee was taking a break after the decision on the sequence of testimony, Al Simpson told me that he thought Clarence should be in the Caucus Room watching Anita Hill as she testified. I agreed that was a good idea; it would make Clarence look strong, and it might unnerve Anita Hill. I also knew that I did not dare even raise that possibility with Clarence. The task was to maintain his psychological edge, and asking him to sit in public view while his character and integrity were attacked was not the way to do it. When we returned to my office, I asked him whether he wanted to stay in my room and watch her testimony. No, he said. I did not argue with him. Once he said no, that was the answer. I wanted him to do what he was comfortable doing.

Allen Moore was present when Clarence refused to watch the hearing from my office. He quotes Clarence as saying, "I'm not watching it. I don't need to see those lies. I know what she is going to say. I just want to go home." In fact, Clarence knew only what Anita Hill had alleged in her written statement. The embellishments in her oral testimony were new material.

After Clarence had left, Al Simpson phoned me at my office. The hearing was about to reconvene, he said, and Clarence should be there, sitting in a chair looking at Anita Hill. It was too late, I said; Clarence had left for home.

Ginni thinks it was very characteristic of Clarence not to watch Anita Hill's testimony on television. As the deputy marshal drove them back to their house, she praised Clarence for his statement. When they reached home, Clarence pulled out a cigar, played his favorite music on the stereo, and talked with the deputy marshal while Ginni went upstairs to watch the hearing alone.

Clarence explains his refusal to listen to Anita Hill's testimony: "I couldn't take it. . . . There was so little left of me, that every time I hear these charges, they just destroy me inside, and I can't take it. . . . I was adamant she was lying and I wasn't going to listen to these charges. This wasn't a lawyer listening and taking notes on somebody else's fate, this was me. As far as I was concerned, she could say anything she wanted with respect to my doing or saying these things, they were all lies and I wasn't going to sit here and destroy myself listening to that. . . . I knew what my limits were, so I came home."

From time to time, Ginni came downstairs to report on the hearing. She told him that Senator Specter was doing a good job; that Anita Hill had testified that Clarence had told her of a character in a pornographic movie named Long Dong Silver; that she had testified also that Clarence had remarked to her about finding a pubic hair on a Coke can. When Ginni told him about "Long Dong Silver," Clarence said, "Is it a joke? Was there a joke or something that used that in it?"

She describes him as being "disgusted" and "flabbergasted" by the reports. As the charges became more specific, Clarence seemed to become more comfortable. Now there could be no room to suppose that he had said something or done something that was innocently intended but misconstrued. This could not be a question of mistake. This was plainly wrong.

Mike Luttig remembers talking to Clarence on the phone several times that afternoon. At one point Mike asked, "Well, are you watching her?" Clarence said, "No. I have heard enough lies." Larry Silberman remembers that he was in his courthouse chambers that Friday afternoon, and that Clarence called him every half-hour or forty-five minutes to find out what he thought. Larry says, "It was funny in a grim way. . . . I couldn't watch any more than he could."

No one argued with Clarence about refusing to watch Anita Hill's testimony, but Ken Duberstein thought it was a mistake. If senators asked Clarence if he had watched and he said "no," they would be incredulous.

Those who busily rewrote history in the aftermath of the Hill-Thomas hearing portrayed the Judiciary Committee, and especially Arlen Specter, as being overly aggressive and even brutal in questioning Anita Hill. More than a year later, an article in the *Washington Post* referred, without citing any evidence, to the Senate's "clumsy treatment" of Anita Hill.[52] Again, without citing any evidence, *Post* columnist Mary McGrory asserted in December 1992 that "the Senate disgraced itself" in the hearing.[53] In August 1993, an article in the *New York Times Magazine* spoke of "the rough, inquisitorial treatment Hill suffered at the hands of some Senators two years ago."[54] One wonders what the revisionists would have said had Anita Hill been subjected to questioning by experienced counsel in a court of law. Supporters of Clarence Thomas who have had legal training, including myself, reach exactly the opposite conclusion of the revisionists: we think that with all the protections of law, Anita Hill could and should have been subjected to far more searching questioning.

I have the greatest admiration for Arlen Specter and for what he was able to accomplish with only three and a half hours of preparation the night before. But he was, as he states, functioning as a senator and not as any advocate. He was doing what a lawyer is not permitted to do: looking out after his own interests.

Larry Thompson says that Anita Hill was "never asked challenging questions. She was never asked in a probing, sifting way to explain inconsistency." He refers, for example, to what a trial lawyer could have done in examining press reports of her early dismissal of phone logs of her calls to Clarence.[55] He thinks that more attention should have been given to details in her testimony that were not contained in the FBI report and that the FBI agents who interviewed her should have been called as witnesses and asked whether they had said during the interview that she should be as specific as possible.[56]

Orrin Hatch has a similar opinion: "Arlen Specter did a very good job under the circumstances. He was limited in what he could do, and he was limited by the political situation. He knew that all of those liberal groups were out there and all the liberal media were out there just waiting for anything that looked like it would be a scourging cross-examination of her. Nobody could say that he mistreated her or did anything that was excessive. But had, let us say, an Arthur Liman been the designated questioner of Anita Hill and Hoerchner or any of those witnesses, there was enough there, there were enough questions there and enough things that Anita Hill would have had a very, very rough couple of days. And when that type of a top-flight lawyer finished, I don't think many people would disbelieve Clarence Thomas."

When Anita Hill began testifying, Arlen Specter thought it might be possible to reconcile her statement with Clarence's denial. Here, again, was the theory of misconstrued intentions. Arlen's mind changed during her opening statement to the committee. Noting what he calls "the disparity" between Anita Hill's written statement and her statement to the FBI on one hand and her oral testimony on the other, Arlen says, "I was somewhere between surprised and astounded. . . . It became apparent to me that there was no reconciliation and that I had grave questions as to her credibility." He adds, "She was just an extraordinarily well-prepared and well-coached witness, so that there was a quality about her of disingenuousness as to what she was saying."

During the hearing, Arlen accused Anita Hill of "flat-out perjury." She had denied a newspaper story that a Senate staffer had told her that if she came forward, Clarence might withdraw. After the lunch break, she admitted that she had had such a conversation. Arlen thinks it "highly likely" that during the break, she had been advised by a lawyer that if she recanted during the proceeding she would not be prosecuted for perjury. Recalling her denial of the conversation with a Senate staffer, Arlen says, "That really bothered me very, very, very, very, very much." As for his claim of "flat-out perjury," Arlen says, "That's what I felt. And I think politically I went way too far for my interests."[57]

Larry Thompson shares Arlen's view that Anita Hill seemed well prepared and well coached: "I thought everything was too contrived. She had nice, neat, pat responses to everything, and that is a signal that a witness has been prepared by a lawyer."

Ken Duberstein thought there was something wrong with Anita Hill's testimony. An observer of American politics, he was reminded of candidate Michael Dukakis in the 1988 presidential campaign mechanically answering a debate question on how he would feel if his wife were raped. Ken recalls, "I was looking for emotion. Instead, I got a clinical recitation of grotesque acts." When others told him she was a credible witness, he wondered what he was missing that others saw.

As Mike Luttig listened to Anita Hill's testimony, it seemed to him that her story "had been constructed." The specific details of her oral testimony were especially significant to him, because he had not noticed them in the FBI report. Two FBI agents had interviewed Anita Hill—one male, one female. According to Mike, the FBI told Anita Hill that "they needed all the nitty, gritty details." The female agent's role was to make the interviews more comfortable for the witness. If the subject matter became embarrassing, the male agent could leave.

That details requested but not confided in private to FBI agents were disclosed to an all-male panel before television cameras led Mike to consider that the whole story was a fabrication.

By the middle of Friday afternoon, we did not know how much longer Anita Hill would be testifying. We did know that it was important for Clarence to return to the committee that day to refute Hill's testimony before the late news and certainly in time to make the morning newspapers. We called Clarence at home and asked him to come to my office so that he would be ready to return to the hearing room on the completion of Anita Hill's testimony.

I wanted Clarence in my office at least an hour and a half before returning to the committee. That would allow enough time to brief him on Anita Hill's allegations so that he would be prepared to respond to them and to help him get in a good emotional condition to face the committee.

At five o'clock that afternoon, I was in my office room with Sally, Ken, Fred McClure, and Allen Moore, watching Anita Hill on television, when Clarence arrived and poked his head through the door. Seeing that we were watching Hill testify, Clarence immediately said, "I'm not watching it." He turned and left. I turned off the television, cleared everyone out of my room, and made it available to Clarence and Mike Luttig.

Mike spent about forty-five minutes alone with Clarence, reviewing notes of Hill's testimony he had scrawled on a yellow pad. In his review, he was conscious of the need to be a calming influence, to offset the chaos that surrounded Clarence. As Mike reviewed the specifics of the testimony, Clarence seemed calm, but after each major allegation, he would say, "I just can't believe this," or "Why would she be doing this?" or "Why would she say this?"

Clarence seemed calm, Mike says, but he was "horrified" that such charges had been made about him on national television. Mike counseled him not to think about his embarrassment but to keep focused on the hearing. After reviewing the charges, Mike started through each one a second time, asking Clarence how he would respond to each one. Clarence said that this second run-through would not be necessary. He would categorically deny every bit of Hill's testimony. He would continue to say nothing bad about Anita Hill: "I am not going to attack her personally. I am not going to say anything bad about her. I am just going to tell the committee that this didn't happen."

Mike says that he spent most of the forty-five minutes trying to strengthen Clarence, counseling him not to lose control of himself before the committee. He reminded Clarence that he was a sitting court of appeals judge and that he could not lose control in a way that would cause people to say that he did not have the temperament to serve on the Supreme Court. By clear implication, if not in words, Mike let Clarence know that it would be a mistake for him to attack the committee. Although he understood the confrontational approach, especially after hearing Anita Hill's testimony, Mike held the opposite position: "Particularly in that environment, you should be more solicitous of the committee and the Congress as a whole, because, in effect, it has your future and life in its hands."

By the time Mike had finished his meeting with Clarence, it appeared that it would be at least three hours before Clarence would testify. Clarence asked Ken Duberstein if he had to do so that night; he was tired. But the lateness of the hour and Clarence's fatigue were less important to Ken than a timely rebuttal to Anita Hill's testimony. He told Clarence that he must speak to the committee that night, but not for long. He would ask Joe Biden for one hour.

Ken phoned Jeff Peck and asked for an hour that night. Peck suggested that the committee break for the day and return on Saturday morning when everyone would be fresher. Ken remembers saying: "Look, you have a choice. Either you let Clarence testify because he wants to for an hour tonight . . . or we will recommend to Clarence that he come upstairs and hold a press conference outside the Senate Caucus Room and respond to each one of her specific allegations, one by one, and say that he wanted to tell the committee that but they told him to cool his heels until Saturday morning and he didn't want to wait."

Within ten minutes, Ken received a response from the committee: "Let him come up here at nine o'clock, and he can testify for an hour."

Clarence's physical appearance left no doubt of his exhaustion. His eyes were red, his movements were slow. Janet Brown offered to take us to her apartment for dinner, but Clarence declined. Ginni thought that he should get some sleep, so I turned off most of the lights in my room and suggested that he stretch out on a couch. But Clarence could not sleep, nor could he eat anything except an apple. I asked him if he wanted to be alone with Ginni in my room, but he said that he wanted me to stay with them. We sat in the semidarkness, Clarence often standing up, rubbing the back of his neck, then sitting again. He said, "I'm confused, Jack." Rubbing his neck, he said, "It's like a weight on the back of my neck." He was confused by his meeting with Mike Luttig.

Mike's was good advice, kindly advice, lawyerly advice—but it was the opposite of the advice I was giving Clarence. Mike led Clarence point by point through Anita Hill's charges, asking Clarence for his response; I was telling him to defend nothing. Mike was suggesting that he not attack the committee; I was saying that if he attacked Congress, he would be a national hero. Mike was advising him to be solicitous to the committee, for his future was in its hands; I was reminding him that he did not care whether he served on the Supreme Court. Perhaps neither approach was better than the other, but they were mutually exclusive, and Clarence, understandably, was confused.

Orrin Hatch came into the office to see Clarence. Orrin spoke about what could be done to win the votes of wavering Democrats. It was an important subject but not the subject for the moment. It had become clear to me that the more Clarence worried about the confirmation vote and the more he cared about being on the Supreme Court, the weaker he became. His strength came in giving up his concern about his own future and fighting for a cause that was bigger than himself.

Because any reference to strategy to win confirmation unnerved Clarence, he may have made more out of an incidental reference to winning support from senators than Orrin Hatch intended. Orrin has his own clear recollection of the discussion.

Because he had the principal responsibility among Republican senators for questioning Clarence, Orrin thought it essential to make contact with his witness before the committee reconvened. Immediately after Anita Hill finished testifying, Orrin went to my office, where he found Clarence pacing the floor, "mad at everybody, mad at everything." Orrin remembers making three points to Clarence. First, he remembers telling Clarence to "get rid of the handlers and be yourself. Tell how you feel." Second, he recalls saying, "Don't take any crap from anybody, including me," to which Clarence replied, "Don't worry." Third, he said, "Now I am going to ask you some questions about antiblack, white racist, negative, stereotype language." To that, Clarence responded, "I hope you do."

Orrin did pursue a line of questions on stereotype language the following day. The idea for this tack came to him while watching two blacks discuss the Thomas/Hill controversy on a television talk show. Orrin's idea was that Clarence would not have used the language attributed to him for a reason aside from its tastelessness. The language portrayed a racist stereotype of a black male. It was inconceivable, thought Orrin, that Clarence Thomas, a proud man, would present himself to a woman as a racist stereotype of a black male. To do so would undercut everything Clarence stands for.

After Orrin Hatch left and Clarence and I were alone in my office, Clarence began to think out loud about what he would say when he returned to the committee. I had one thought in mind: whatever he said had to be authentic Clarence Thomas. He had to go to the committee room and tell the American people exactly what was on his mind. So for most of three hours, Clarence paced, sat, paced, sat, and let words come out that gave expression to what he felt.

First he wanted to make a strong denial of Anita Hill's allegations.

I said that this was very important. When something is not true, say so, immediately and clearly. Then he wanted to tell the committee what was in his heart.

I remember precisely where Clarence was when he first spoke what would be the most memorable words of the hearing. He was sitting in the middle of the couch on the south wall of my office, and he said, "You know what this is, Jack? This is a lynching. This is a high-tech lynching." The idea was his. The words were his. No person put them in his mind. I said, "Clarence, if that is how you feel, then go upstairs and say it." I suggested that he write it down, and he did.

It was exactly what he felt, and he said it with power, even in my office. He had heard tales of lynching as a boy in rural Georgia. He had read a book on lynching while in law school. He knew that claims of sexual misdeeds by black men gave rise to lynchings. This was not a hanging out in the woods; this was on national television. It was, indeed, a high-tech lynching.

Clarence's statement to the committee was, "As far as I am concerned, it is a high-tech lynching for uppity blacks who in any way deign to think for themselves." The word *lynching* was rooted in his lifelong interest in the subject. The reference to "uppity blacks" may have had its origin in a *Wall Street Journal* editorial shown to Clarence by John Mackey in the early weeks of the confirmation process. Mackey was a Justice Department veteran of the unsuccessful battle to get Bill Lucas confirmed as assistant attorney general for civil rights. At the time, the *Wall Street Journal* editorialized that Lucas, a black conservative, was being punished because he was "a black who dared to think for himself."[58]

As had been the case on the previous day in Clarence's family room, my own role was that of a prompter. I encouraged Clarence to think out loud, to express his feelings. Occasionally, I interjected a word or a phrase but told him to use his own words and to reject mine if they were not appropriate. My suggestions were usually more combative than his, and fortunately he did not use them. If any senator's question seemed judgmental, I suggested that he say, "Judge not that you be not judged, Senator. I deny that these charges are true, but even if they were, would you apply the same standards to members of the Senate that you apply to me?" Of course, such a remark would be in the nature of dropping a nuclear bomb on the hearing. Clarence did not use my idea. He was more restrained than I.

Two other suggestions I made were not used by Clarence in public. The committee did not try to get into matters unrelated to the charge of sexual harassment, thereby observing the limits imposed by Chairman Biden. If it did, I advised Clarence to say, "I'm not going to get into my personal life, and I'm not going to ask you what movies you watch or what you do in your bedroom." If asked to take a lie detector test, I advised him to say that he would do so when members of the committee took lie detector tests about the leak.

As Clarence was putting his feelings to words, Ken Duberstein was dealing with a psychological setback he had seen on television. Two networks had suggested that the White House was gloomy about Clarence's prospects and that the president was considering withdrawing the nomination. Ken reached the White House chief of staff John Sununu at home and secured a strong presidential statement of confidence in the nominee.

Ken remembers how Clarence seemed that night: "Determined, angry, convinced, compelled, ready to lay down the gauntlet and make sure every one of those senators understood that he was telling the truth and that he was not going to be party to giving them the opportunity to destroy him; that he was going to tell the truth, and if that made them uncomfortable, too bad."

Ken remembers that while waiting to testify that evening, Clarence asked, "How can the committee believe her? . . . When is Biden going to be fair and rule some of this stuff out of order? Why doesn't he stop this lynching?" According to Ken, Clarence believed that the committee, and especially Chairman Biden, should speak up for him.

That is what Clarence thought Joe Biden had pledged on the floor of the Senate. If the committee did not believe the charges were sufficient to slow the nomination in the first place, how could it allow such outrageous statements to go before the country without defending the nominee? Clarence says about the committee, "They all allowed me to be destroyed and no one had the guts—you know what it reminded me of, Jack? It reminded me of when I was in the seminary and guys would yell racial slurs and nobody would stand up. It always bothered me, not so much that the person yelled the racial slurs, but nobody would say, stop it. That's wrong. The way I felt about that committee was nobody was standing up and saying no. I mean the Republicans were fighting, but Biden, the chairman of the committee, who prides himself on fairness, wasn't standing up and saying this is wrong.

"So when I went up there I was exhausted and I was not going to tolerate them. They had wronged me. They had wronged this country. They had bastardized their own process. They had distorted it. It was a joke. No one should be put through that in this country. I wasn't going to let them off the hook.

"They weren't going to get off the hook and make me or this country believe that what they were doing was fair. . . . They wouldn't let us use the FBI reports, they wouldn't let us subpoena her, anything about her, they didn't even want us to touch her. She had to be treated with kid gloves. There were no procedures. There were no rules of evidence. There were seven people there who had voted against me."

Ken Duberstein remembers that before Clarence left my office for his second appearance of the day before the committee he said, "If you thought I did well this morning, tonight is going to be even better."

Larry Thompson recalls that Clarence had a "big, beaming smile."

Clarence returned to the Senate Caucus Room. "I had already pretended in the first hearing. I wasn't going to pretend anymore," he recalls. "This process was not fair."

Clarence's opening statement to the committee that evening went right to the points he wanted to make.

I would like to start by saying unequivocally, uncategorically that I deny each and every single allegation against me today that suggested in any way that I had conversations of a sexual nature or about pornographic material with Anita Hill, that I ever attempted to date her, that I ever had any personal sexual interest in her, or that I in any way ever harassed her.

Second, and I think a more important point, I think that this today is a travesty. I think that it is disgusting. I think that this hearing should never occur in America. This is a case in which this sleaze, this dirt was searched for by staffers of members of this committee, was then leaked to the media, and this committee and this body validated it and displayed it in prime time over our entire nation.

How would any member on this committee or any person in this room or any person in this country would like sleaze said about him or her in this fashion or this dirt dredged up and this gossip and these lies displayed in this manner? How would any person like it?

The Supreme Court is not worth it. No job is worth it. I am not here for that. I am here for my name, my family, my life and my integrity. I think something is dreadfully wrong with this country, when any person, any person in this free country would be subjected to this. This is not a closed room.

There was an FBI investigation. This is not an opportunity to talk about difficult matters privately or in a closed environment. This is a circus. It is a national disgrace. And from my standpoint, as a black American, as far as I am concerned, it is a high-tech lynching for uppity blacks who in any way deign to think for themselves, to do for themselves, to have different ideas, and it is a message that, unless you kow-tow to an old order, this is what will happen to you, you will be lynched, destroyed, caricatured by a committee of the U.S. Senate, rather than hung from a tree.[59]

Standing at the back of the Caucus Room, Ken Duberstein heard the most powerful testimony he had ever heard in his life. He thought Clarence's reference to a high-tech lynching for uppity blacks was "right on target." Clarence was saying that he was not afraid to be his own man and that he was being lynched for that reason.

As we returned to my office that night, Ken and I were ecstatic. There was a general feeling among his supporters that Clarence had taken the offensive and the committee was under siege. Ken remembers telling Clarence, "You hit a home run. In fact, you hit a grand slam."

Saturday, October 12

In addition to the Clarence Thomas ordeal, Nancy Altman had a second cause of distress in the autumn of 1991. Her brother, Bob, law partner and protégé of Washington's super lawyer Clark Clifford, was appearing before the House Banking Committee in its investigation of what was known as the BCCI scandal.[60] It was a matter for which he was subsequently prosecuted and acquitted, and at the time of the Thomas-Hill hearing and since, it tormented the close Altman family. For fear that her brother's notoriety would rub off on Clarence Thomas, she decided not to read her prepared statement at the women's news conference she herself had organized on Thursday. Now she could hold her tongue no longer. She was determined to read her statement not to the media but to the committee, and she was determined to do so with a large panel of women. It mattered not that the committee had drawn up its lists of witnesses and she was not on it or that character witnesses would not be allowed to testify.

Nancy called me at home early Saturday morning. She was convinced that the key to success was the testimony of women; many women throughout the country were pro–Anita Hill, and it was important for women who knew Clarence to testify. I agreed and told her that she should work with Janet Brown and Ricky Silberman to pull together a panel of women; I would do my best to see that the committee would let them testify. When I arrived in the office Saturday morning, I enlisted Janet Brown in Nancy's effort, asking her if she could help find women who would give brief statements for Clarence.

Nancy believes that Clarence's thoughtfulness toward her, even in

the midst of his own crisis, validated her commitment to him. She remembers one break in the hearing when Clarence returned to my office visibly exhausted. Nancy had come to the Capitol with Jan, her
sister. Although Jan was a stranger to Clarence, he made an effort to
make her feel welcome and at ease for being in the office.

On another occasion, Nancy wanted to say something to Clarence,
and I was trying to keep people out of my office room so he could have
some quiet. Clarence saw that I was trying to exclude her and said,
"Nance, what's going on? Do you have something to talk to me
about?" Although he had never met Nancy's brother, Clarence asked
after him even in the midst of his own testimony, and expressed concern about how Bob's troubles were affecting Nancy's parents. He was
attentive to someone else's problems even during the worst hours of
his own ordeal.

Riding to the Senate that morning, Clarence saw evidence that his
testimony had a positive effect on the public. Motorists who recognized him in the marshal's car honked their horns and gave him a
thumbs up. When Clarence reached my office, Ken Duberstein relayed a message he had received on the phone from John Sununu. The
president had asked Sununu to give Clarence a message: "Tell Clarence that I felt very positive about last night. I am very upbeat, and
keep going." When Ken showed his note of the phone call, Clarence
smiled, shook his head, and said, "We're going to hang in there."

Orrin Hatch, the Republicans' designated questioner that day,
came to my office to say that he was so proud of Clarence he could
hardly sleep the night before. He was ready for the hearing to begin.

Arlen Specter came to the office about twenty minutes before the
hearing was to reconvene. He said that he thought the longer Clarence
was before the committee the better, and that he had a number of
questions to ask about inconsistencies in Anita Hill's testimony. Clarence, who was tired and hopeful that his ordeal would end by noon,
recalls that Arlen's interest in prolonged questioning "did not gladden
my heart."

At the start of Saturday's hearing, Clarence remembers, "I wasn't as anxious. I just wanted to get it over with. I was adamant not to lose any ground with these guys and not to let them bully me."

As agreed, Orrin Hatch asked Clarence about racial stereotypes. Was not the language that Anita Hill attributed to him in keeping with the most offensively racist stereotype of a black male and therefore especially unthinkable for him?

That subject was no surprise to Ricky Silberman, who remembers discussing it with Clarence three or four years earlier. Their conversation, which had taken place in the chairman's office at EEOC, had centered on Clarence's concern about raising a black son as a single parent. He said only discipline would keep a black son safe. Ricky quotes Clarence, "Never mind birth control, this business about condoms in schools, what you ought to tell kids, what I tell Jamal is don't! I tell him don't and if he does I'll kill him." Ricky continues, "And he talked about it, the racial, sexual stereotypes. And how dangerous it is for black men and had been historically. And how that was something that black men were always afraid of."

Mike Luttig also remembers that Clarence had talked to him about the matter of stereotype before Orrin Hatch raised the question.

Clarence's memory of being told that the subject of racial and sexual stereotypes would be raised at the hearing is somewhat different from Orrin Hatch's. He believes that Orrin did not mention it to him on Friday night, but that on Saturday morning Mike Luttig told him that Orrin intended to ask about it and that Orrin called me on the phone before the hearing and I relayed the information to him. Clarence also believes that he had a phone conversation with a black friend, Tony Welters, perhaps late on Friday night, in which Welters said that he should "do something about the way in which they're smearing me with sexual innuendos." However it was first broached with Clarence in connection with the hearing, it was a subject familiar to him. Speaking of Orrin Hatch's line of questions, he says, "I think he was absolutely right."

Sally remembers that after he testified about the sexual stereotype of black men she told him, "Clarence, that really took guts." He responded, "Sally, I did it for the young men."

Ken and I were well aware of one strategic problem: how to explain the testimony of Anita Hill. The simplest explanation was pursued by many of Clarence's friends and was abandoned only grudgingly by all of us: that both Clarence and Anita Hill were telling the truth and that this was a question of mistaken intentions. Now there could be no doubt that that explanation was unavailable. The statements of Clarence Thomas and Anita Hill were flatly contradictory and wholly irreconcilable. One of them was not telling the truth. We believed Clarence.

The media, the public, and senators were asking the same question: why would Anita Hill not tell the truth? The public might believe that the nominee would have ample reason for lying to the committee, but what could be the motive of Anita Hill? What reason was there to think she was making up a story?

The first help in providing some understanding literally walked through the door of my office room on Friday afternoon. It was one of Mike Luttig's Justice Department lawyers who had been watching the proceedings in my commandeered legislative correspondents' room across the hallway. Anita Hill had just told the committee of Clarence's alleged remarks about a pubic hair on a Coke can. Luttig's assistant announced that the Hill statement was not original material; he remembered a similar line in the novel *The Exorcist*. Could Anita Hill have borrowed part of her testimony from fiction?

The second help came from Clarence's successor as chairman of the EEOC, Evan Kemp. Anita Hill had taught employment discrimination law at Oral Roberts University Law School, and in the literature of that field, Long Dong Silver was a known character. In fact, a sexual harassment case from the same judicial circuit in which Anita Hill resided involved a man who had made reference to Long Dong Silver. Evan Kemp knew of the case and passed this knowledge on to us. Could this too be borrowed material?

Orrin Hatch first learned of the Long Dong Silver law case when he arrived at his office on Saturday morning. He had known of *The Exorcist* passage the day before, and although he thought it was a possible explanation for Anita Hill's statement about pubic hair, he decided not to use it. Orrin was concerned that if he did, people might think he was overreaching. But in his mind, *The Exorcist* story, combined with the Long Dong Silver case, was a different matter from *The Exorcist* story standing alone. Orrin thought, "This is just too cute," and decided to use both items in his questioning of Clarence.

In addition to the possibility that Anita Hill had borrowed her story, another factor persuaded Orrin to raise the issues of *The Exorcist* and the Long Dong Silver law case: neither of these details had been mentioned in Anita Hill's written statement to the committee, in her own reedited version of her statement, or in her interview with the FBI.

Before the hearing began Saturday morning, Ken Duberstein told Orrin to hold the book, *The Exorcist*, up when he questioned Clarence about it. Ken thought that if he did, a photograph of Orrin holding up the book would be on the front pages of Sunday's newspapers. Ken believed that *The Exorcist* revelation was very important and that a newspaper picture of the book would effectively demonstrate a possible explanation of how Anita Hill's testimony had been developed.

Larry Thompson was impressed with the Long Dong Silver law case, less so with *The Exorcist*. He thought that the case was particularly helpful in attacking the credibility of Anita Hill.

For me, Orrin Hatch's line of questions about *The Exorcist* and the Long Dong Silver case was the most important part of Saturday's hearing. Together they showed that Anita Hill's allegations were in her own mind; the events had not really happened. Two possible explanations occurred to me: that she lied or that she was deluded. In either event, the book and the law case strongly suggested that her story was based on things other than the words or actions of Clarence Thomas.

None of us can put himself in the mind of another person. For his part, Orrin Hatch chose to reject both the perjury and fantasy theories of Anita Hill's testimony. He thinks that she believed she was telling the truth but that she was under heavy pressure from interest groups and was coached by experts to make her story more vivid. Orrin believes that an "entourage of feminist lawyers and feminist special interest groups" followed her wherever she went. In his words, "Unethical lawyers can put words into the mouths of witnesses all the time, and they get so they think these are their own words."

Who knows? What I did think at the time and what Orrin Hatch thought was that he had made a significant point during Saturday's hearing.

Because the Capitol Police had received a bomb threat for the Russell Building, Saturday's lunch break was unusually long. As they had promised, the Laws had been in the Caucus Room praying silently throughout Clarence's testimony. That day Steven offered a prayer he attributed to Voltaire. As one Democratic senator was questioning Clarence, Steven prayed, "Lord, please make my enemies look ridiculous." He claims that his prayer was answered. Now, during the long lunch break, the Laws and Charles James walked the hallways of the Russell Building praying for Clarence.

I was not so prayerful. An ABC reporter had handed me a note asking whether Clarence would agree to take a polygraph. I asked Steve Hilton to return my handwritten reply to the reporter. It was the answer I had suggested Clarence give if asked that question: first the members of the committee and the staff must submit to polygraphs about the leaks.

During the lunch break, Fred McClure told Clarence that the White House switchboard was inundated with calls of support. I decided to take my own poll. Because it was Saturday, my office was not staffed with receptionists answering calls from the public. I went into the reception room and asked a constituent who had dropped by if she would please take fifteen or so phone calls and keep a tally of opinion on the hearing. I got the report and slipped Clarence a note just as he began testifying: in my sample, the calls were 100 percent pro Clarence.

======

Lee Liberman remembers that after Anita Hill testified, the White House counsel's office spoke with four or five psychiatrists who independently mentioned the same hypothesis for Anita Hill's story. The hypothesis was known as erotomania, a rare delusion of some women that particular men in positions of power, such as supervisors or political figures, have romantic interests in them. According to the psychiatrists, a woman with erotomania might be quite specific in describing fantasized behavior by a man and would be so convinced that the behavior had occurred that she could pass a polygraph.

Larry Thompson became aware of the erotomania hypothesis that Saturday while reading a newspaper article quoting a psychiatrist named Dr. Park Dietz on the subject. He had then called a psychologist friend in Atlanta who confirmed that erotomania is a recognizable medical condition. Next he called people who had been prosecutors and had experience with psychiatrists. They knew Park Dietz and confirmed that he was highly regarded; he had examined some well-known suspects, including the man who shot President Reagan, John Hinckley.

Elizabeth Law, whose employer, Gary Bauer, knew of Park Dietz, made contact with him as he was attending a high school reunion in Pennsylvania and then turned him over to Larry Thompson. Dr. Dietz told Larry that since he had not examined Anita Hill, he could not diagnose her condition. He did say that he was familiar with erotomania and that he could describe how it manifests itself. He said that he thought he would be performing a public service by doing so, and that he was willing to come to Washington the next day.

During breaks in the hearing, my job was to step outside the Caucus Room and make myself available for comment to the media. This is what is known as being a "spin doctor." It is always used after presidential debates when supporters of the candidates go to a large media room to declare that their candidate won. So it was after each break in these proceedings. Both sides headed for the cameras, as I did after Clarence finally completed his testimony Saturday afternoon.

Putting it mildly, I was pumped up. Clarence had met his challenge with amazing strength. He was powerful throughout his testimony although on Saturday he was much less combative than on the day before. Clarence had risen from the dead. The American people were behind him. Whether or not he would win confirmation, he was victorious.

When I went before the television cameras outside the Caucus Room, I remembered the country and western song Clarence spoke of at his home three days earlier. I would tell the country about it, for it well expressed the sense of freedom from the need to succeed that made his powerful testimony possible. To the best of my recollection, I said, "Clarence Thomas's view of the Supreme Court is, 'Take this job and shove it.'"

I also recall walking down the Russell Building marble stairway to my office on the floor below the Caucus Room talking to Bob Adams of the *St. Louis Post-Dispatch* after I left the cameras. He asked me if I thought my support for Clarence would damage my relationship with my Senate colleagues. My answer, while excessive and really not true, captured my euphoria of the moment: "I don't give a damn."

The scene outside my office resembled a pep rally, the kind of reception World Series winners get when they arrive at the home town airport. Clarence was there, and Ginni and Ken and Mike, and the women supporters and the Laws and dozens more. It was a victory celebration, for Clarence had won.

Clarence describes how excited I was: "You yelped: 'We did it, we did it! We did exactly what we wanted to do. I don't know whether you'll get confirmed.' You said, 'But you did exactly what you wanted to do. The American people are in an uproar!'"

I spoke to the crowd. I told them that I had quoted Clarence to the cameras, "Take this job and shove it." The crowd cheered. I told them that when a reporter asked about my relationship with my colleagues, I said, "I don't give a damn." The crowd cheered again. I said, "This is a clear case of good versus evil." They cheered again.

In his typically quiet way, Mike Luttig said something Clarence thought beautiful: "The first hearings you had to be coached. You had to be because that was the game. This hearing, you had to do it. The American people had to see you. You were defending your honor and your name and you could not be coached to do it. You had to do it."

After the pep rally in the hallway, Allen Moore came into my office and said to me, "You know, Clarence has recovered his manhood."

After Clarence's testimony, Ken Duberstein thought that Clarence had turned the corner and would win confirmation. He thought Orrin Hatch had done a brilliant job questioning Clarence. Despite Ken's optimism, he knew that the hearing was not yet over and that "there was still some heavy sledding yet coming."

Now Bob Dole and Orrin Hatch came up with the same idea that Bob expressed over the telephone late that afternoon and Orrin said in my office: it was important for Clarence to be in some public place. He had been alone too long. He should see the people, and he should be seen. Orrin announced that he and his wife, Elaine, were taking the Thomases and the Danforths out to dinner. He picked a large steak house in northern Virginia, Mortons of Chicago. By coincidence, Bob Bork and his wife, Mary Ellen, were at Mortons that same evening together with Ted Olson, a party in a well-known Supreme Court case Clarence had been questioned on in his first round of hearings, *Morrison* v. *Olson*.

Bob Bork was very pleased by Clarence's aggressive approach to the committee. I visited with him briefly before we sat down to dinner. He said that he was putting out the word that the only way the Democrats could save themselves from disaster was to confirm Clarence Thomas.

The six of us ordered dinner. Clarence, who could eat only an apple in my office, chose a huge porterhouse steak. He was exhausted but obviously happy. We spoke of the hearing and of what lasting effects it might have on the country.

Perhaps the euphoria of the evening made us too optimistic, but we talked about whether the ordeal of Clarence might change the way in which the Senate confirms presidential nominees. We did not speak about structural reforms in the confirmation process but rather of the healthy consequences that might flow from public attention to Clarence's troubles. Clarence was not the first person to be savaged in Senate confirmations; another was in the restaurant with us that night. Was it too much to hope that at long last Americans were alert to what was happening, that they were sick of it, and that this public reaction would have a preventative effect in the future?

We talked also of the civil rights coalition and whether this event would have any effect on the alliance between blacks and women's groups. We spoke of how the problems of blacks and women were not the same and of the possibility that the alliance did not well serve the needs of blacks. I said that women's organizations had made it difficult to reach an agreement on my civil rights bill that would be satisfactory to blacks.

Sally and I told Orrin that he had done a magnificent job that day. I was especially complimentary of his questioning about *The Exorcist* and Long Dong Silver. Win or lose the confirmation vote, Clarence felt that he had reached the American people.

The management of Mortons told us that six different tables had offered to pay our dinner bill. Orrin Hatch paid it. Although shocked by the $350 bill, he says that no one could take that privilege from him.

We stood up to leave, and, as we did, the entire restaurant rose and broke into applause for Clarence Thomas.

Futility and Victory

Sunday, October 13

Having finished his testimony, Clarence felt gratified. Old friends called him—people he had known in college or law school or at EEOC—and all their messages were similar: "That's the guy I knew from law school." "That's the guy I knew from college." "That's the Clarence Thomas we all know and love."

Ken Duberstein was pleased as well. As he arrived at the Russell Building at noon on Sunday, he saw a group of Thomas supporters who were happy and excited and thought, "They, too, think we have turned the corner."

I had work to do that morning, an appearance on "Face the Nation" with several other people, both pro- and anti-Thomas. Arlen Specter was there with his wife, Joan, who told Sally that Arlen might have ruined his political career but he had done the right thing.

My appearance on "Face the Nation" was the beginning of my effort to destroy the credibility of Anita Hill. In the past four days, I had had a deeply spiritual experience. There would be no spiritual content in what would follow. When I put my hands on Clarence's shoulders on Friday morning and said, "Go forth in the name of Christ, trusting in the power of the Holy Spirit," I acted as a minister. Now I would begin acting like a street fighter. Having done my best to support Clarence Thomas, I turned my attention to Anita Hill.

No question about the propriety of doing this crossed my mind. The whole controversy was a question of credibility. Clarence Thomas or Anita Hill was telling the truth; the other was not. I was convinced that Clarence was telling the truth, and I thought it essential to persuade the country that Anita Hill was not.

The comments of two Democratic senators the previous day had underscored the importance of challenging Anita Hill's credibility. Howell Heflin and Pat Leahy had asked what motive she would have for lying.[61] It seemed to me that someone should address that question. If the country thought that truth was the only explanation for Anita Hill's story, it would not believe Clarence.

I reasoned that there were two possible explanations for Anita Hill's telling a false story. One was that she was lying—intentionally committing perjury before the Judiciary Committee and before the world. The other was that she believed in good faith that she was telling the truth when, in fact, she was not. In short, she could be deluded. Of the two, the delusion theory seemed gentler by far. Her statement might not have been made in bad faith; it might simply have been wrong. Moreover, it was not a theory I had spun out of thin air. During Friday and Saturday, psychiatrists had phoned the White House suggesting the possibility of fantasy in the mind of Anita Hill, and I was fortified in my thinking by Hill's apparent borrowing of testimony from *The Exorcist* and the Long Dong Silver case.

On the basis of this reasoning, I decided to discuss the possibility of delusion during my appearance on "Face the Nation." What better place to challenge the credibility of Anita Hill than on national television? What's more, I tried to enlist Bob Dole in my effort.

Bob, who was about to appear on another Sunday morning talk show, called me just before airtime to ask what points I was emphasizing. I said that there was a possibility that Anita Hill was fantasizing rather than lying and that the fantasy theory was very important.

Of course, I had never met Anita Hill. I had no expertise in psychology or psychiatry. I was not in a forum where my comments could be challenged successfully. I was in a fifteen-minute segment of a talk show, and I was accusing a perfect stranger of having a psychiatric condition.

I was on the first segment of "Face the Nation." One of Anita Hill's lawyers appeared on the second segment and blasted me as a racist and sexist for raising the possibility of fantasy. When I learned of this, I thought the charge against me was so outrageous that its unfairness might hurt the cause of Clarence's opponents. I thought it was an extreme reaction to what seemed to me a reasonable conjecture that there was something in Anita Hill's mind besides perjury.

Rob McDonald, my administrative assistant, was uncomfortable as he watched me on "Face the Nation" and as he watched a sidewalk interview with me after the show. It might be necessary for someone to raise the fantasy explanation, but he did not want it to be me. He thought it was uncharacteristic of me to offer what amounted to a professional opinion on a subject I knew nothing about. Worse than that, Rob says, "You were about as far in the gutter as I can ever remember seeing you."

Later that morning, I read a newspaper article that bolstered my confidence in the fantasy theory. It quoted Dr. Park Dietz as saying, "It would be tragic if that possibility were left unexplored," and there are "many thousands of people who incorrectly believe that famous people have done something to them."[62]

When I arrived in my office just before the hearing reconvened, Senator Hank Brown was there with his chief of staff, Bill Brach. During Friday's hearing, John Bliss of Senator Brown's office was sitting on the dais next to Dick Day of Senator Simpson's office. Day had a memorandum of a phone conversation with a man who claimed that his son had been a law student of Anita Hill's. According to Bliss, the memo said that the son had stories to tell about Hill, the gist of which was that he believed her to be a "left-wing radical feminist . . . who has made certain racist statements in class." Because Simpson's office did not have the time to pursue the matter, Bliss volunteered to do it.

Bliss and others in Brown's office spent Friday and Saturday phoning former law students of Anita Hill's. Bliss estimates that they talked to twenty-five to thirty former students. Some students told them that she was "an ardent feminist, some said radical," and some told them more as well, including an alleged incident involving pubic hair and an alleged reference by her to Long Dong Silver.

The moment Hank Brown told me of his staff's interviews with the former law students, I was certain that the course of events would change dramatically and soon. Until Clarence completed his testimony, my only goal was to help Clarence gain sufficient strength to face the Judiciary Committee. But even if he were exceptionally strong in his testimony, it would be a contest between two credible witnesses in which it would not be possible to establish beyond anyone's doubt that one of the two was telling the truth. It would be a he said–she said contest in which the public would pick sides on the basis of political philosophy or gender. Now there was a new possibility: to establish Clarence's credibility beyond a doubt by destroying the credibility of Anita Hill. If it was not possible to bring the former law students to Washington by the end of the day, it was certainly possible to obtain their affidavits and present them to the American people through the Judiciary Committee. Getting those affidavits became my obsession that afternoon. I knew that Anita Hill was going to be demolished.

In my mind, this was not simply a matter of getting the dirt on Anita Hill, although that did not bother me. I thought that the stories of the law students were consistent with the idea that Hill's testimony was based on a delusion. Such behavior by a teacher toward students, if true, seemed to demonstrate that she had a mental problem that, in my entirely amateur opinion, could fit with the concept of erotomania. Most telling, I thought, there were parallels between the former law students' stories and Anita Hill's testimony against Clarence Thomas relating to pubic hair on a Coke can and Long Dong Silver.

Clearly I was far more concerned about procedural fairness for Clarence than about procedural fairness itself. I wanted Clarence to be represented by counsel who could cross-examine Anita Hill and all other witnesses. But I wanted to obtain damaging affidavits from her former law students and release them to the public without any cross-examination at all. At least Arlen Specter, Orrin Hatch, and the other committee Republicans had the opportunity to cross-examine live witnesses appearing against Clarence. There is no possibility of cross-examining an affidavit; it is simply a sworn statement, not tested in any way for its probity. The person signing it can head for the hills and avoid any questions. The person about whom it speaks can deny it but not question it. In my quest for affidavits, I was showing no concern at all about fairness to Anita Hill.

For five hours on Sunday afternoon, obtaining the affidavits was my passion. My failure to get them was my great frustration.

I pressed Mike Luttig to get the Justice Department to help take statements from the law students, but the Justice Department did not want to get involved. I told Ken Duberstein that we should find some lawyers to help us. Nothing happened. I asked Fred McClure if the White House could find some supporters of the president in Oklahoma who could help get statements. I received a phone message from an Oklahoma Republican who said he would be happy to help Clarence Thomas, but there was no follow-through.

I got the idea that if we already knew of some law students who had shocking things to say about Anita Hill, we might be able to find more. I reached Senator Don Nickles, an Oklahoma Republican, and told him that we needed to recruit people who would make calls to former Hill law students to see what they could find out. Nickles said that he had a person on his staff who said that Hill was a poor teacher, but that was not what we needed. We needed to find out whether Anita Hill had a sexual problem that might cause her to fantasize. Nickles said he would call back. He never did.

Hank Brown said that he would try to get affidavits from three law students. Where were the affidavits? I went to the Caucus Room to press Hank Brown. By late afternoon, he produced one affidavit, which was clearly inadequate. Drafted by someone on Brown's staff and sent out for signature, it consisted largely of opinion about Hill's teaching ability.

Senator Al Simpson phoned the former law student whose father had called his office. The young man confirmed the stories about Anita Hill but declined to put his statement in affidavit form, saying that his father had advised him against coming forward.

Peter Leibold, my legislative assistant, remembers my growing frustration on Sunday afternoon. "You were very agitated all day Sunday that Brown had said he could get this stuff, and that nobody was delivering. And who was going to be responsible for delivering this stuff? If it was all out there, if we were wasting all of these man hours trying to get them, that somebody had to get them and push them out into the public domain, and nobody was doing it. Sunday, you were incredibly agitated that these things were being promised and they were not delivered on. You were very concerned that people were not finishing their jobs."

No one else in Clarence's support group came close to the intensity of my enthusiasm for the law student stories. Larry Thompson thought they were important stories, going to the nature of Anita Hill. Arlen Specter thinks that, if true, they would have been "extremely damaging to her credibility if not absolutely destructive." However, he is much more cautious than I was in assessing the stories of the law students. He does not know what the law students would have said or how Anita Hill would have responded. Nor does he know the course grades Hill gave the law students. I merely wanted to get the affidavits and release them to the public; Arlen believes that the law students should have been brought before the committee and questioned about their alleged experiences.

Other Thomas supporters were decidedly cool to the idea too. Orrin Hatch says: "If they were unwilling to come forward and testify, I was unwilling to give any credibility to what they had to say. Even though it wasn't a court of law, I felt that there should have been a certain amount of fairness, and that would not have been fair." Orrin adds that the "media would have had a field day" criticizing the use of statements by law students who were not willing to come forward against a complaining witness who was.

Mike Luttig describes the law students' stories as "far-fetched" and says that at the time he thought they were "politically motivated and

probably made up." In any event, Mike says, "I could not get involved
in that directly because it would be so time consuming."

My legislative director, Jon Chambers, advised me that use of the
law students' stories might be damaging to Clarence, and Lee Liberman thought their use could result in the loss of his confirmation.

The strongest negative views on the subject were held by Ken
Duberstein. Ken strongly urged me not to use the stories unless there
was overwhelming, convincing evidence. A single affidavit did not
meet that test. Nor, in his mind, did use of the stories well serve the
Senate. It would be sinking to a depth to which Ken did not want us
to go, and, if used, there would be reverberations. He recalls telling
me, "Jack Danforth, that's below you."

Ken thought Clarence would win without the law students' stories,
and that if we used the stories, the public would see it as "piling on."
He was concerned as well that the media would descend on the students, and that if they began to retreat from their statements, it would
hurt our cause. He thought that the media response would be, "Even
Jack Danforth has been sucked into this process of slime. . . . Will
they not stoop to any level to destroy this woman?"

My Senate staff had little access to me that weekend. I was in the
Caucus Room or in my own office; they were in theirs. What little they
saw of me, feverishly pursuing the stories of former law students, they
did not like.

Professional staff people in Senate offices are bright and idealistic.
Most of them have advanced degrees, usually law degrees or masters',
and most of them could be making more money elsewhere. They are
in their twenties and thirties, interested in public policy, and see the
Senate as a place to make America better by shaping law. They answer to a single senator, and their own sense of worth and their own
prestige is closely related to the standing and performance of that person. If their senator succeeds, they succeed. If their senator is respected, they are respected.

Jon Chambers, my legislative director, was in his late twenties at the time. With a master's from Columbia University, he had started in my office as a legislative assistant and had risen to become my chief policy adviser. He was concerned on two scores, to the point of seriously considering resigning from my staff. He went to my administrative assistant to share his concern and to discuss the possibility of resignation.

Jon's first concern was that I was hurting myself politically—that because of my activities at that time, the public would see me as someone who had lost perspective or had done something unforgivable or not understandable. The second concern had to do with character—as Jon says, "with dirt-digging and purposeful character assassination." Jon continues, "There was something that I saw in you that I didn't think existed and didn't identify with you, but would always from then on identify as being a part of you."

Rob McDonald, in his early thirties, had been with me for ten years. He had run my St. Louis office and was now my administrative assistant, the top staff person in my office. His recollection of the weekend, if accurate, would remove any argument that although I was acting in a questionable way, at least I believed my actions were in the service of a worthy cause. In Rob's words: "I can remember one conversation with both of you [Sally and myself] in which you both appeared in absolute agreement that if Clarence was defeated, Jack Danforth would be blamed and this would be awful and that this was one of the most crucial and important points in your career and that we had to win. The essence of the conversation that I drew was that we had to win at any cost."

For several reasons, I do not think Rob's recollection is correct. First, although I had told Ginni, "It is my fault," and it was in the sense that I was the cause of Clarence's coming to Washington in the first place, I never thought anyone would blame me for Clarence's losing the confirmation. Second, I had decided to retire from politics well before the Thomas nomination and had discussed the decision within my family, so any political consequences of my actions were not important to me. Third, such a remark would not have squared with other things that I was saying at the time, for example, telling Jon

Chambers, "It doesn't matter what happens to me." Finally, neither Sally nor I share Rob's memory. If Rob is correct that I did make such a statement, perhaps I was being dismissive, brushing off his expressed concerns about the political consequences of my actions. But that is conjecture.

Rob's more general comments about that day deserve mention: "It was extremely uncharacteristic, and it was looney. But the whole damn thing was looney and the atmosphere that this took place in was so unbelievable. To see the things that were being talked about on nationwide television in a Supreme Court nomination were unbelievable. Your actions were wild and erratic and uncharacteristic, but so were many, many, many people's actions in the whole thing." Rob continues: "You didn't sleep, you didn't eat. You ate Pepto Bismol tablets like M&M's. You were not stable about it. You did the job, and you did a helluva job, under tremendous pressure, but you were pretty frazzled."

Peter Leibold had graduated from Yale Law School three years earlier and had established himself as a star in my office. He agrees that when I began the quest for affidavits from law students, I crossed the boundary of propriety. Peter describes the situation as it existed before Sunday and as it changed: "We had the high ground because it was wrong calling people to dig up the dirt on Clarence Thomas. That was what was wrong with the system. That [when I made a speech against the attack on Clarence] was when you were at your best. It is wrong on a nominee to call the EEOC and simply ask for the dirt on the nominee. By Sunday and Monday you began to focus all on the result; that you have been wronged so you've got to win. The only way to beat these people is to win. And if we beat them it will send the message that we disapprove of what they did, and maybe they won't do it again because they didn't profit from it. I can understand all of that rationale. But as we moved closer and closer to doing exactly what we condemned, I was very worried about it. . . . It's the whole ends justify the means. . . . It undercuts your whole statement about the process, and that was my concern Sunday and Monday."

Peter continues, "You know your training as a lawyer, you've got to do it. You represented a client, Clarence Thomas, who was being put into a forum where he had no protection whatsoever. If there are no rules and regulations being used, no protections, no due process protections or anything else being used to defend your client, then adequately defend your client. If you look at this as a large-scale legal proceeding, we were playing within the rules. We were, because there were no rules. But when you look at it from your philosophic position which was 'This is wrong. . . . This process has destroyed an individual,' then there are problems. Because then you couldn't use that attack and attack the process the way you did unless you were willing to say, 'This is the process and I am going to participate in it as aggressively as I can . . . because I'm powerless right now to change it, and all I want to do is win.' "

In my view, if the pursuit of bizarre tales of former law students was beyond the bounds of propriety, the development of a psychological explanation for Anita Hill's charges was clearly within those bounds. Fantasy was a gentler explanation than perjury, and the psychological theory did not require the aggressive pursuit of former law students who would submit their colorful charges by affidavit. Clarence Thomas's supporters had never heard of erotomania. Psychiatrists contacted us, and psychiatrists were willing to appear before the committee as witnesses and to subject themselves to cross-examination. This does not mean that erotomania was a likely explanation in the opinion of all Thomas supporters—Orrin Hatch and Lee Liberman were not persuaded by it—but it was an explanation thought plausible by reputable psychiatrists. It did not depend on flaky statements by former law students, only one of which was ever put in an affidavit, or any other written form.

Mark Paoletta was still in his office on Friday night when the White House switchboard routed a call to him from a man who said he was a psychiatrist who had watched Anita Hill's testimony. He described the symptoms of erotomania. To me, it seemed a plausible explanation.

By Sunday afternoon, two psychiatrists were in my office. One was

Dr. Dietz. The second was thought by Larry Thompson to be credible but not useful as a witness because he was a personal friend of the Bush family and might be attacked as being biased. The two psychiatrists had not examined Anita Hill and could not make a diagnosis, but they could describe the symptoms of erotomania.

On Sunday, Larry Thompson interviewed Dr. Dietz, whose credentials as a potential expert witness he assessed as being "exceptional" and "impeccable." In Larry's judgment, Dietz would have been an "outstanding" witness. He would not have appeared as an advocate for one side but as an expert who could have described the condition of erotomania without purporting to diagnose Anita Hill.

But whether Joe Biden would allow Dr. Dietz to testify before the committee was uncertain, so Larry asked Dr. Dietz to prepare a written statement. Neither Larry Thompson nor anyone else on the Thomas team had any input into the drafting of the statement. It was entirely the product of Dr. Dietz, and in the opinion of Larry Thompson, it was "superb."

Ken Duberstein is more inclined to attribute Anita Hill's charges to the influence of Susan Hoerchner, and perhaps James Brudney of Senator Metzenbaum's staff, than to the theory of delusion, but he thought there might be some medical explanation for her testimony, and he saw Dr. Dietz's statement as entirely different from the stories of law students. Ken believed that Dietz was a renowned psychiatrist and was insistent that neither Larry Thompson nor anyone else on the Thomas team lead Dr. Dietz in the preparation of his testimony. In contrast, Ken describes the law student stories: "You have one student sending in an affidavit, after six hours of us pacing the floor. I didn't think that was compelling testimony, nor was that sufficient corroboration."

Ken, Larry, and I agreed that Dr. Dietz was an excellent resource who could help explain Anita Hill's charges. The question was how to use him, especially if he was not permitted to appear before the committee. Jon Chambers recalls discussions about the possibility of my taking Dr. Dietz before the bank of cameras outside the Caucus Room so that he could present his views to the public. To Jon Chambers, it was inappropriate to use Dr. Dietz or to insinuate that Anita Hill was mentally unbalanced. As far as Jon was concerned, all Dr. Dietz knew was what he had seen of Hill on television. Jon recalls telling Rob McDonald that he would resign from my staff if we persisted with what he calls "this psychiatry business."

Dr. Dietz did not appear before the committee, and no use was made of his statement that day.

As the world watched Sunday's hearing on television, panels of witnesses testified—Anita Hill's friend and confidante Susan Hoerchner, Thomas supporter John Doggett, and various others. I saw it only in glimpses. I was busy tracking down former law students or dealing with whether additional witnesses would be allowed to testify.

Larry Thompson had found lawyer's work to do. He discovered that no one was interviewing witnesses who would appear on behalf of Clarence, to find out in advance what they would say and to prepare them for potential questions. He and Dick Leon, a lawyer and Clarence's friend from college days, volunteered for the task.

For Senator Alan Simpson, one of the important developments of Sunday afternoon occurred during the testimony of Susan Hoerchner. Hoerchner was Hill's principal corroborating witness, testifying that Hill had told her a decade earlier of being harassed by her supervisor or by Clarence. When Hoerchner began her testimony, Simpson remembers thinking, "Something is very strange about this woman. Wooden, with lidded eyes, looking into just blank." As she was testifying, Simpson took a phone call from his son who practices law in Wyoming. The son said that a client had told him that Hoerchner had filed her own claim of sexual harassment, against a senior judge in California, and, in Simpson's words, it "absolutely destroyed him." Within minutes, Simpson confirmed the information from his son.

When Simpson got his chance to question Hoerchner, he asked

whether she had ever brought a sexual harassment claim. Her answer was evasive and gave no indication that she had. Later, he confronted her with a sexual harassment claim she had filed against a Judge Foster in California. In the confrontation, Simpson stated that Judge Foster had resigned in a widely publicized case.[63]

Describing Hoerchner, Simpson says, "This was the woman who started it all. This was the woman who, when she heard that Clarence Thomas was nominated, she knew that this was the end of pro-choice America. . . . This was the lady. You are going to do this for the women of America, and you are not going to be fainthearted. And she worked on her and worked on her and worked on her."

Ken Duberstein remembers watching Susan Hoerchner on television, thinking, "She was coming across as somebody who would not be trusted by the American people." When Simpson questioned her about her own sexual harassment charge against a judge in California, Ken speculated that that charge might be the prototype for Anita Hill's charge against Clarence Thomas.

I saw little, if any, of the testimony of John Doggett, but I was aware that he testified that Anita Hill had chastised him, saying he should not "lead women on."[64] That Anita Hill was given to fantasy seemed an increasingly likely possibility.

Characteristically, Clarence watched the Washington Redskins game on television, not the hearings. Larry Silberman was home, also watching the Redskins. Larry recalls that every forty-five minutes or so, Clarence called him to ask his reaction. Larry said repeatedly, "Clarence, I'm watching the game the same as you are. I don't know what's going on."

That afternoon, Clarence's phone rang. It was the White House switchboard saying that Mrs. Anwar Sadat, widow of Egypt's late president, was calling him. Her voice came on the phone telling Clarence that he was an international hero, with people all over the world cheering him. Ginni recalls that Clarence was amazed both by the message and by the messenger.

Before Anita Hill testified on Friday, a former partner of Wald, Harkrader and Ross disclosed to Boyden Gray that Hill had left the firm involuntarily, as a result of ethics and competence problems; however, the former partner did not have first-hand knowledge of the circumstances. This information did not seem critical to the White House until Hill testified that no one at the law firm suggested that she leave its employ. At that point, the circumstance of Hill's departure from the law firm became critical. If she had left involuntarily, as Boyden Gray had been told, she had lied to the committee, and if she had lied about one fact, that would call into question the veracity of her entire testimony.

The White House counsel's office and the minority staff of the Judiciary Committee then made phone calls to lawyers who had worked in the firm at the time of Hill's employment. A second lawyer was found who had the same story but, again, no first-hand knowledge. The minority staff believed that the best way to determine whether there was any truth to the story was to subpoena the employment records of the law firm.

As the White House counsel's office and the minority staff were attempting to follow up on this new information, Nancy Altman continued to insist that a panel of women be allowed to testify on behalf of Clarence. She, Janet Brown, and Ricky Silberman had done their job: they had assembled a group of nine women to testify, who had prepared written statements and were waiting in Rob McDonald's office for their chance to go before the committee. Now it was my turn to fulfill my part of the bargain: to see if the committee would hear them. Their appearance would be no small feat; the witness list was closed, and the women might be considered character witnesses and, as previously agreed, off-limits.

I left my office and went to the Caucus Room to ask Joe Biden if the women could testify. The discussion started with me on one knee whispering to Joe about the women. All I was asking for was one hour so they could testify. He was very reluctant to extend the hearing at all but suggested that he and I step into the adjoining room. There he told me that I would have to work out any arrangement for women witnesses with Ted Kennedy. I also asked Joe about issuing a subpoena for the law firm's employment records. His initial response was that the custodian of the documents would have to be subpoenaed to bring them to the committee. Thereafter, he decided that no subpoena would issue.

From Joe Biden's request that I work out witness list issues with Ted Kennedy, it was my impression that Ted was acting as the Hill team's representative in dealing with the committee. Joe has since told me that, as chairman, he saw himself in the role of a judge. In order to provide balance to my advocacy of new witnesses on behalf of Clarence, Joe thought that Ted Kennedy should make sure that the hearing not be weighted against Anita Hill.

Ted and I met in his office, where I told him we wanted an hour for the nine women to testify. In fairness to Anita Hill, he said, if we were given one hour, her side should be given the same amount of time. The Hill witnesses would be character witnesses plus an expert on the psychological aspects of sexual harassment. I responded that Joe Biden and I agreed that there would be no character witnesses and that I did not consider our list of women as such. Rather, they would be testifying to material fact—how, in their experience, Clarence had treated people who worked with him. Further, several of the women could testify from first-hand experience about the relationship between Clarence and Anita Hill on the job. With respect to an expert witness, I said that any expert would consume a substantial amount of time in questioning. Also it was our position that the committee should subpoena the employment records of the law firm because we believed they would show that Hill did not leave the firm voluntarily. Ted promised he would get back to me with a response to my request at the next break in the hearing.

———

During the next break late in the afternoon, Joe Biden asked that the committee meet privately in Ted Kennedy's office. There, Joe announced his decision on my two requests: the panel of women would be allowed to testify, provided that each witness limit her remarks to three minutes and that the entire panel consume no more than one hour, including questions from the committee, and the committee would not issue a subpoena. I asked Strom Thurmond to ask that the committee be polled on the question of the subpoena. The chairman was sustained on a party-line vote.

We then discussed the possible psychological aspects of the matter. Al Simpson, Hank Brown, and I told the senators what we knew of the former law students and their stories. I said that a psychiatrist was available to testify and raised the possibility that Hill was deluded. Joe Biden passed out a photocopy of a handwritten letter from a psychiatrist speculating that Clarence may have been abused as a child and perhaps that had caused sexual harassment. I responded that obviously one of them had a psychological condition, but that was not the point. The point was to determine how someone could testify to something that was not true. The committee should not be interested in general issues of mental health; it should be interested in explaining the possibility of false testimony by reason of delusion. Finally, Joe ruled that the committee would not receive testimony relating to psychiatry or any statements of law students, but any senator who wanted to raise such points was free to do so on the floor of the Senate.

The next point of discussion was whether Angela Wright would testify. Strom Thurmond, Al Simpson, and Orrin Hatch favored her testifying, thinking that she would be such a weak witness that she would taint the case against Clarence. Hatch would have insisted that other former employers of Wright testify in rebuttal. At that point, I was of two minds: I thought that her testimony could be easily impeached, but I wanted the ordeal to come to an end.

Joe Biden, of course, was reluctant to close the door on a complaining woman who wanted to testify. During the meeting in Kennedy's office, a Judiciary Committee staff member phoned Angela Wright's lawyer to determine her preference with respect to appearing. When the staff person hung up the phone, he reported to the committee, "She is not going to testify."

As the meeting broke up, the end of the hearing was in sight. It would conclude with the testimony of Clarence's women supporters that night, except that Anita Hill and Clarence Thomas would be given the chance to return for rebuttal the next day. Our psychiatrist, Dr. Dietz, would not be allowed to testify, but that did not disturb me. No senator had been precluded from putting out evidence in his own way, and since the ultimate jury was the American people, I could release Dietz's statement together with any material from the law students without the committee's help. The chairman himself had acknowledged that fact.

But what is possible is not always fair. The fair way to raise issues was before the committee, where charges or theories of behavior could be open to question by the senators. Late Sunday afternoon, the finish line was in sight, and I was racing toward it, content to dump into the public record anything not covered in the hearing.

There could not have been a more dramatic change in my own sense of what was right and what was wrong. For days, I had complained with righteous indignation about the unfairness of the proceeding against Clarence Thomas. Just minutes before, I had asked the Judiciary Committee to issue a subpoena and expand the witness list—in short, to accord due process to my friend. Now I was relieved that the hearing would soon end—relieved not to be bound by procedural rules, relieved that my case against Anita Hill could be placed before the public without bothersome challenges to its merits by questioning members of the Judiciary Committee. I was the same person who had prayed with the nominee in his home and in my office and in a bathroom. It was as if my sense of right and wrong could be switched on and off like a light as circumstances required.

Arlen Specter, in contrast, thought that we were moving too fast. He said we should not rush to finish the hearing by the following day. Too much was happening that was not adequately explored: the circumstances of Hill's leaving the law firm, the law student stories, the reference to Long Dong Silver in a court case. All those matters deserved attention. There was a second reason for Arlen's concern: fatigue. The committee was moving too quickly, and its members were too fatigued to do an adequate job. I did not agree with Arlen at the time. I do now. Then I wanted the end to come. Now I believe that a more deliberate process would have been more orderly, fairer, and more comprehensive in developing the case for Clarence.

The Thomas team was unanimous in its view that the law firm's employment records were of exceptional importance to our case. Larry Thompson had felt so strongly about it that on Friday afternoon he phoned his law firm in Atlanta to request legal research on whether records of prior employment were subject to discovery in a sexual harassment case in federal court. Larry asked for research on a second subject: what about medical records in the same kind of case? Anita Hill's written statement said that in February 1983 she had been hospitalized with stomach pains, caused, she thought, by stress on the job. Did her medical records support her story? The legal research confirmed that the employment and the medical records were clearly available to a defendant in a sexual harassment lawsuit under the Federal Rules of Civil Procedure. In his memorandum of the legal research, Larry concluded: "In these proceedings Judge Thomas has been denied fundamental fairness as well as information that could be obtained by any defendant in a routine sexual harassment case with much less at stake than in these proceedings."

Speaking of the employment records, Larry says, "We didn't get that, and I think that was critical. I have to believe that there was a reason why we didn't get them and there is a reason why they were resisted."

Mike Luttig shares the view that the circumstances under which

Anita Hill left the law firm were important to Clarence's defense and that the committee's vote on the subpoena deserves special note. He says, "I think that that vote not to get those records was significant. Because it is not an ordinary situation where neither side knows what they will find. Or somebody on the other side knew what was there from the people." When asked whom he meant by "somebody on the other side," Mike acknowledged that he was referring to the committee or the committee staff.

Orrin Hatch describes both the employment records and the medical records as "critical" to Clarence's defense, believing that they would have absolved him. For that reason, he argued in Kennedy's office for a subpoena of the employment records. Having lost the vote on the employment records, he gave up on the medical records as a lost cause.

Hatch thinks that if Hill's medical records had made any mention of sexual harassment, they would have been placed in evidence by the Hill forces. He refers to the vote denying the subpoena of employment records as "power politics." He thinks that Democratic committee staffers and anti-Thomas interest groups knew the records would have absolved Clarence and that "they couldn't dare let those employment records come in."

Ken Duberstein believes that the employment records were "obviously fundamental" in showing that the reasons Hill left the law firm contradicted her testimony. In Ken's words, had the true story been placed before the committee, "that certainly would have begun to seriously unravel her story."

Evidence of Anita Hill's departure from the law firm became available that night, but with the list of witnesses now closed, not in a form that could be submitted to the committee.

John Burke had been a partner at Wald, Harkrader and Ross when Anita Hill worked there. By coincidence, he was now a neighbor of Mike Luttig in McLean, Virginia, although they were not personal friends. In Mike's words, "I hardly knew him at all." Burke was on a business trip on Friday when he learned that Anita Hill had testified that no one had asked her to leave the law firm. Later on Friday, John Burke phoned Mike Luttig's home and left a message for Mike to return the call. When Mike did, Burke asked him to keep what he had to say completely confidential, and Mike agreed. According to Mike, Burke told him that he was sympathetic to the political views of the opponents of Clarence Thomas, but someone had called him when he was out of town and told him of Hill's statement. Mike describes Burke as "pretty upset about it." Mike says that Burke told him "in so many words" that he had tried to bring his information to the attention of the committee as soon as Anita Hill testified and that the committee "deep sixed it." Burke's information is that while at Wald, Harkrader and Ross, he personally had met with Anita Hill and told her that her work was not up to the standards of the firm and that she should start looking for work elsewhere.

Because Mike had pledged confidentiality, he had kept Burke's information to himself. Now, unable to subpoena the firm's employment records, we had no other way to bring to the light the error in Hill's testimony. Sitting in my office at 8:30 Sunday night, Luttig phoned John Burke.

Assuring Burke that he had respected his confidentiality, Mike put me on the phone with him without telling me his name. I said, "I am not supposed to know your name, and I don't know your name." He said, "I have no problem with that. My name is John Burke." When I asked him to tell me what he knew, he responded that he had heard that Hill testified that nobody had suggested that she leave the firm; in fact, he had suggested that she leave the firm, so, in his words, she was "lying." I said, "I know that you don't want to come forward, but this is clearly very important information and it is very important for you to come forward even if you don't want to." He said, "Well, I can't say 'no' to a senator. What would you like me to do?" I asked him to come to my office and make out an affidavit, which would be used in the cross-examination of Hill the next day.

John Burke arrived at my office at nine o'clock wearing blue jeans and a brown leather jacket, and for the next three hours, we talked and reviewed the transcript of Hill's testimony. Burke dictated a draft of an affidavit to my secretary, Judy Dassira, who is also a notary. He edited the draft and it was retyped. By midnight, I had the affidavit of John Burke, a statement made under oath that flatly refuted Anita Hill's sworn testimony.

Confident that the affidavit was vital in challenging Anita Hill's credibility, I was now concerned about getting it before the committee. After that night, the only witnesses who could testify before the committee were Hill and Thomas, and neither of them was required to testify. The Burke affidavit could be used to impeach Anita Hill, but only if she appeared before the committee. It occurred to me that the Republicans on the committee might not want to leave anything to chance. We might want to take the initiative by requesting that Hill appear the next day so that she could be confronted with Burke's sworn statement. With that possibility in mind, I wrote a note to Arlen Specter, attached it to the affidavit with excerpts from Hill's testimony, and hand-delivered it to Arlen, who, at midnight, was about to begin questioning one of the witnesses. I sat in one of the staff chairs next to the dais as Arlen conducted his questioning and then read the material I had handed him. As I was waiting for Arlen, four or five senators on the committee asked me whether Clarence would want to testify if Anita Hill did not. I said that the only way I could get him to come to the committee again would be to bring him there in a bag.

After Arlen had read the affidavit, he and I went into the hallway outside the Caucus Room. Now Arlen was the one who sought to move the process forward without delay. It was not necessary to have Hill testify in order to make the Burke statement public, he said; all we had to do was release it the next day.

In Lee Liberman's mind, the Burke affidavit was enough to win the confirmation vote for Clarence. Other matters, including the stories of law students, should be left alone.

At midday Sunday, the expected happened: the Hill camp announced that she had taken and passed a lie detector test. I had seen it coming for days and had mentioned it to Mike Luttig and Ken Duberstein. Within an hour, we were ready with our response.

Because they are not reliable, polygraphs are inadmissible in court, and, under federal law, they cannot be used by employers to screen potential employees.[65] Civil liberties advocates, including members of the Judiciary Committee, are on record attacking the use of polygraphs. Soon after the Hill camp made its announcement, we released a quotation of Senator Kennedy condemning the reliability of polygraphs.[66] We did not believe that liberal supporters of Anita Hill would credibly put stock in her taking of such a test. Ken Duberstein viewed the release of a polygraph as "their last, desperate shot."

The possibility of erotomania provided an explanation of why a polygraph might be especially unreliable when taken by Anita Hill. If she were suffering a delusion, it would be possible for her to tell with absolute honesty a story that was not true.

Hank Brown states that he is less skeptical about the reliability of polygraphs than other members of the Judiciary Committee. For that reason, he sought his own expert on the subject, a man who had served the government in various intelligence capacities for nearly twenty-five years and who, Brown believed, was the leading expert on the subject in the Washington area. Brown says that the expert gave him several reasons to discount the Hill polygraph. First, the questions asked Hill were formulated in ways that would permit her to be evasive but literally truthful. Second, it was significant that the actual tapes of the polygraph were not available for inspection. Third, he said, the person who read Hill's tape "was thought to be more of a political polygraph taker rather than someone who was viewed as independent and reliable."

From the outset, Ken Duberstein thought that, regardless of what Anita Hill had done, Clarence should not take a polygraph. Ken's reasons went beyond his beliefs about the unreliability of the tests. He did not think a sitting federal judge should take a polygraph. He asks, "Are we going to hook up everybody to a polygraph machine who is nominated for any job, let alone a judicial job? What have we come to as a society?"

Larry Thompson was less certain. He agreed that it would be inappropriate for a federal judge to take a lie detector test but thought that it might be useful in defending Clarence. At least, he should raise the issue with Clarence and let him decide this matter that might be crucial in determining his fate. Feeling uncomfortable even approaching the subject with Clarence, Larry confided in one person he felt comfortable with and who was close to the nominee: my wife, Sally.

Sally thought that Clarence should take a lie detector test. Two nights earlier, she had raised the subject with me as we were driving home. She reasoned that if Anita Hill was fantasizing, she might pass a polygraph. Then Clarence should take one too. My response: "No, that's stupid."

Sally recalls what happened: "Larry was just terribly distressed about what to do for Clarence. He said, 'There is only one thing that I can think of and I don't want to do it.' That was to suggest that he take a lie detector test. He didn't really even want to say it. . . . He said, 'I know someone who is very, very good at this. He's in North Carolina. I could call him up.' But, he said, 'I hate to ask Clarence to do it. I just can't bear the idea of asking Clarence to do it. But if it would help Clarence, it would be a good thing to do. And if Clarence is so nervous and so upset then he probably wouldn't pass the test anyway. And the tests aren't really all that great.' I said, 'Well, you know, what if he didn't pass the test, we just wouldn't have to tell anybody that he had taken the test.' . . . So he went to call his friend."

As Larry spoke to his friend in North Carolina, alerting him that he might have to come to Washington on short notice, Sally came into my office to tell me of the plan. She recalls my answer: "I don't want to know anything about it. I don't want to hear you speak to me about it again. If you do something like this, you are on your own."

Clearly, I had given less than a strong no. If Clarence passed a lie detector test, that would be an effective response to Anita Hill's test. But lie detectors are unreliable, and Clarence was far from at ease. I did not want to be told that he had taken the test and failed.

Sally returned to Larry, who, after talking to the man in North Carolina, had broken down in tears. The polygraph man was to arrive on a USAir flight at 9:48 the next morning and administer the test in our home. Now Larry and Sally met in the hallway, and Larry asked, "Who is going to approach Clarence with this?" and then answered the question himself: "I can't make myself do it. So Sally, you're going to have to do it." Sally agreed.

She asked some people to leave one of my office rooms and punched the phone number. She recalls, "My heart was beating really, really fast because I felt so terrible about doing it. I was so nervous, I punched the wrong numbers." She tried again and Clarence answered.

Sally continues, "I said, 'Larry asked me to call you and tell you he was going to talk to you at ten o'clock about something.' He said, 'You sound concerned, is it something really bad?' I said, 'Clarence, I'm not concerned, I'm just extremely nervous because I've never made a phone call like this before.' He said, 'Is it about a polygraph?' I said, 'Well, I guess, yes. I guess it's something about that.' He said, 'No, I will not take a polygraph test.' "

Sunday afternoon, soon after learning of Anita Hill's polygraph, Larry Silberman was worried. A half-dozen or more women who were supporters of Clarence phoned Larry to tell him that the new development had put them in despair. Their concern became Larry's concern. Minutes later, Clarence called with his usual question, "What do you think?" Larry broke the news of Hill's polygraph. At that point, Larry thought that for Clarence to refuse to take the test might cost him the confirmation. He recalls saying, "You've got a terrible choice. I think it would be profoundly wrong and unprincipled to offer to take a lie detector test, because you would convert this confirmation process into a real circus. . . . It's an unprincipled thing to do, but you might go down because of this. . . . So if you don't offer it, you have got to know what the cost is."

Immediately after talking with Larry Silberman, Clarence phoned Mike Luttig. Clarence stated firmly that he would not take a lie detector test. As Mike characterizes the conversation, "It was just further degradation and he had nothing of his own humanity left." Clarence said that it would be a "spectacle" for a sitting federal judge to take a lie detector test. Clarence recalls telling Mike, "I'm not going to be further humiliated. This was the end of the line and that's it. No other federal judge or any other nominee would ever forgive me if I did it."

As promised by Sally, Larry Thompson phoned Clarence at ten o'clock. Clarence's answer was, "It is not worth it, Larry. I'm not going to be further disgraced by this whole thing." He added the same fighting response we discussed in anticipation that a senator might ask him to take a polygraph: "You tell them I'll be next in line if they take one as to who leaked."

Nancy Altman remembers the crowded camaraderie of the women who packed Rob McDonald's office from eight o'clock Saturday morning until after midnight Monday morning. All told, she estimates there were twenty or twenty-five women who were present during at least part of the weekend; some she knew, many she had never met, but all had worked with Clarence and had shared an experience similar to her own. Nancy says they were there "because of both what they felt about Clarence as a person and what they thought about what was happening and the injustice of what was happening." She adds, "It completely belied the idea of Clarence Thomas as someone who would be using his power over women."

But camaraderie was not their reason for crowding into Rob's office. They wanted to speak up for Clarence, and in Nancy's mind, they were being "filibustered out" of the Caucus Room. Nancy recalls her feelings on Sunday afternoon: "I really had the sense that [the testimony of other witnesses] was going on because we were being kept out. I realize now that that is a kind of paranoid view of the whole thing. But I, at one point, was saying to the other women, 'I think we should storm in there. I think we should walk in there with placards. We have something to say.' "

By late afternoon, some of the women left Rob's office and went to the cameras outside the Caucus Room to try to get media coverage of their opinions. Then I emerged from Senator Kennedy's office with news that they would be allowed to testify but for no more than one hour, beginning at one o'clock Monday morning. Eight women who had waited through the weekend for their time to speak finally had their chance.

Just before they went before the committee, Nancy Altman's emotions were close to the surface. She asked Allen Moore, "How can I deliver this? I don't think I can get through it." Allen gave advice that he thought might distract her from her nervousness: "Pretend all the senators are nude."

Sally and I sat in the Senate Caucus Room just behind the eight women,[67] to give them moral support as they testified. At one o'clock on Monday morning, after three full days of drama, the atmosphere in that massive room was far more of exhaustion than of tension. The room seemed less packed; some of the media had left, and some senators were no longer in their seats. Anxious to leave, no senator asked questions of the panel. Yet the testimony, succinct and pointed, spoke from personal experience of the character of Clarence Thomas.

Some panel members knew Clarence but not Anita Hill.

Janet Brown testified:

A number of years ago, I was sexually harassed in the workplace. It was a demeaning, humiliating, sad and revolting experience. There was an intensive and lengthy internal investigation of this case, which is the route that I chose to pursue. Let me assure you that the last thing I would ever have done is follow the man who did this to a new job, call him on the phone or voluntarily share the same air space ever again.

Other than my immediate family, the one person who is the most outraged, compassionate, caring and sensitive to me was Clarence Thomas. He helped me work through the pain and talk through the options. No one who has been through it can talk about sexual harassment dispassionately. No one who takes it seriously would do it.

Nancy Altman began her testimony:

My name is Nancy Altman. I considered myself a feminist. I am prochoice. I care deeply about women's issues. In addition to working with Clarence Thomas at the Department of Education, I shared an office with him for two years in this building. Our desks were a few feet apart. Because we worked in such close quarters, I could hear virtually every conversation for two years that Clarence Thomas had. Not once in those two years did I ever hear Clarence Thomas make a sexist or an offensive comment, not once.

I have myself been the victim of an improper, unwanted sexual advance by a supervisor. Gentlemen, when sexual harassment occurs, other women in the workplace know about it. The members of the committee seem to believe that when offensive behavior occurs in a private room, there can be no witnesses. This is wrong.

Other panel members told the committee what they had observed while sharing the same workplaces with both Clarence Thomas and Anita Hill. Lori Saxon, who had worked with both at the Department of Education, said:

My office was just down the hall from Anita Hill's during her tenure at the Department of Education.

I never saw any harassment go on in the office. The office was run very professionally. Clarence Thomas and Anita Hill were always very cordial and friendly in their relations. There was never any evidence of any harassment toward any of the female employees. I dealt with Anita Hill on a daily basis in performing my duties. She was happy in her position and she liked working for Clarence Thomas.

Anna Jenkins, who had worked at EEOC, testified:

I had daily contact with Anita Hill and Judge Thomas. We shared a suite of offices consisting of a reception area, conference room, kitchen, and five offices. Judge Thomas' conduct around me, Anita Hill, and other staffers was always proper and professional. I have never witnessed Judge Thomas say anything or do anything that could be construed as sexual harassment. I never witnessed him making sexual advances toward any female, nor have I witnessed him engaging in sexually oriented conversations with women.

I have witnessed Judge Thomas and Anita Hill interact in the office. At no time did the relationship appear strained nor Anita appear uncomfortable with the relationship.[68]

During Sunday evening, Ken Duberstein received a phone call from Jeff Peck telling him that Anita Hill did not want to return to the committee for further testimony. If she did not return, would Clarence do the same? Ken thought Peck's call was good news. Anita Hill would have been very sharply cross-examined, and, in Ken's words, "It would have gotten very nasty. I think the American people were satiated by Sunday night."

Although Duberstein and I agreed that enough was enough, and I had told that to the committee by way of a written note handed to Duke Short, I had not gone through the formality of checking with Clarence. I was certain of his response, but at the end of the testimony of the eight women, Joe Biden asked me to call Clarence. I could reach only his answering machine.

As I left the Caucus Room to make the call, Joe Biden excused the panel of women. Not wanting to destroy the drama of the moment, Janet turned to the other women and said, "Don't move and don't laugh. Don't engage in any levity. Just sit here until this is all over." Pat Johnson, one of the panel and nine months pregnant, gave Janet a slight smile and said, "My skirt's falling down. Do you mind if I jack it up?" Janet said, "No, that's quite all right."

Hank Brown views the panel of women as "the most persuasive witnesses" on Clarence's behalf. Larry Silberman thinks that any other political figure in the United States would have been more vulnerable to a charge of sexual harassment than Clarence because no one else could have mustered the number of women who testified for Clarence.

Janet Brown explains, "I don't know too many people that would inspire anyone to do what at the end of the day by all of those women was a completely selfless act. There was nothing in it for them. They wanted to stand up for Clarence."

At about 2:00 A.M. the hearing adjourned. Neither Clarence Thomas nor Anita Hill would return for further testimony. Janet Brown, her husband, Mike Brewer, and Pam Talkin, one of the panel, were outside the Russell Building, on the northwest corner of Delaware and C streets when chairman Biden emerged. Joe thanked Janet for the panel's testimony and walked on to Mike Brewer and Pam Talkin. Mike Brewer recalls that Biden said how hard it is to deal with purists and how impressed he was with the women. He added that he, Joe Biden, did not believe Anita Hill.[69]

Monday, October 14

Rob McDonald remembers my frustration during the late hours of the hearing. After a day of struggle, we had secured three documents— the affidavits of one former law student, John Burke, and Dr. Park Dietz—that I thought either damaging to Hill's credibility or explanatory of how she might have made a false statement while believing it was true.

In less than forty-eight hours, the Senate would vote on Clarence's confirmation. The issue would be one of credibility. Clarence Thomas and Anita Hill had made irreconcilable statements to the Judiciary Committee. One of them was not telling the truth. If the Senate, and ultimately the public, believed Anita Hill, Clarence would lose the vote and be disgraced. If the Senate and the American people did not believe Anita Hill, Clarence would win the vote and be vindicated. Because the credibility of the two adversaries was being weighed by the country, I thought it my job to show that Anita Hill was not telling the truth. I wanted to present what I thought was relevant evidence to the public—evidence that was not presented to the committee and the sort of evidence that Joe Biden had agreed any senator was free to present after the hearing.

It was not my desire to "get" Anita Hill out of anger or vindictiveness. My intention was to present documents that refuted her credibility in a contest where credibility was the sole issue. To members of my Senate staff, I was unprincipled, and I had to be stopped. In my mind, I was an advocate, contesting the only relevant point in controversy under the only rules at hand.

Jon Chambers, my legislative director, disagreed with me. He thought that my value system was distorted and told me as I walked to my car in the early hours of the morning that he opposed what he called the "end justifies the means" approach I was taking. I told Jon, "Well, we just disagree on that." For the next twelve hours, I made an effort to get the three affidavits into public circulation. For the same twelve hours, my Senate staff worked successfully to slow me down.

Rob McDonald recalls that before leaving the Capitol early Monday morning, I gave my news secretary, Steve Hilton, two assignments: to arrange a news conference the next day for Dr. Dietz and to release the affidavit of John Burke. My understanding was that Hank Brown's office would release the affidavit of the former law student.

Steve Hilton and Jon Chambers were in upbeat moods when they reached the office on Monday morning. Steve had seen only positive news on the morning wire: strong support for Clarence, and at least one Democratic senator had made a statement that he would continue to support the nominee. Steve thought that the dissemination of polling information would create positive momentum for the vote, and he set to work gathering the data, making sure it was circulated.

Jon Chambers was in a giddy mood. The hearing was over, and, after a little sleep, he was remembering humorous moments in the proceedings. The ordeal was ending, and Jon looked forward to my turning myself to more happy causes and in a less angry spirit. My midmorning phone call ended the joyful mood of the office.

I slept late on Monday. When I woke up, I phoned Ken Duberstein, who told me that Steve Hilton had made the decision not to hold a news conference for Dr. Dietz. I immediately dialed my office, reached Rob McDonald, and exploded in anger. What, I asked, was being done about the Dietz news conference? Nothing. What was being done about the Burke affidavit? Nothing. Jon Chambers joined Rob on the speaker phone. Everything was going well; Clarence was ahead in the polls; the office had made the decision to do nothing. Perhaps some other senator would release the Burke affidavit; the Dietz statement was speculative and not helpful to Clarence. All of this would damage my reputation, so the office—Rob McDonald, Steve Hilton, and Jon Chambers—had decided to ignore my direct order of the previous night.

I think that most of my professional staff have thought of my office as a relaxed, happy place to work. Not that morning. I was furious. I (still at home) told my staff (in the office) that they were sitting on their duffs. I told them that if I wanted anything done in my office, I had to do it myself. I told them that Dietz must have a news conference and that I would have my own news conference to release the Burke affidavit.

After that conversation, Rob McDonald told Steve Hilton to proceed with the Dietz news conference. Still convinced that the Dietz approach was neither helpful to Clarence nor in keeping with my style, Steve proceeded in the most indirect and purposefully feckless manner possible. Rather than calling our own news conference for Dr. Dietz, Steve counseled Dick Leon to hold a news conference with Dietz at a place off Capitol Hill. The tactic worked; only one media person attended. That day, Jon Chambers destroyed all copies of the Dietz affidavit he could find in my office.

Jon Chambers did not want me to release any of the affidavits, but he thought John Burke's statement was least damaging to me. Even so, Jon tried to take the statement out of my hands, calling the offices of Judiciary Committee Republicans to see if they would release it instead. Jon had no takers. At last, I had a news conference scheduled for midafternoon, but even then, Jon proceeded with his go-slow approach. As I headed out my office door for the Senate press gallery, I asked for copies of the Burke affidavit. They were not available. Jon had slowed down their reproduction.

Responding to my phone call to the office and to a midday conversation with me, Peter Leibold called Hank Brown's staff to inquire about progress in getting the former law students to put their stories in affidavit form. There had been no progress. Only one person was willing to sign an affidavit, and Brown's staff thought that a single statement, without corroboration, was not sufficient basis for its release.

My disposition did not improve as the day progressed. Peter Leibold, who had been watching the five o'clock news, came into my office to tell me that a Washington television station had just reported that Janet Brown, whom they identified as a Clarence Thomas supporter, had been sexually harassed while she was employed in my office. That was the last straw in the media's coverage of Clarence Thomas and sexual harassment for me. Allen Moore, who was in my office when Peter came in, describes me as "hair-trigger angry."

Steve Hilton was on the telephone with the producer of the news program when I stormed into his office and grabbed the phone from his hand. Steve describes me as "shouting mad." I told the producer that I had been libeled and that if the television station did not correct the statement in the six o'clock news, "I'll sue your ass." I gave him Janet Brown's phone number so they could check the story.

Under the law, it is very difficult for a public figure to sue for libel and win, but I did not have to press the point. The station made the correction on the six o'clock news. For me, it was an hour late, and it did not make up for a mistake that the station would have avoided by competent journalism. They ran a story without bothering to check with me, Janet Brown, or anyone else. Charges of sexual harassment are sensational, and where there is sensation, there is little room for accuracy or decency.

Monday was Columbus Day, and in the morning Elizabeth and Steven Law went to the Thomases' home. Clarence was relaxed. "He seemed light," Elizabeth said. Clarence acknowledged that God had directed his words during the hearing. Elizabeth remembers that Clarence said, "Don't be sorry for me. We need to pray for our country. This isn't about me. This is about our country and what the process has come to and what our government has come to."

Concerned that Clarence would not be confirmed, Larry Silberman phoned Arnon Siegel, one of Clarence's clerks on the court of appeals. If Clarence were defeated, he would continue to serve on the court of appeals, but would he have law clerks to help him with his work, or had his clerks made other plans and not been replaced by the departing judge? "If he is defeated, I will stay for the year," said Siegel. "That's a fine young man," thought Larry.

On Monday, Ken Duberstein learned of an unusual occurrence during the Judiciary Committee's deposition of Susan Hoerchner. The deposition was attended by Janet Napolitano, a lawyer for Anita Hill who interrupted the deposition to confer with Hoerchner. After the interruption, Hoerschner changed her testimony in two important respects.

Before the conference, Hoerchner testified that sometime before September 1981, Hill told her by phone of "sexual harassment by her boss." The date was important and damaging to Hill's story because Hill did not begin working for Clarence until August 1981 and testified that Clarence first asked her for a date approximately three months after her work commenced, which would be November 1981. Thus, Hoerchner's original testimony would indicate that the "boss" Hill complained of was someone at Wald, Harkrader and Ross. After conferring with Hill's lawyer, Hoerchner said, "I don't know for sure" when Hill told her of the alleged harassment.

Also, before conferring with Napolitano, Hoerchner had testified that "very recently" Hill had told her that she, Hoerchner, was the only person Hill had told about the alleged harassment. This, too, was damaging to Hill's story for it would mean that no one else could corroborate the claim. After conferring, Hoerchner testified that her conclusion was based on what the FBI told her, not on what Hill said.

After receiving this information, Ken called a senior staff person for the Judiciary Committee and told him he was under great obligation to tell Chairman Biden of the interruption and changes in Hoerchner's deposition. Ken recalls that when he told the staff person, the response to each of the two changes was a colorful and emphatic expression of dismay.

When I went to bed on Monday night, I was optimistic that Clarence would be confirmed. I counted forty-one certain Republican votes and four certain Democrats. Adding likely but not sure votes, I thought he would end up in the mid-fifties.

Tuesday, October 15

In the evening, the skies opened, but the day of the vote was beautiful: blue sky, balmy weather, and a festive atmosphere outside the Capitol Building, almost as if it were a presidential Inaugural. The sidewalks at the intersection of Delaware and Constitution were crowded with partisans of both sides but largely Thomas supporters who were singing or chanting cheers. Television crews worked the crowd, trying to get sound bites from whomever came along.

For me it was a day of phone calls to doubtful senators and keeping track of who was going to the Senate floor to announce a position. It was a day of wheel spinning combined with excitement that soon it would all end.

I made one office visit, to a senator who is always fair but had voted against Clarence for the court of appeals. David Pryor was the chairman of the Committee on Aging, and he had opposed Clarence because of lapsed age discrimination cases at EEOC. I told David that there had to be some point in time when the handling of the age discrimination cases would be forgiven. Then I appealed to him in a way I thought he would understand.

The *New York Times* had editorialized that Anita Hill had raised a doubt about Clarence, and that in case of doubt, the nominee should not be confirmed.[70] I argued that this was just the opposite of how it should be. If doubt was all it took to defeat a nominee, then there would be no end to mud slinging in the future. All the interest groups would be invigorated in their efforts to find dirt on nominees. What had happened to Clarence Thomas was unfair, and unfairness should not be rewarded. Doubts should be resolved in favor of the nominee. I thought it was a strong argument, but David Pryor nevertheless voted against confirmation.

By late Tuesday morning, I was optimistic but not confident. Fifty senators had not announced their intention to vote for Clarence, but I thought that enough were leaning his way to give him the victory. I was counting on forty-one of the forty-three Republican senators, with only Senators Packwood and Jeffords announced against confirmation. Just before lunch, Bob Dole told me of two problems I did not know I had: the votes of Senators Cohen and Rudman were in doubt.

Every Tuesday when the Senate is in session, Republican senators meet for lunch in Room S211 of the Capitol, just off the Senate floor. I was called out this Tuesday for a phone call from White House chief of staff John Sununu inquiring about the vote count. I am told that in my absence, Ted Stevens from Alaska made a nice speech about me, and when I returned from taking the call, my Republican colleagues gave me a very warm round of applause complete with shouts of approval. I asked for recognition and said that while I appreciated the applause, what I really wanted was their votes; I was counting on forty-one Republican votes, and if I did not have them, I had a real problem. I asked any Republican who was in doubt to let me know. At that, Bill Cohen signaled to me, pointed to Warren Rudman and to himself, then to me, and mouthed, "After lunch."

After the luncheon adjourned, I sat at the end of a table with Bill Cohen and Warren Rudman. We were joined by Al Simpson. Cohen said that he had a hard time believing Clarence and that he did not think he was a great nominee. Warren Rudman said that he was having difficulty coming to a decision on how to vote and that he would have to take an hour or so to think it out by himself. I said to both of them, "I've got a real problem if you vote the other way." Bill Cohen said he would let me know if he decided to vote against Clarence.

I returned to my office and phoned Bob Dole to ask if he could talk to Cohen and Rudman. "Bob," I said, "we could lose this. We need these two, and their votes are essential." Dole thought it best not to pester Rudman but said he would phone Cohen. He touched base with me after talking to Cohen and related that he did not know what Cohen would do. He suggested that I call him. I did. When I finished the call, I still did not know how Cohen would vote, I did not know how Rudman would vote, and I did not know if Clarence would win.

I jotted down some notes on what I would say in the closing debate, mainly the same point I made to David Pryor. If any senators still had doubts as to how they would vote, it was important to resolve those doubts in favor of the nominee. To do otherwise would demonstrate that the creation of doubts through personal attacks was an effective way to defeat a confirmation. The fight against Clarence Thomas would become the standard of the future for opposition to controversial nominees, and that would be a tragedy for America. After making my notes on what I would say at the close of the debate, I headed for the floor for the final hour of speeches before the scheduled vote.

When I reached the Senate floor, the debate was in progress. Bill Cohen was speaking, announcing his vote for Clarence. Sam Nunn announced his affirmative vote as well. That made fifty. We had reached our goal. Victory was certain.

When the roll call was completed, Clarence had fifty-two votes. Several senators came up to my desk on the center aisle of the Senate and congratulated me. Bill Cohen and Warren Rudman came—Warren with an intense, almost angry look on his face. He said, "Bill and I just an hour before decided together that this was how we were going to vote, and you are the only reason we voted this way. We voted for you." I said, "Well, for whatever reason, I'm glad I had your vote."

To avoid the crowd and the media, I ran down a back staircase behind the Senate Chamber. A tourist asked if I knew who won. I walked through the tunnel to the Russell Building and then to my office. I met Sally, and we drove to the Thomases' as it started to rain.

Clarence Thomas, just confirmed as an associate justice of the U.S. Supreme Court, was soaking in a bath, reading, when Ginni told him the result of the vote. He shrugged at the news.

They had stayed at home all day listening to religious music on the stereo. One song that had special meaning to them that day was, "He that is in us." They did not watch the Senate debate on television, nor did they watch the vote. Late in the afternoon, Fred McClure called Ginni to ask if she and Clarence would like to come to the White House to watch the vote with President and Mrs. Bush. When Ginni asked Clarence, he said he was not interested and would rather stay at home. Ginni summarizes Clarence's attitude: "Clarence had said he was ready for it to go either way and it was like he was uninterested in it going either way."

A friend called Ginni to tell her that the Senate had voted confirmation. Clarence describes how he felt when he learned of the vote: "Not blasé, but not happy. I felt I had been abused. I just felt like I went through something that shouldn't have ever occurred. It was like pulling a thorn out of your finger. You know, you're relieved to have it out, but someone put it there and it shouldn't have been there to begin with. So you don't feel any pleasure, you don't feel any joy. You're just relieved that it is out. And you can start a healing process and that's the way I felt."

Clarence says that he had two additional thoughts: he was glad that the interest groups that opposed him were not rewarded for their efforts with victory, and he believed that God had made it clear that his confirmation was God's will.

Allen Moore, who arrived at the Thomases' house fifteen minutes after the vote was announced, worked his way through the crowd standing

in the rain and through security, to join Ginni, Clarence, and Butch
Faddis inside. Clarence seemed relieved and happy, but not ecstati-
cally so. Allen encouraged Clarence to jot down some notes for a short
statement to the media and to his supporters outside. Later, Strom
Thurmond arrived and encouraged Clarence to go outside and speak
to the media. So with Strom at his side, Clarence stood under an umbrella in the glare of television lights and said that a time of healing
had begun. Senator Trent Lott's son, a Domino Pizza employee, arrived with a stack of boxes announcing that they were "Supreme piz-
zas." A gracious congratulatory message from Joe Biden left on
Clarence's answering machine was greeted by a less than gracious
response.

Sally and I arrived, then Steven and Elizabeth Law, then the Duber-
steins and other friends. Sally remembers it as a "warm and loving
time, but not a crazy, joyful time." We went into the living room, stood
in a circle, and held hands. I offered a prayer of thanksgiving.

Sally says that at one point during the evening Clarence shook
his head back and forth and back and forth and said, "I just always
will be absolutely baffled at what made this thing happen and
what made her do this. She was always a very nice person. We always
had a fine time together. We were friends. I just cannot understand
it. She was a tough woman, but she was a good person. It just baf-
fles me."

That night, Clarence told me that he thought that someday the truth
would come out.

In Ken Duberstein's presence, Clarence said that at their first meeting
a day or two after the president had announced the nomination, Ken
had warned that "they are going to throw the kitchen sink at you."
Clarence said, "That's the only time Ken Duberstein ever lied to me,
because it wasn't the kitchen sink; it was the kitchen, it was the
house, it was the foundation. They threw everything at me!"

Ken remembers his own feelings that night: "I felt very proud that
Clarence Thomas had been confirmed. I felt shell-shocked by the sys-

tem and how bad things had become in the Senate. I was revolted by interest group politics." Ken also remembers a comment he made that night with reference to me: "Believe me, the saint of the Senate is far less saintly now than he was four months ago."

Afterword

As October 1991 retreats into history, it does not fade from the memories of the American people.

Most times when I am in public places, strangers ask me about that week and ask how Clarence is doing.

My answer is that he is doing fine. The booming laugh is still there, as is the earnest expression on his face when he asks after his friends. He loves his job on the Supreme Court and is working hard at it. He is proud of his productivity on the Court and of the quality of the opinions he has written.

He and Ginni have built a new house in a secluded area of northern Virginia. He continues to refuse to read newspapers but otherwise keeps track of what is going on in the world. Some friends think he is too secluded, but I think his need for privacy is both understandable and consistent with his past. He has started to travel a bit, to make appearances at gatherings of lawyers and other events, and he enjoys that.

Shortly after taking his place on the Supreme Court, Clarence told what he learned in his confirmation experience:

"It showed me just how vulnerable I am. . . . It showed me how vulnerable any individual is. . . . It showed me that I was no greater than any other person and that I could be destroyed and that I had to rely on God, not myself. And that humility is, I assure you, permanent.

"It also showed me something that I will never lose, and that is that that 2 percent or 1 percent or 0.2 percent can always be used to destroy a human being when there are no barriers, when there is no perspective and no context.

"It also taught me, on the good side, the goodness of the American people, that they are, by and large, far better as a group than their representatives and the interest groups who are playing the representative and the media who reports to them, that they are a far better lot.

"It taught me something about my wife. It taught me about her strength. It taught me how good she is, how committed she is to me and how much she loves me, and it has brought us closer. It taught me about my friends. There is nothing more wonderful than to have good friends. . . . The Janet Browns, Nancy Altmans, Pam Talkin, Ricky Silberman, all the people who just stood up.

"I have been taught about the protections that we have as individuals in society so these things don't happen. The importance of the appropriate forum; that you don't get divorced before Congress; that you don't fight battles about whether somebody molested their kid in front of Congress and the national audience. That's not the right forum. There are no procedures. There are no safeguards. There are no protections. There is no way to test the validity of statements, the accuracy of statements, the reliability of statements. There are no rules of evidence.

"I can say at bottom that the person that came out of that process, and I will see the total product years from now, but is different from the person who went into it. . . . I have still got to go through a lot of healing, but I think I am a better person.

"I don't carry an ideological burden. I don't carry a vendetta or anything like that. . . . I think I will be a better judge in the sense that I feel liberated, in the sense that I am not here to please anyone."

I suggested that some might expect Clarence to "take it out on" interest groups that had opposed his confirmation now that he was on the Supreme Court. He answered: "No. They think I'm as bad as they are. . . . These people think I am as without principle as they are; that when they don't like somebody, they attack them. They get even. They try to destroy them. . . . So they expect that I am going to do the same thing they did. I am not going to do that. Then I become just like them. And the worst thing, my worst punishment, could be to be like them. I'm never going to be like that, and they know it. And maybe that's their protection, that most people in this country are not like that."

Shortly after Clarence's confirmation, Elizabeth Law expressed her anger toward people who had opposed Clarence. She remembers his response: "We need to forgive all of these people."

Orrin Hatch and Clarence had lunch together soon after Clarence took his place on the Supreme Court. Clarence told Orrin that a laborer in a work uniform at the Court came up to him and gave him a hug and welcomed him to the high bench. Other laborers vigorously shook his hand and told him they were glad he was there. Clarence told Orrin, "I am going to be a meat-and-potatoes justice just for them."

From the time the FBI visited his home, Clarence has thought of the charge of sexual harassment as "a stain that won't come off." That thought was prescient, for, indeed, the stain has spread. At the end of the hearing, two of three Americans believed Clarence Thomas. According to the *Washington Post,* by the end of 1992, the public believed Anita Hill by a margin of 53 percent to 37 percent.[71] Anita Hill became the cause of the feminist movement, and Clarence became its demon. When Hill addressed female state legislators from around the country, those present twirled napkins and pounded tables in approval.[72] When Clarence addressed the annual meeting of the Missouri Bar in September 1993, the National Organization for Women picketed the meeting.[73]

The stain was spread with the help of the media, and it reached members of the Judiciary Committee, especially those who had supported Clarence. Liberal columnists portrayed the questioning of

Anita Hill as abusive[74] and television shows lampooned both Clarence and the committee.[75] Oliver Stone amended the script of his docudrama *JFK* to add Arlen Specter's name to the assertion that an obscure but "ambitious junior counselor" when the Kennedy assassination was investigated was a liar. The film was released during Arlen's reelection campaign, and the inserted mention of his name was the cause of boos and hisses in movie theaters.[76] The *New Yorker* magazine transformed a planned profile into a lengthy diatribe against Alan Simpson.[77] Orrin Hatch is confident that the reason the press has attempted to implicate him in the BCCI scandal is, in part, a payback for his involvement in the Thomas-Hill hearing.[78]

Others have written of the relentless effort to get the dirt on Clarence Thomas, which began as soon as his nomination was announced.[79] Obviously, I was not included in the councils of these who opposed him. Nor do I know what was in the mind of Anita Hill. To the best of my knowledge, I have never seen her in person, much less known enough about her to explore her psyche. What I do know from personal experience is not the cause but the effect—the result of an effort to destroy, or in Clarence's word "kill," a human being.

And it works. It works perfectly. If a small army of interest groups, staffers, investigators, and lawyers sets out on a mission to destroy a person and if they are aided by the media, that mission will succeed.

The result is to take from a human being that which makes life worth living: self-respect, the respect of others, the chance to enjoy a day without a stakeout on the front lawn, even the ability to eat and sleep. If that is life, then Clarence is correct: the result of the mission to destroy is death. It is to take a good, kind, happy person and reduce him to a sobbing soul, driven into the fetal position.

The Thomas-Hill drama proves that a mission of destruction succeeds, and if it succeeded in the case of Clarence Thomas, it can succeed for anyone. The methods used to destroy Clarence Thomas are not the exclusive possessions of the political left. If they can be used by liberals to destroy a conservative nominee, they can be used with equal effectiveness by conservatives to destroy liberals. Conversely, if it was wrong for liberals to do it, it is equally wrong for conservatives to do it.

In the days before the hearing, I told Clarence to take on the Congress, that in so doing he could become a national hero. I told him that the American people had contempt for Congress and that they were waiting for a champion who would stand up to it. This, I think, was good advice for the occasion. If Clarence was to acquit himself, he had to turn tables on the committee.

It may have been good advice for the occasion, but it ran contrary to what I believe about the relationship between the American people and their elected representatives. Healthy skepticism about government is an important aspect of our national character, but there is a significant difference between healthy skepticism and toxic cynicism. Skepticism allows Americans to have a sense of reality about what government can do for them. Cynicism is the notion that government is no longer We but They, and that They—those in charge—are trying to serve themselves by disserving us.

Cynicism is clearly the national mood. It is fostered by thirty-second campaign commercials and a surfeit of investigative reporting. It is manifested in the phenomenon of Ross Perot—the notion that average Americans must stand united against the inept and corrupt politicians who have turned against us in their selfish need to get elected.

Years before the Thomas nomination, during some now-forgotten debate, I had joined other senators in making remarks that tended to disparage the Senate. The most zealous guardian of the dignity and traditions of the Senate, president pro tempore Robert Byrd, took me aside. Gently and without specific reference to me, he used a phrase I have often recalled. He spoke of senators who "soil their own nest." He was right then, but in October 1991 I did it again.

In the year before I announced my own retirement from the Senate, other senators who had made the same decision used their announce-

ments to express their dismay with the institution. It has been important to me to make it clear that I do not share that dismay. Service in
the Senate has been the highest honor of my life, the fulfillment of a
childhood dream. No institution is perfect, and the Senate surely has
its faults. Its members, like those of any other body, run the gamut of
character and competence. But the Senate is a great institution that
serves our nation well and represents well the interests and hopes of
the American people. The large majority of senators are bright, competent, honest, and diligent.

Clarence Thomas had every reason to be indignant. So did I. A
great injustice was taking place in the Senate itself. It was essential
that Clarence give voice to his indignation, that he speak from the
heart. As for me, rage is difficult to control. Insofar as my own rage
was directed to the Senate and insofar as I encouraged Clarence to do
likewise, more so by far than he actually did, I believe that I went
too far.

Yes, the Senate should have voted, as planned, on October 8. That
vote should have confirmed Clarence by a comfortable margin. Joe
Biden should have been forceful in dismissing Anita Hill's story, and
the pro-Thomas Democrats should not have withheld their votes.
However, I completely understand why events occurred as they did. It
is not true that members of the Senate refuse to listen to their constituents. When the public speaks, senators have an acute sense of hearing. Women's organizations were shouting into the ears of Democratic
senators: "Delay the vote!" "Hold another hearing!" "Stop Clarence
Thomas!" These groups are a significant constituency of that party,
and the senators listened. They could not proceed as though nothing
had happened.

In constitutional terms, Clarence Thomas was deprived of life without
due process of law. For a proud man, the humiliation he experienced
was a far more severe penalty than that faced by most defendants in
civil or criminal cases. Yet he did not have the protections accorded
defendants in courts of law.

This is not to say that Joe Biden was unfair in conducting the hearing. He was in a difficult situation, and he handled it as well as he could.

The problem is that a Senate committee is not a court, and a trial by television before the American people is not a trial by jury. There was no judge. There was no statute of limitation. There were no rules of evidence. There was no right to subpoena documents. Unlike a court of law, inadmissible evidence—the lie detector results—was put before the ultimate jury.

Before the hearing began, Clarence had not seen Anita Hill's written statement. He never saw the FBI report. He, and the rest of the world for that matter, first heard the stories of Long Dong Silver and pubic hair on the Coke can when Anita Hill testified on Friday afternoon.

Most important, there was no representation by independent counsel and no right of counsel to cross-examine the accusing witness. A member of the Senate is not an independent counsel, but even the senators were hampered by lack of time to prepare questions.

A challenge to Hill's testimony about the termination of her employment by the law firm was never made. By the time I knew of John Burke's existence, the witness list was closed. Anita Hill never returned to testify further, so there was no chance to cross-examine her on the subject.

Al Simpson thinks that if Arlen Specter and Orrin Hatch had been given three weeks to prepare, the results of the hearing would have been more clearly in Clarence's favor. I agree and believe that instead of trying to schedule the hearing as soon as possible, I should have advocated more time for preparation. On the other hand, I do not know that Clarence would have agreed to prolonging his agony any longer. Also, at the time, we thought that delay was the tactic of the interest groups.

In the future, when a nominee's character is put in question, much more attention should be paid to procedural due process. At the least, the nominee should be represented by legal counsel who should have the right to subpoena evidence, take depositions, and cross-examine witnesses. Counsel should have adequate time to prepare.

In the absence of a legal process for conducting Clarence's defense, I was willing to turn to an extralegal process: the attempt to gather material wherever I could and dump it into the public domain. Are there former law students with nasty stories? Find them and release their statements to the media. Is there a psychiatrist with a theory of delusion? Call a news conference and introduce him. Is there a former employer who disputes the accuser's testimony? Take his affidavit to the press gallery.

Unfortunately, it was a practice that did not end with the Senate's vote on confirmation. For months thereafter, I was intent on peddling my theories about Anita Hill to whoever would listen. Clarence had been confirmed, but he had not had his day in court. If he had, I thought, no fair-minded person would doubt his innocence. He had been denied due process. He had been denied an adequate defense. Still, his enemies were attacking him. Still, I was trying to defend him.

The development of adequate procedures to protect the accused in Senate proceedings is essential, but no rules of procedure will substitute for public outcry in the face of injustice. Women members of Congress made the front pages of newspapers as they stormed the steps of the Senate on their way to the majority leader's office, but voices of outrage were few on behalf of Clarence Thomas. The media covered the spectacle with obvious glee. Few were heard to say that last-minute charges and leaks to the press and trial without rules were offenses to even minimal standards of fairness. Indeed, the rationale at the time was that the episode, however outrageous, served the useful purpose of calling the public's attention to the problem of sexual harassment. Yes, but every accusation calls attention to something.

America's standards of fairness will never be fully embodied in rules, however carefully drawn. There will always be some new form of indignity that the rule makers have not thought of. But however novel the circumstance, a breakdown in fundamental fairness will always be an affront to American justice to which Americans are obliged to speak, starting with their politicians and starting with their press.

Was I justified in what I tried to do to help Clarence that Sunday and Monday? If Rob McDonald is correct in his recollection, the clear answer is no, for then I would have been no more than a politician fighting to save his own skin with whatever weapon was at hand. But I honestly do not believe Rob was correct. I truly believed then, and I truly believe now, that I was fighting for a good cause: Clarence Thomas.

Yet to believe in a good cause does not justify using every means to advance that cause. The interest groups and the staffers who opposed the nomination thought they were serving a good cause. Throughout history, all kinds of atrocities have been committed in the names of causes thought to be good. If there is any lesson to be learned from the Thomas-Hill matter, it must be that service of a good cause does not justify the wanton destruction of a person, whether that person is Clarence Thomas or Anita Hill.

In my mind, there is a distinction between a good cause and a just cause. A good cause can be one's own creation, whatever one perceives to be worthwhile. A just cause is how one responds to injustice. Throughout the Thomas-Hill controversy, I believed in Clarence Thomas. To me he was a good cause. But more than that, I believed he was the victim of a horrible injustice.

On the evening of July 1, the day he was nominated, I phoned Clarence from the Shrine Club in Kirksville, Missouri, and told him to read Romans 12. It is St. Paul's advice not to be overcome by evil but to overcome evil with good. It is a basic Christian doctrine, the law of love, and it is a doctrine I readily set aside on Columbus Day weekend, 1991. I thought that this was no time for meekness or mildness.

This was a time for war, and we had to win that war or a terrible injustice would be done.

So I took Clarence into a bathroom and punched the button of a tape player, and a song came on that is rarely heard anymore in Christian churches. It is considered far too bellicose for today's believers. Onward Christian soldiers, marching as to war!

And when Clarence left my office for the Caucus Room, it was not as a martyr with his eyes fixed on heaven. It was as a warrior doing battle for the Lord.

So that Sunday and Monday I fought for Clarence. I fought dirty in a fight without rules.

And I fought ineffectively, for nothing I did in those efforts to destroy the credibility of Anita Hill had any bearing on the outcome. That outcome was determined no later than Friday night when Clarence returned to the committee to testify, and, perhaps on Wednesday afternoon when we prayed in his home.

For all my efforts to get affidavits and put them in public circulation, Hank Brown says that the most significant event of the last day of the hearing was the testimony of the panel of women. That is a statement of surpassing hopefulness, for it shows that the ordeal of Clarence Thomas was more than a breakdown of justice; it was a victory of love.

My various connivings bore no fruit at all. What bore fruit was the love of Janet Brown and Nancy Altman, of the Laws and the Jameses and the Silbermans, of Butch Faddis, and so many more who stood by their friend. Ultimately, what bore fruit was the love of God.

Days after his confirmation, Clarence told me that his victory occurred not on Tuesday when the Senate voted but on the preceding weekend when he testified. I think it occurred the previous Wednesday afternoon when Clarence decided he did not have to win confirmation—not for the job, not even to save his name. I think it occurred when he acknowledged his weakness and turned to God as the sole source of his strength and of his destiny. When prayer is answered, the appropriate response is, Thanks be to God.

On October 18, a magnificently sunny day, Clarence took the oath of office in a White House Rose Garden ceremony. In his brief remarks, he paraphrased Psalm 30, which he had read in the dark hours of his ordeal. The psalm begins:

> *I will exalt you, O Lord,*
> *because You have lifted me up*
> *and have not let my enemies*
> *triumph over me.*
>
> *O Lord my God, I cried out to You,*
> *and You restored me to health.*
> *You brought me up, O Lord, from*
> *the dead;*
> *You restored my life as I was*
> *going down to the grave.*
>
> *Sing to the Lord, you servants of His;*
> *give thanks for the remembrance of His holiness.*
>
> *For His wrath endures but the twinkling*
> *of an eye, His favor for a lifetime.*
>
> *Weeping may spend the night, but joy*
> *comes in the morning.*

During the summer of 1991, Clarence lived in fear that people would kill him. In all but the strictly physical sense, the person I saw on Wednesday afternoon, October 9, was dead.

Less than forty-eight hours later, on the morning of the third day, Clarence Thomas walked into the Senate Caucus Room, took his seat at the witness table, and commenced his testimony. Clarence had risen.

Alleluia!

Notes

1. Romans 6:5

2. Matthew 26:51; Mark 14:47; Luke 22:50; John 18:10

3. See, e.g., speech to the Federalist Society, University of Virginia, March 5, 1988, p. 13, ". . . as Ollie North made perfectly clear last summer, it is Congress that is out of control!"; speech to the Gordon Public Policy Center, Brandeis University, Waltham, Massachusetts, April 8, 1988, p. 4, "Congress is no longer primarily a deliberative or even a law-making body"; speech to the Tocqueville Forum, Wake Forest University, April 18, 1988, p. 7, "The [Supreme] Court has used [the due process and equal protection clauses] to make itself the national school board, parole board, health commission, and elections commissioner among other titles."

4. Associated Press, July 5, 1991

5. The identification of destruction of a person's reputation with murder is made in Jewish and Christian teaching. "Anyone who humiliates his fellow in public; it is as if he has spilled his blood." *Babylonian Talmud,* Tractate Bava Metzia, 58b. In the New Testament, the prohibition against killing is extended to insults. Matthew 5:21–22.

6. Henry David Russo, "Pro-Choice Activists Call 1987 Speech Antiabortion," UPI, July 3, 1991.

7. Cheryl Arvidson, "Court Pick Sidesteps Farrakhan Stir," *Dallas Times Herald,* July 13, 1991, p. A1.

8. Laurence H. Tribe, "Natural Law and the Nominee," *New York Times,* July 15, 1991, p. A15; "A Higher Law for the High Court," *U.S. News & World Report,* July 22, 1991, p. 50.

209

9. "Periscope," *Newsweek,* July 29, 1991, p. 4.

10. Marilyn Gardner, "The Judge Who Judged His Sister," *Christian Science Monitor,* July 30, 1991, p. 13.

11. David G. Savage, "Thomas' Church a Center of Anti-Abortion Activity," *Los Angeles Times,* July 11, 1991, p. A14.

12. Legal opinions were provided by Professor Geoffrey C. Hazard, Jr., of Yale Law School and Professor Ronald D. Rotunda of the University of Illinois College of Law. The reasoning of Professor Rotunda is set forth in "Points of View," *Legal Times,* August 26, 1991, p. 20. The opposing views of Professor Monroe Freedman of Hofstra University Law School appear on the same page.

13. The identity of the groups and their method of operation have to be pieced together from other sources. See David Brock, *The Real Anita Hill* (New York: Free Press, 1993), chaps. 1–2. See also "A Distressing Turn," *Washington Post,* October 12, 1991, p. A1, which reports, "Within days after President Bush announced Thomas' nomination, liberal activist groups began the search for ammunition they hoped could defeat him. An informal coalition that included [Arthur] Kropp [president of People for the American Way], Kate Michelman of the National Abortion Rights Action League, Nan Aron of the Alliance for Justice and others began holding almost daily strategy sessions, at first restricting their probes to exposing what they viewed as his track record as a rigid Reagan administration ideologue."

The *Post* story goes on to explain that the interest groups then delved into such subjects as Clarence's travel records, his divorce and alleged wife beating, and his supposed favoritism to me in the Ralston Purina case. It reports that People for the American Way "assigned four full-time staffers, several interns and four other field organizers to anti-Thomas activities." The story adds that Supreme Court Watch, described as "a project of the liberal Nation Institute," uncovered the Ralston Purina case and then issued a news release accusing Clarence of unethical conduct. It reports that the national secretary of the National Organization for Women made "repeated efforts to confirm the rumors" that Clarence beat his first wife.

In a column printed in his newspaper on October 10, 1991, "Open Season on Clarence Thomas," *Washington Post* writer Juan Williams stated that throughout September he had received phone calls from staff members working for Democratic senators on the Judiciary Committee. He believed that he was called because he had written several articles, including a long profile, on Clarence and knew the nominee. Among other things, the callers asked whether Clarence had ever taken money from the government of South Africa, whether he had criticized civil rights leaders, and whether Clarence had filed improper travel expense statements. According to Williams, finally one exasperated voice said: "Have you got anything on your tapes we can use to stop Thomas?"

Williams continued: "The desperate search for ammunition to shoot down Thomas has turned the 102 days since President Bush nominated him for a seat on the Supreme Court into a liberal's nightmare. Here is indiscriminate, mean-spirited mud-slinging supported by the so-called champions of fairness: liberal politicians, unions, civil rights groups and women's organizations. They have been mindlessly led into mob action against one man by the Leadership Conference on Civil Rights."

A detailed account of the efforts of Senate staffers to secure a statement from Anita Hill and transmit it to the media is the subject of *Report of Temporary Special Independent,* 102d Cong., 2d sess., S. Res. 202 (Washington, D.C.: U.S. Government Printing Office, 1992).

14. Tony Mauro, "Abortion Rights Group Sees Thomas as a Foe," *USA Today,* July 3, 1991, p. A2.

15. As chairman of EEOC, Clarence Thomas persuaded the solicitor general to file a brief in the Supreme Court case of *Meritor Savings Bank* v. *Vinson,* 477 U.S. 57 (1986). The solicitor general argued and the Court held that sexual harassment constitutes a hostile workplace environment and violates Title VII of the Civil Rights Act of 1964.

16. While chairman of EEOC, Clarence appointed women as executive director, chief of staff, legal counsel, chairman of the Executive Resources Board, director of the Office of Federal Operations, and director of training.

17. "Comparable worth," strongly opposed by the Reagan administration, has been defined as "the concept of paying the same salaries for jobs in which women predominate as for different jobs in which men predominate, but which require comparable skills, knowledge and responsibility." "House Authorizes Comparable-Worth Study," *Washington Post,* October 11, 1985, p. A25.

18. Brock, *Real Anita Hill,* pp. 85, 86.

19. "Despite Achievement, Thomas Felt Isolated," *Washington Post,* September 9, 1991, p. A1.

20. For the number of hours Clarence Thomas testified see *Report,* Committee on the Judiciary, Nomination of Clarence Thomas, 102d Cong., 1st sess., Exec. Rept. 102–15, Additional Views of Senators Thurmond, Hatch, Simpson, Grassley, and Brown, p. 158.

21. Since 1948, the Senate Judiciary Committee has requested the opinion of the ABA Standing Committee on Federal Judiciary for every federal ju-

dicial nomination. The committee conducts interviews, consults law school professors, and examines the legal writings of Supreme Court nominees and rates nominees well qualified, qualified, or not qualified. Of the fifteen committee members, twelve voted that Clarence Thomas was qualified to serve on the Supreme Court, two found him not qualified and one member did not vote. See *The ABA Standing Committee on Federal Judiciary: What It Is and How It Works* (Chicago: American Bar Association, 1991).

22. "Thomas' Judges: A Collection of Speed Readers," and "Thomas in the Coliseum," *Wall Street Journal*, September 5, 1991, p. A14. The *Wall Street Journal* states that "Judge Thomas has now provided the Judiciary Committee with more than 32,000 documents, disclosing everything from the name of the gym where he works out (Ironworks in Alexandria) to the fact that he belongs to the International Churchill Society."

23. The First Amendment to the Constitution states, "Congress shall make no law respecting an establishment of religion."

24. There is a distinction between the term *sexual harassment* as it is popularly used to characterize the alleged conduct of Clarence Thomas and the meaning of that term for purposes of applying the Civil Rights Act of 1964. In its popular use, *sexual harassment* means sexually offensive language in the context of employment. It is an open question as to whether offensive language alone, in the absence of some threat to employment or to benefits, constituted sexual harassment at the time Anita Hill worked for Clarence Thomas. Anita Hill never alleged any threats or promises, let alone any economic impact predicated on them.

   The principle that language alone could be sufficiently severe or pervasive to alter the conditions of the victim's employment was not recognized by the Supreme Court until 1986 in the case of *Meritor Savings Bank v. Vinson*, 477 U.S. 57 (1986).

   Even under the test laid out in *Meritor* and explained further in *Harris v. Forklift Systems*, 114 S. Ct. 367 (1993), it is highly doubtful that Anita Hill's allegations constitute sexual harassment within the meaning of the Civil Rights Act. *Meritor* found that the "mere utterance of an . . . epithet which engenders offensive feelings in an employee" does not sufficiently affect the conditions of employment to implicate Title VII. *Harris* expanded *Meritor* somewhat by holding that tangible psychological injury is not necessary to a sexual harassment claim. Under *Harris*, one can only determine whether an environment is "hostile" or "abusive" by looking at all the circumstances. "These may include the frequency of the discriminatory conduct, its severity, whether it is physically threatening, or a mere offensive utterance; and whether it unreasonably interferes with an employee's work performance." The Court has been unwilling to label infrequent, offensive utterances that do not interfere with an employee's work performance as sexual harassment.

25. *Hearings Before the Committee on the Judiciary of the United States Senate*, 102d Cong., 1st sess., on the nomination of Clarence Thomas to be associate justice of the Supreme Court of the United States, October 11, 12, 13, 1991. pt. 4, p. 37.

26. Andrew S. Fishel, former management director of Office of Civil Rights, Department of Education, to Senator Biden, October 10, 1991, printed in ibid., pp. 416–417.

27. *Congressional Record*, September 27, 1991, p. S13865.

28. Transcript of Executive Session of Senate Committee on the Judiciary, September 27, 1991.

29. In an interview on January 10, 1994, Joe Biden told me that his intentions in making his statements on the day of the committee vote differed from our interpretations of his meaning. He told me that Anita Hill seemed credible to him, but that he feared that her allegation would be made public not by her own accusation but by rumor. In that case, Clarence would not have a fair chance to defend himself. Biden calls his public statements warnings to those who might resort to rumor that, if they did so, he would defend Clarence.

30. See Garry Sturgess, "Senate Mulls Thomas' Controversial Case," *Legal Times*, September 30, 1991. The courthouse leak was criticized by Judge Buckley in his concurring opinion in *Lamprecht v. FCC*, 958 F. 2d 382 (D.C. Cir. 1992), at 403.

31. See Code of Judicial Conduct, adopted by the House of Delegates of the American Bar Association in August 1990, canon 3, sec. 9, *ABA/BNA Lawyers' Manual on Professional Conduct* (Chicago: ABA, 1993). Generally judges may not make public comments on a pending proceeding where the comments "might reasonably be expected to affect its outcome or impair its fairness." The canon does allow judges to explain the procedures of the court. At the very least, comments about the status of deliberations on a specific case would have given rise to charges of violation of both the Code of Judicial Conduct and the established practice of the court.

32. Joe Biden has told me that he does not doubt that he said something along the lines of the Thomases' memory of the phone call but that his remarks were made in the context of his concern that Clarence would be attacked by rumor and not by Anita Hill. In such an eventuality, Biden

would insist that his own vote against Clarence had been based on philosophical differences, not on questions of character.

33. Joe Biden does not believe that he told Ken Duberstein that he would issue a statement endorsing Clarence's character. He has told me that on October 6 he did not believe it appropriate, as chairman of the Judiciary Committee, to make a public statement of his thoughts on Clarence's guilt or innocence. His personal view was that Hill's allegation was "on the face of it, a credible charge."

34. Timothy M. Phelps, "Ex-Aide Says Thomas Sexually Harassed Her," *Newsday*, October 6, 1991, p. 7.

35. U.S. Senate, *Report of Temporary Special Independent Counsel*, 102d Cong., 2d sess., S. Res. 202 (Washington, D.C.: U.S. Government Printing Office, 1992), p. 19.

36. *Congressional Record*, October 7, 1991, pp. S14495, S14496.

37. Photocopies of the phone logs appear in *Hearings*, pp. 170–179.

38. See *Hearings*, p. 346. Diane Holt testified that in addition to the phone calls noted on the message slips, Hill made five or six phone calls when Clarence was in the office, and the calls were put through to him.

39. Since giving me the scrap of paper, Jim Cannon has discovered that the prayer was offered by Sir Jacob Astley, an English Royalist soldier, before the Battle of Edgehill on October 23, 1642, and that his words were, "O Lord! thou knowest how busy I must be this day: if I forget thee, do not thou forget me." Robert Andrews, *The Columbia Dictionary of Quotations* (New York: Columbia University Press, 1993), p. 722.

40. The case of Judge Walter Nixon was heard by the Senate on November 1, 1989, and Judge Nixon was removed from office on November 3, 1989. See *Congressional Record*, November 1, 1989, S14493–S14517, November 3, 1989, S14633–S14639.

41. John Tower, formerly a Republican senator from Texas who served as chairman of the Senate Armed Services Committee, was President Bush's initial selection for secretary of defense. After being subjected to charges of excessive drinking, womanizing, and giving "at least the appearance of profiting from public service" through his work as a defense consultant, Tower was defeated on March 9, 1989, by the Senate by a vote of fifty-three to forty-seven. See Helen Dewar, "Senate Kills Tower's Nomination as Defense Chief, 53–47," *Washington Post*, March 10, 1989, p. A1. For the record of the Senate floor debate, see *Congressional Record*, March 2–March 9, 1989 (March 2, S1949–S1985; March 3, S2096–S2146; March 6, S2162–S2185; March 7, S2211–S2229, S2238–S2252; March 8, S2295–S2346; March 9, S2411–S2466).

42. *Congressional Record,* October 8, 1991, pp. S14537, S14538.

43. During the confirmation proceedings for Ruth Bader Ginsburg, the next Supreme Court nominee after Clarence Thomas, the Judiciary Committee did schedule an executive session for the purpose of hearing any personal charges against the nominee. There were no such charges.

44. The Civil Rights Act of 1991, P.L. 102–166, 105 Stat. 1071–1100, passed the Senate on October 30, 1991, and was signed by President Bush in a Rose Garden ceremony on November 21, 1991. It strengthened civil rights laws relating to employment by overruling at least five Supreme Court decisions.

45. *Congressional Record,* October 8, 1991, pp. S14568, S14569.

46. 1 Samuel 22:1. Steven Law believes that David's experience is expressed in Psalm 57.

47. 42 U.S.C. S2000e-5(e) creates a 180-day statute of limitations in Title VII employment discrimination cases, including sexual harassment cases.

48. Job 11:6.

49. John 9:2.

50. See *Hearings,* pp. 443–551, for the transcript of Angela Wright's deposition.

51. Ibid., pp. 5–10.

52. Eric Pianin, "Senate Inquiry on Packwood Signals Sea Change in Attitude," *Washington Post,* December 7, 1992, p. A1.

53. Mary McGrory, "Squirm Time in the Senate," *Washington Post,* December 6, 1992, p. C1.

54. Trip Gabriel, "The Trials of Bob Packwood," *New York Times Magazine,* August 29, 1993, P. 32.

55. The *Washington Post* reported that "Hill called the telephone logs 'garbage' and said she had not telephoned Thomas except to return his calls." Helen Dewar and Ruth Marcus, "Thomas Vote Put Off a Week to Probe Allegation," *Washington Post,* October 9, 1991, p. A1.

56. FBI special agents John B. Luton and Jolene Smith Jameson filed statements on the discrepancies between Anita Hill's interview with them and her testimony before the committee. Their statements are reproduced in *Hearings,* pp. 125, 126.

57. See *Hearings,* pp. 64–67, 116–118, for Senator Specter's questioning of Anita Hill on this point and p. 230 for his assertion that her testimony was "flat-out perjury."

58. "The Price of Apostasy," *Wall Street Journal,* August 2, 1989, p. A14.

59. *Hearings,* pp. 157, 158.

60. The BCCI case involved the acquisition of First American Bank in Washington by the Arab-owned Bank of Credit and Commerce International. In August 1993, Robert Altman, who had been president of First American Bank, was acquitted of one count of banking fraud and three counts of filing fake documents by a jury in New York City. Sharon Walsh, "Altman Acquitted on BCCI Counts," *Washington Post*, August 15, 1993, p. A1.

61. *Hearings*, pp. 241, 242.

62. Barbara Vobejda, "Who's Telling the Truth? Experts Say Answer May Never Be Known," *Washington Post*, October 13, 1991, p. A30.

63. *Hearings*, pp. 324, 332.

64. Ibid., p. 555.

65. 29 U.S.C. S2001 et seq.

66. While debating the Polygraph Protection Act on the Senate floor, Senator Kennedy referred to a study by the Office of Technology Assessment and said of the polygraph: "One of the interesting points that is raised by the OTA is who passes it? Who fails it? If you are an altar boy, you probably will fail it. You would have a sense of conscience, and potential guilt. But who passes it? The psychopaths, the deceptive ones." Senator Kennedy continued, "OTA points out that if you are mean, scheming, lying, a child pedophile, you will pass the test." *Congressional Record*, March 2, 1988, S1703.

    In debating the same legislation, Senator Metzenbaum said of polygraphs, "Careers are crushed and reputations are ruined because of these intimidating, unscientific and inaccurate tests." *Congressional Record*, June 9, 1988, p. S7505.

67. On Sunday afternoon, nine women were prepared to testify. By one o'clock Monday morning, attrition claimed one potential witness.

68. *Hearings*, pp. 586–592.

69. Mike Brewer and Pam Talkin recall Joe Biden's saying that he did not believe Anita Hill. Biden recalls meeting members of the witness panel on the sidewalk but does not remember making any comment on Hill's credibility.

70. "Against Clarence Thomas," *New York Times*, October 15, 1991, p. A24.

71. *Washington Post*, ABC News poll, December 11–14, 1992; Richard Morin, "Harassment Consensus Grows," *Washington Post*, December 18, 1992, p. A1.

72. Gwen Ifil, "Conference Lauds Anita Hill, Exultantly," *New York Times*, November 17, 1991, sec. 1, p. 28.

73. "Women's Group Protesting Thomas Appearance," Associated Press, September 29, 1993.

74. See, e.g., Anthony Lewis, "Time of the Assassins," *New York Times*, October 14, 1991, p. A19, and "Slash and Burn," *New York Times*, October 18, 1991, p. A31; Richard Cohen, "Thomas' Missed Chance," *Washington Post*, October 15, 1991, p. A23; Ann F. Lewis, "The Feminists Will Strike Back," *New York Times*, October 16, 1991, p. A25; Tom Wicker, "Waltz of the Democrats," *New York Times*, October 20, 1991, sec. 4, p. 15.

75. Brock, *Real Anita Hill*, p. 11.

76. "New Film Fires a Bullet at Specter's Re-Election," *Philadelphia Inquirer*, January 5, 1992, p. A-1.

77. John Newhouse, "Taking It Personally," *New Yorker*, March 16, 1992, pp. 56–78.

78. At the request of Senator Hatch, the Senate Ethics Committee investigated published reports of contacts between his office and the Bank of Credit and Commerce International. On November 20, 1993, the committee reported that it found "no credible evidence that Hatch had violated any law or Senate rule." The committee said that it did not find "any reason to believe that the senator engaged in any improper conduct." The action of the committee and the background of the matter are reported in Helen Dewar, "Panel Clears Hatch of Wrongdoing in BCCI Case," *Washington Post*, November 21, 1993, p. A5.

79. See note 13.

Index